About the Author

Sheka Tarawalie is a distinguished Sierra Leonean journalist with over two decades of experience. An English Honours graduate of the country's premier university, the 1827-established Fourah Bay College, he founded *The Torchlight* newspaper and was more well-known for his 'Black Tank' column. He endured persecution: sent to jail, declared 'wanted', went into hiding, and eventually into exile in the UK. He afterwards took up a political appointment as Press Secretary to the President; later to become Deputy Minister. And now he is out with his first book on all that.

Tarawalie has written reviews on books such as British author William Fowler's *Operation Barass: the SAS Mission in Sierra Leone*, Gbanabom Hallowell's *When Sierra Leone was a Woman* and Edward Turay's *The Prophecy of a Father* – all about Sierra Leone. He was also acknowledged as proofreader in Dr. Abass Bundu's *Democracy by Force?*

He did a post-graduate course in Journalism at the University of Lincoln (UK) during which he presented literary papers.

POPE FRANCIS, POLITICS AND THE MABANTA BOY

A Journalist's Journey With God And Humanity

Sheka Tarawalie

Matador
9 Priory Business Park,
Wistow Road, Kibworth Beauchamp,
Leicestershire. LE8 0RX
Tel: 0116 279 2299
Email: books@troubador.co.uk
Web: www.troubador.co.uk/matador
Twitter: @matadorbooks

ISBN 978 1789018 158

British Library Cataloguing in Publication Data.
A catalogue record for this book is available from the British Library.

Printed and bound by CPI Group (UK) Ltd, Croydon, CR0 4YY
Typeset in 11pt Sabon MT by Troubador Publishing Ltd, Leicester, UK

Matador is an imprint of Troubador Publishing Ltd

An ordinary man trying to make sense of the world around him

Dedicated to the ever-loving memory of my younger brother, Hudson Tarawalie, who went ahead to meet the Lord;

And also to my Mabanta school brother Francis Koroma (Bio-Chemist) and my journalistic brother Tatafway Tumoe, both of whom did the same.

I posthumously call them 'the three Hebrew boys'.

Contents

Acknowledgements

Many sacrifices were made to make this work a reality. And many people, in diverse ways, helped me in the process.

I would specially thank my wife, Rose, for being the strongest pillar – after God – in making it happen. She endured with me both in Sierra Leone and in England: she saw and bore the sometimes crazy moments of becoming emotionally detached even when it should be time for holidaying or resting. She even helped in typing sections of the manuscript laboriously, considering my hard-to-understand handwriting ("You write like a doctor," she kept complaining in diligence). Thank you dearest. We both would hope our children – John Sheka, Catherine, and Marie – would come to appreciate this work.

Of course, the source of my existence – apart from God – are my parents, Rev. John Sheka and Mrs. Marie Tarawalie, who laboured and laboured on this field for it to yield this fruit. God bless you.

I will surely thank, posthumously, Rev. Dr. Y.M. and Mrs. Matilda Kroma, who grafted me into their family, by the grace of God, and watered the plant to bear fruit.

I thank my intertwined Tarawalie and Kroma siblings and extended family members (we have all types of uncles, aunties, cousins, nieces, nephews, brothers and sisters – you may never stop counting) who put up with me despite at times finding me hard to understand. Your being there alone was a great source of inspiration. The joy we have shared – and continue to share – is precious.

I also thank Rose's eldest sister, Maria Jones. She was in hospital when I showed her the manuscript in London; a week or so later she was asking about it when back home. You don't play pranks with your sister-in-law – especially if she is from Paul Kagame's Rwanda.

I must also acknowledge the contribution of Richard Lance Keeble, Professor of Journalism at the University of Lincoln and Visiting Professor at Liverpool Hope University, both in the UK. Some while back, I had a stint on a course at the University of Lincoln as an exiled journalist; and he was one of my lecturers. After a break in communication for more than ten years, Prof. Keeble did not ignore me when I reconnected with him. Rather, he indulged me by reading the manuscript line by line, making invaluable editing changes, and encouraging me to endure to the end. Thank you, sir.

I would also thank Professor Tim Unwin, formerly of the Commonwealth Telecommunications Organisation, whom I first met while I was serving as Deputy Minister of Information and Communications. He became my ICTs 'godfather' and we had fruitful times in Sierra Leone, Rwanda, Uganda, Mauritius, and England. Most memorable was when I visited after the 2018 elections and he took me to the historic Athenaeum in central London. An 1824-founded club of intellectuals named after the Greek 'goddess of wisdom' Athena (whose statue stands at the top of the portico), I think there is no category in the Nobel Prize that at least one of its members has not won. There I showed him the manuscript of this book; he was impressed and nudged me on. He gave me his latest book

Reclaiming Information & Communication Technologies for Development with an autographed message: "Sheka, My 'godson' – it has been wonderful to catch up again. You have taught me so much. I pray that God will indeed reveal His plans for the new stage in your life, and will guide you in His way. You have so very much to contribute to us all. With very best wishes, Tim. London 18th May 2018." I remember the joke with Tim saying I could possibly be the first-ever Sierra Leonean to have visited the Club. There is a huge painting, among others, of William Wilberforce inside the Athenaeum.

Later-generation Wesleyan missionaries, Paul and Eila Shea (siblings), need to be thanked also. Their parents, Alton and Aileen Shea (commonly known as Pa Shea and Ya Shea), were missionaries at the Gbendembu Bible School (recording studio section) in the 70s when I was born there. It was through his studio that my father would become a radio evangelist, as his Temne messages were recorded and aired over Radio ELWA (Eternal Love Winning Africa – station burnt during the war, revived after), based in Liberia and broadcasting to the sub-region. Paul and Eila themselves followed the parents' missionary footsteps – the brother in mainstream, the sister as a nurse at the once-famous Kamakwei Wesleyan Hospital. However, I only got connected or re-connected with them when I was in England and read an online article titled 'From Houghton to West Africa and Beyond' written by Paul. I wrote to him in admiration of the article and asked whether he was the Paul Shea that my parents used to talk about. Indeed he was.

In his reply, Paul had this to say: "You have a rich heritage even though the finances on this earth were poor. When I think of the number of highly educated and brilliant pastors' children from Sierra Leone, I realize that the country has tremendous resources and talent. I remember a British

Member of Parliament or some big position once said, 'I would rather my son be a faithful minister of the Gospel than the Prime Minister.' I know you and your family suffered much in the small corners where God called. But faithful ministry to the powerful news of Jesus can change a world." And what pricked me more, vis-à-vis the writing of this book, was when Paul, now a professor at Houghton College (USA) which sent some of the earliest missionaries that would die in Sierra Leone, wrote: "I wish more history were compiled on the Church in Sierra Leone. Various ones from Marion Birch to Don Kinde were working on it from the US side. I wonder if you or another Sierra Leonean would like to write a new history from the Africa viewpoint. It would be of tremendous value."

That was in October 2006, way before I ever imagined I would meet the Pope or even be a government functionary. I started taking notes since then. And when Paul gave me the contacts for his sister, Eila, my probing began with her. She gave me the years of their family's missionary work in Sierra Leone. She also told me about John Ayers and Will Boardman (both graduates of Houghton College and in their twenties), plus the first victim a six-year-old, all of whom died and were buried alongside others at Kunsho, Sierra Leone. Today, one of my parents' most-prized possessions is a three-generation family photograph of the Sheas which I received in England through the post from Pa Shea himself.

Philip Neville, editor of *Standard Times*, and my Makeni and FBC buddies, Alfred Ben Kargbo, Dr. Michael Kizito Kargbo, Alhaji Bangura (Banco) and Ibrahim Jalloh (Jallomy) also encouraged me to go on with the idea. Thanks gentlemen.

The current Speaker of the Parliament of Sierra Leone, Dr. Abass Bundu, has to be thanked. While we sojourned in The Gambia in similar circumstances of having suffered the heavy-handedness of the previous SLPP government, Bundu wrote a book, *Democracy by Force?*, and (staying in the same house) gave me the opportunity to proofread all of it. I learnt a lot on how to write a book under no supervision (because a university dissertation is a kind of book). I believed I could do it. Bundu supported my book-writing when I showed him the manuscript.

I must thank those who responded to my crosschecking of facts relating to chapters in which they were mentioned – the Rev. Andrew Dawson, Don Ignazio Poddighe, Jo Anne Lyon, Rev Momodu Conteh, Martina Kroma, Martina Gjergja, Clare Taylor, Kinglsey L. Ighobor, Lans Gberie, Mansoor Hassan, Bob Pounder, David Oglaza, Edward M. Turay – and at the same time buoyed me up to go ahead and get the book published.

I am indebted to Professor Fr Joseph Turay, Vice Chancellor/ Principal of the University of Makeni, and the Reverend John A. Baminhoma, National Superintendent of the Wesleyan Church of Sierra Leone, both of whom skimmed through the manuscript and wrote a well-appreciated Foreword to the book.

In a special group are former President Ernest Bai Koroma and current President Julius Maada Bio, who, with all their busy schedules, found time to read and make comments accordingly. Thank you, Your Excellencies.

This work is wholly mine, and I take full responsibility for its contents.

ST

October 2018

Foreword

Making politics 'the most noble and highest expression of love and charity'

By Joseph Turay and John A. Baminhoma

Writing about the Church, the Pope, his country and himself from a secularist perspective, Sierra Leonean journalist Sheka Tarawalie has brought something new into the world in *Pope Francis, Politics and the Mabanta Boy*. Delving into the history of his country, and making discoveries hitherto unknown to most Sierra Leoneans, he has stirred the sensibilities of many intellectuals to scratch beneath the surface.

Tarawalie, the son of a Wesleyan pastor, has made us realise that there's much more that binds us together than separates us.

We believe that this book has the capacity to change certain world-views about religious bigotry, fundamentalism, tribalism and politics. It brings out the power and value of education. Sheka has inadvertently made himself a role-model for generations yet unborn either in Sierra Leone or the world at large.

There was a time when many in the world were wondering why Sierra Leone, once known as 'the Athens of West Africa', has not been producing writers like Ghana and Nigeria, which originally had their source of education from Sierra Leone. Now we know we have, wittingly or unwittingly, been waiting for Sheka. He has done us proud.

Having had a cross-denominational secondary education from the Wesleyan-oriented Birch Memorial to the Catholic St. Francis in Makeni, he has encouraged us to make moves for closer ecumenical fellowship. Christians, Muslims, Jews and free-thinkers would find edification in this book. It has gone deep into history and discovered the tapestry of humanity that binds us all together. He has just broken the glass ceiling on anti-Semitism: if anyone wants to blame the Jews for the death of Christ, then the rest of us would be blamed for the death of His disciples! And many Muslims would appreciate this work because it has tried to put their religion into perspective.

Mabanta village, once only known for derogatory things in its neighbourhood, can never be the same again owing to this book. Something good – perhaps something great – has come from Mabanta! His portrayal of his people's traditions and customs in a most dispassionate and sincere way will only help in endearing this book to scholars and non-scholars alike.

For Sheka to have gone into the complexities of African politics and come out unsullied is a great testament to his moral fibre. He has come out clean – perhaps cleaner. He has left a legacy of integrity for future aspiring politicians and public servants. The diligence he manifested during his tour of duty impressed us all. He never lost his faith; he never left his God. He has proven that you can be in the world but not of the world.

We believe this book will be of immense importance to peace-makers around the world, not least the United Nations, whose admiration for Sierra Leone's religious tolerance is touched on by Sheka.

Tarawalie has thrown a challenge not only to his fellow journalists (we can hardly recall any Sierra Leonean journalist writing a 'personal experience' book published by established international publishers in contemporary times) but also to many other Sierra Leoneans to write books that will have an international appeal.

This is an invaluable work relevant to educationists, especially those in the departments of literature, history, religious and peace studies. It is our desire and hope that it will eventually be incorporated into the curricula of educational institutions. Indeed, every library in the world deserves a copy of this book.

By getting the endorsements of former President Ernest Bai Koroma and current President Julius Maada Bio (both from different political parties), Sheka has made the book more appealing to all Sierra Leoneans, irrespective of political links or lineage. This is a class act! This is real-time history! And it couldn't have come at a better time as now, when the government of Sierra Leone has put much premium on education. We hope and believe that this book will help further inspire the advancement of education in Sierra Leone.

Asylum-seekers and refugees around the world, plus the body lobbying for their welfare – the UNHCR – will find this book useful and perhaps personal. Persecuted journalists and people who just want to contribute to nation-building and peace-building have a handy handbook.

The British people will love this book: they are portrayed as a most hospitable and loveable people through their humanitarian and charity work. The Salvation Army, Refugee Action, Oldham Unity, Boaz Trust and many more must, through this book, realise that their work is not in vain – it has not gone unnoticed.

Sheka has written a most fascinating book about his encounter with one of the most influential leaders in the world: Pope Francis – through 'Love Bridges', an Italian charity working in Sierra Leone. His journey through his experiences of an African village, an African faith mediated through cultural lenses shaped by his world, is a fascinating reading for anyone interested in the encounter of faith, culture and religion. Faith is discovered and expressed within a specific cultural milieu. We are products of the experiences that shape our lives' journeys.

Sheka comes across as one who understands very well that our God transcends borders, colours, religions and divisions. God calls us all to bring love to humanity everywhere. The Church is presented as a divine and a human institution filled with grace but also a vessel in earthenware prone to sin and in need of God's mercy.

The author's journey leads him to maturity in faith and love for the divine working in human institutions. The book points out the possibility of Churches working together for the good of their communities and their members. Ecumenism is possible and dialogue with other religions is a must in Africa and the world in the midst of a clash of civilisations.

We also encounter a politician who tries to make sense of religion and his faith. Africa needs such politicians who can work for the common good. Politics should not be seen as a 'dirty profession' but in the words of Pope Paul VI 'the most noble and highest expression of love and charity'. The author could be pointing towards that direction.

Every Christian should find oxygen in this work. Each Wesleyan and each Catholic must read it!

Sheka has displayed inspirational writing skills in this book. It is very educative. For example, the revelation it projects on the issue of the poro secret society and members of chieftaincies in the Mabanta community, the Catholicism of the Church, the transformation and expansion of the Church – beginning from the protest of Martin Luther – are some of the issues many will learn from this text.

And the question that now perplexes us: couldn't Sierra Leone have just produced its own Wole Soyinka or Chinua Achebe or Adu Boahen or V.S. Naipaul?

Time will tell.

Prof. Fr. Joseph Turay, Vice Chancellor and Principal,
University of Makeni,
and the Rev. John A. Baminhoma,
National Superintendent,
Wesleyan Church of Sierra Leone

Prologue

Not Writing From A Position Of Self-Righteousness

By socio-historical pecking order, I was meant to be either a farmer or a palm-wine tapper or at most a second-hand clothing trader (the general profession of my kindred). When my mother married my father, she knew she was pitching her future with a man of that stock and the children to come thereafter would follow suit. But God in His infinite mercy reached down and changed the story. And now this book.

I have not written it from a position of strength, but of weakness. I am not standing on a pedestal of perfection, neither on a platform of self-righteousness nor of judging others. But in trying to unravel the world around me, I have written this book from a resource of faith, in the knowledge that what is called salvation is really available to all. And it's free. It has nothing to do with religion *per se*. God is real.

Even one of the world's most renowned scientists, Albert

Einstein, apparently subscribed to this view. When asked whether he believed in the historical existence of Jesus Christ, according to Walter Isaacson's book *Einstein: His Life And Universe*, the trailblazing scientist retorted: "Unquestionably! I am a Jew, but I am enthralled by the luminous figure of the Nazarene. No one can read the Gospels without feeling the actual presence of Jesus. His personality pulsates in every word. No myth is filled with such life." It was Einstein's belief that science itself points to the existence of God: "That deeply emotional conviction of the presence of a superior reasoning power, which is revealed in the incomprehensible universe, forms my idea of God… Everyone who is seriously involved in the pursuit of science becomes convinced that a spirit is manifest in the laws of the universe – a spirit vastly superior to that of man, and one in the face of which we with our modest powers must feel humble…"

"There are people who say there is no God. But what makes me really angry is that they quote me for support of such views," Einstein, the Nobel laureate credited for his contribution to the creation of the nuclear bomb crucially used by America in ending the Second World War, was quoted by the former *Time* magazine editor Walter Isaacson.

But this actually is not a religious book. I have generously quoted from the Bible because I am a Christian. Inasmuch as I relate to my faith, I have also made references to the Koran as well as to several secular and literary works plus newspapers, magazines and other sources. I am just telling my story. I am not preaching. I am not a pastor. My father is. I may be later. But not yet. I'll, however, accept this book is a testimony. This is my testimony. In literary form. I have consequently bundled myself into Church history: in recounting my labyrinthine Christian journey – together with the democratic journey of a nation – in a secular world. I have tried to bring out the traditions and culture of my native people and how they have been responding to 'external' influence.

In going through the pages of this book, you will find out that I am a very imperfect fellow, a sinner, a mere mortal like all of us. But in the knowledge that there is a God, and that His love is unconditional, I would hope that those who read this book will, like me, come to the conclusion that it is better to believe in His existence than not. After all, believing is one of the easiest things to do! For faith is lurked in the DNA of every human.

This book is about the story of an encounter – a meeting. Me, meeting the Pope. It's just a work of art. I've tried my best to narrate events as they are – but, of course, they are just as I see them. And you may wish to see them otherwise.

Throughout the ages, men have tried to make sense of the world they find themselves in. Why not me? I am not craving for a place in history, but everybody can be a part of history. If one's God-given talents are not utilised to benefit others, then it profits one nothing, I believe. The creativity of writing was not acquired from the excellent educational institutions I attended – they were passageways. It had always been there, from God. For the edification of others. It is my hope that this book will edify you even as a work of literature or as a historical document. And I hope it will serve as an eye-opener to coming generations in mainly Developing World countries.

It was local BBC Correspondent Umaru Fofana, when I was a government minister and he was the journalists' association president, who asked me during a conversation with colleagues about my future in politics. I replied: "I am a journalist on loan to politics." I hope this book will help clarify that statement and generate a debate around journalism, politics, education and nation-building in Sierra Leone – the world's geographically roundest country, according to Argentinean mathematician

Gonzalo Ciruelos' 2016 algorithm study (using Natural-Earth dataset minutely describing the perimeters/borders of all countries) which saw the Vatican curiously being the 4th roundest and the 2nd most rectangular country at the same time.

Though this book very much seems like a religious text due to the central personalities involved, you will find out that I have not glorified even the Pope. I have not venerated the Church either. It's a normal human story – with pitfalls. Therefore, Christians, Muslims, Jews, those on the fence and even absolute non-believers should try to go through it with open minds before making conclusions. It is not my autobiography *per se* (imagine if I didn't meet Pope Francis, how my story would have looked like). I would like this book to be read by celebrities (even if by accident), musicians, artists, the down-trodden as well as the powerful, and find something worth comprehending.

One of my greatest delights was the twin-discovery (at least at the level of what was being taught in Sierra Leone's educational institutions) I made while researching about my country – about her first recorded contact with outsiders and the origins of the tribes. Futa D'jallon was after all not the place where humanity began. And Christianity is not exclusively "the white man's religion"! The Bible was not originally written in English – it was translated as it has been done into Mende, Krio, Temne, Arabic etc etc.

The book could well look like a history of the Church. But it's not that straightforward. I would rather admit it's an attempt at portraying how God can work in the affairs of men. It could also appear as a story of the Vatican. Not really. Though I am a journalist, yet I can't claim to be a writer in the category of Dan Brown or John Thavis or Andrew Greely who have all written well-publicised books about the Vatican (fiction or factual).

I'll rather just be me. I'll just sum it up with the age-old truism that, learning (education) is better than silver and gold.

Anything is possible – if you only believe.

To God be the glory!

Chapter One

Meeting The 'Most Powerful' Man On Earth

For a boy from Mabanta to meet the Pope is a miracle! Accept it or not, that's how I see it. Because I am 'the boy from Mabanta', and I know where I'm coming from, and I know where I'm going as far as relating the events that led to this great encounter is concerned.

From that perspective, therefore, to say you are going to meet the Pope at the Vatican and it happens is an extraordinary occurrence – a miracle I should say again. To me, at least; and perhaps to the many people of different nationalities from across the world who flocked to pose with me to take pictures and 'selfies' immediately after (or because) I met him.

Of course, for those priests and other officials who work closely with the Pope at the Vatican on a daily basis, meeting him cannot be a miracle. To them, the Pope is just another human being (though obviously revered by them as well), a mere mortal who at times laughs and at times gets angry. The Pope's cleaner, his cook and other domestic staff are clearly not affected by the awe and aura surrounding him.

To the rest of mankind, Christian or not, the Pope is not an ordinary human. He is arguably the most powerful human being on earth. Great world leaders like the UN Secretary General and the President of the United States of America pale into 'second best' in the presence of the 'holy father'. Therefore, even if he is not the most powerful in terms of raw political power, he certainly is the most revered!

America virtually came to a standstill when Pope Francis visited in 2015; and the then-President of the United States (known also as the leader of the free world), Barack Obama, in welcoming the Pope in glowing terms in a 12-paragraph speech, called him either 'Holy father' or 'Your Holiness' in eight of those paragraphs. The US Congress gave him a standing ovation. America, the most powerful nation on earth, the world super power – being a Christian nation with millions of Catholics – added spice and glamour to the authority of the Pope. On the same trip, Pope Francis became the first pontiff to address the opening of the United Nations General Assembly. Welcoming the Head of State of the Vatican, then-Secretary General Ban Ki-moon, could not have been more deferential: "Your Holiness, your views move millions. Your teachings bring action. Your example inspires us all."

We remember how the Pope's mere 'chance' encounter with the then-Democratic Party presidential hopeful Bernie Sanders created a media buzz in the US in 2016. With no photo opportunity and the Pope himself dismissing it as just a handshake and nothing more, Sanders came away with hyperbolic descriptions of the Vatican meeting, describing Pope Francis as "one of the great leaders in modern world history". Sanders went further, telling the media, "I just conveyed to him my admiration for the extraordinary work he is doing raising some of the most important issues facing our planet and the billions of people on the planet and injecting the need for morality in the global economy."

Of course, mass-selling magazines such as *Forbes* don't regard the Pope as the most powerful person on earth, but view him as 'one of the most powerful', putting him in the fourth position in their 2015 statistical rankings. But I would go beyond the mundane and look at whom the Pope is actually representing. I'm looking at his office. I'm not looking at raw physical power, but on soft power – the influence, the respect, the metaphysical authority which has endured through the ages and still persists. A perfunctory look at his titles would put him on a pedestal: 'Bishop of Rome, Vicar of Jesus Christ, Successor of the Prince of the Apostles, Supreme Pontiff of the Universal Church, Primate of Italy, Archbishop and Metropolitan of the Roman Province, Sovereign of the State of Vatican City, Servant of the Servants of God.'

And certainly this authority was drastically reduced by the Reformation, the split in the Church that gave birth to the Protestant churches including the Church of England. Consequently, the Catholic Church can no longer claim to be the only gateway to heaven. There was a time when the Pope had the singular power to forgive sins – even those of the dead, as he could "shut the gates of hell and open the door to paradise" during the days of the 'holy trade' of indulgences.

Today, every denomination — including the Wesleyan Church to which I belong, and even Joseph Smith's vilified Church of Jesus Christ of Latter Day Saints – claims to posses equal spiritual authority with the Pope, or more. They all claim direct access to God, salvation, and forgiveness of sins, without having to pay for it – through Jesus Christ's death on the cross!

But, the Catholic Church, with the wealth it has acquired over the centuries, and the status it continues to hold in world affairs – even as a permanent observer at the United Nations – gives a special status to anyone occupying the position of Pope. The fact that it's a position that one can occupy until death gives him an edge over other rulers – except perhaps the monarch of the United Kingdom. The Queen also, by British historical tradition, is God's representative on earth as the head of the Church of England. The Pope obviously has greater global religious influence and jurisdiction – though in terms of raw power, by means of her standing as the head of a more geographically bigger political system, the Queen or British monarch is more powerful! Yet, the comparative power-scale still tilts in favour of the Pope when it is recalled that even Great Britain was once a Roman province and the Church of England an offshoot of the Roman Catholic Church!

No doubt a Pope today cannot be as powerful as the medieval Pope before the Reformation. The Catholic Church's participation or collaboration in abhorrent events in history like the Crusades and the Atlantic slave trade lowered its moral authority in the eyes of the world. And today, the never-ending revelations in child sex abuse scandals (including one of Pope Francis' closest advisers now facing litigation in Australia) have rocked the Church and made it look like the opposite of what it should be.

In all this, by virtue of the paraphernalia of the office, the Pope is still the most respected church leader. The investments of the Catholic Church across the world in the areas of education, health, and charity in general could arguably only be surpassed by the UN. Nations become ecstatic whenever the Pope visits. Heads of State, Presidents, Prime Ministers, all types of functionaries pay homage to him. A papal visit to some nations in Africa in 2015 brought the national agendas to a standstill.

The fact that the Pope does not dress like the rest of us in public, by itself puts him in a special category. Even on that November 2015 day when we met at the Vatican – even though the other members of the Catholic Church had their own special ways of dressing – his immaculate white gown matching with the skull cap made him somewhat an extraordinary human: like a white lamb among the black-robed flock.

The man who claims to be the direct representative of God on earth must surely be the most powerful man on earth. Christ has unarguably been the greatest Man to walk on our planet; therefore, the Vicar of Christ must still be the greatest man living. And the cardinals would tell you that any personal encounter with him must first have been ordained in heaven! With 1.3 billion Catholics around the world, spanning all continents, seeing him as their spiritual leader, he's certainly a powerful man. That many a world leader – Presidents, Prime Ministers, even Cardinals – have tried and tried but failed to get an audience with the Pope, with any Pope (past and present), is not a hidden reality. So for a man from Mabanta (a village in rural West Africa) to meet the Pope is a most unlikely event in world history – whether noticed by the world or not. It's my duty to make it noticeable.

If a world survey is to be carried out – for Christians and non-Christians alike – to choose their favourite or ideal icon from an array of the most prominent world leaders inclusive of the Pope, the UN Secretary General, the American President, the British monarch, the Dalai Lama, the Ayatollah, the Saudi King, among others, I have an intuitive inkling, subjective as that is, that the majority would choose the pontiff. For historical legacy, world-wide membership numbers, western-world weight, global humanitarian interventions, neutrality in especially the Second World War, message of peace, and continuing influence in world affairs, the Pope stands on a higher pedestal. It is even more certain with Pope Francis who has been bridging the gap with the Muslim world by going into mosques, visiting Muslim countries, and even taking in Muslim Syrian refugees at the Vatican.

Pope Francis carries a lot of moral authority and aura as the most visible Christian leader. I remember what my colleague on this trip – Alie Wasco, a Muslim – said after we met the Pope: "My Muslim brothers and sisters go on an annual pilgrimage to Mecca and they don't meet anybody except a huge black stone, and they get blessings; we've come on a pilgrimage here and we met a living person. This is so exceptional. We've got great blessings." That, coming from a Muslim, summed it up.

Therefore, to meet such a man, even if by chance – like Bernie Sanders – is worth celebrating. To meet him by appointment is worth trumpeting. To meet at the public square, St. Peter's Square, with live TV cameras and giant screens relaying the event is out of this world. To meet him, talk to him, have a conversation and receive a prepared gift from him is an extraordinary once-in-a-life-time event for me. Many nations and personalities crave for a papal visit to their countries – Sierra Leone has not been fortunate (even with its supposed 1million Catholics), and still counting and waiting.

As a Christian – a protestant Wesleyan, I must emphasise – I would only subscribe that it's the work of God. To be in Rome, the Rome I've been reading about in the book of Romans since a child, as the son of a Pastor, was surreal to me. This was Rome, the seat of Christianity; as Christendom history tells us that Rome was the first among equals, the first in honour of the five ancient patriarchates (Rome, Constantinople,

Antioch, Alexandria and Jerusalem, in that order). This very Rome where Christ's vicar now reigns as Pope was the very Rome that I read about in the Bible to have produced the Roman governor Pontius Pilate who handed over Christ for crucifixion to Jewish leaders. The Gospel has come full circle; my Christian journey has come full circle.

I thought for a moment, if only there was no sale of indulgences, if only there was no Reformation, if only there were no Crusades, if only there was no participation in the Transatlantic slave trade, if only there was no child sex abuse scandal, the Catholic Church would have remained the untainted bride of Christ.

But then I realise, the Pope is also human. The cardinals and priests are also human. We are all human. Our dependence on human strength is ephemeral. Only our dependence on the grace of God offered through direct access by Christ is eternal. Pope Francis could look like the biblical Melchizedek, 'the priest-king'; but he is not Melchizedek!

That means the most powerful man on earth is not really the most powerful! But meeting him, in whatever circumstance, is worth recording. And a CNN-aired 2018 documentary titled, 'Pope: The Most Powerful Man In History' would only go on to reinforce the fact. This is how the world-renown television broadcaster summarises the plot for the series:

> *"Pope: The Most Powerful Man in History, from Glass Entertainment Group and Rearrange TV, is a six-part CNN Original Series that goes inside the Vatican to reveal the true power held by popes throughout the ages. The docuseries explores how 12 apostles became 1.2 billion Catholics today, linking recent news events surrounding the Vatican with their unexpected origins. The premiere episode, "The Rise of the Pope," examines the origins of*

the papacy and how Catholicism, against all odds, spread throughout Europe. Jon Hirsch, Nancy Glass, Randy Counsman, Amy Entelis and Lizzie Fox serve as executive producers."

Chapter Two

Would Anything Good Come From Mabanta?

Apart from the tribes of the Amazon forests and their counterparts in other inaccessible territories around the globe, if there is ever a village that could be seen as refusing to change from its traditions and culture, it is my hometown called Mabanta.

Tucked in a small corner of the world in the Bombali District of northern Sierra Leone, Mabanta is perhaps best known for the practice of the Poro society (I'll explain this in due course) and for producing the local alcohol known as palm-wine or more appropriately 'poyo'.

Just a couple of miles outside of the northern city of Makeni, Mabanta has refused to move along with the times. In fact, its residents embody native conservatism resisting anything foreign, particularly western.

The people, the Temnes, cling to their old ways and use all means possible including witchcraft – another primitive attribute for which the village has also been infamous. Talk about the heart of darkness!

Therefore, in Sierra Leone, when one is referred to as 'Temne Mabanta', it means he /she is the most traditional of the Temne tribe – a tribe which on its own is already known to be the most troublesome and stubborn and warlike. They were the people that 'owned' Freetown (then known as 'Ro Kiamp' or 'Romarong'), Sierra Leone's capital, before it was established as a 'colony of freed slaves' in the late seventeenth to early eighteenth centuries. And the British had to fight seemingly endless battles with the Temnes before the freed slaves could actually and effectively be settled and become integrated as part of Sierra Leone – but not before the natives reportedly buried the head of an ass as a curse for the forceful acquisition of their land!

In a bigger context, the most famous and fearless Temne chief who fought the British colonial administration on a wider geographical scale over the 'hut tax', Bai Bureh, was an embodiment of the Temne character. It is believed that some of his most loyal and fiercest fighters came all the way from Mabanta.

Mabanta, home of anti-western/anti-British fighters; Mabanta, home of poro and bondo secret societies; Mabanta, home of poyo-selling; Mabanta, home of witchcraft. Nothing good would ever come from Mabanta. This notion was not only fuelled by the fact that there was virtually no development in the village, but actually made known via public self-confessions of witches. They publicly confessed that they had not only been eating babies born in the village, especially those they realised were poised to become great, but that it was their ultimate aim to prevent anybody from being educated in the village – to fight against any change. Trials of cases concerning Mabanta witchcraft were a regular occurrence at the Paramount Chief's court at the chiefdom headquarters of Panlap in the 1980s.

Thus, when the former head of the Wesleyan Church of Sierra Leone, Rev. Usman J. Fornah, was preaching at an immaculate and well-attended special service at Mabanta in late 2015 during the ceremony to crown my mother as 'Wesleyan District Woman of the Year', he could not help but re-echo what was the common refrain – the pep talk or locker-room banter in the whole Bombali District and beyond – that is, the once-held belief that nothing good would ever come from Mabanta.

"With what I have seen in this church today, with the welcome accorded me and my wife, and the crowning of Mama Marie as the winner, indeed something good has come out of Mabanta! " he declared to an applauding congregation that included invitees from various churches in the district.

What had Rev. Usman Fornah (who would later be Chairman of the Human Rights Commission) seen? How had he seen it? The answer was encoded in one of his biblical texts for the occasion, Matthew 4:16, in which Jesus was declaring scriptural fulfilment through the words of the Prophet Isaiah: "The people who sat in darkness have seen a great light; those who were living in the land of the shadow of death, on them a light has dawned."

According to the nationally-acclaimed preacher, it was further recorded in the Gospels that one of the earliest disciples Philip, after he found Christ, came to Nathaniel to reveal the great news of having seen "the One Moses wrote about in the law". But Nathaniel – in line with the low esteem in which Nazareth was once held in Israel – condescendingly asked: 'Can anything good come from Nazareth?'

Nazareth – like Mabanta – never had a good reputation. Professor Paul Anderson, of the Department of Biblical and Quaker Studies, George Fox University, writing in the *Huffington Post*, put it this way in a March 22 2017 article:

> *"For one thing, Nazareth was a small village during the days of Jesus, perhaps boasting a population of only a few hundred. For another, Nazareth did not have the greatest of reputations politically. Following the death of Herod the Great in 4 BC, the Roman armory in Sepphoris (four miles from Nazareth) was robbed, and the Romans retaliated by crucifying 2,000 Jews as a disincentive to such revolts. Sepphoris was burned to the ground, and its inhabitants were sold into slavery. Maybe that's where Joseph and Jesus did some of their construction work. Less than a decade later, when Jesus was just a boy, Judas the Galilean instituted a tax revolt, evoking another crackdown by the Romans in which many were also crucified. Therefore, one can appreciate the jaded words of Nathanael in John 1:46: "Can any good thing come from Nazareth?"*

Rev. Forna re-echoed these words and sentiments in his message. To him, it was unfathomable that the women's wing of the Mabanta Wesleyan Church could sing in English! This was a church that was once negligible and thought unworkable by the national leadership as far as attracting membership was concerned.

"And today, it is not only hosting me the head of Church and my wife, but the native women are singing in English, it has produced the 'Wesleyan Woman of the Year', look how beautiful the church building is with new chairs, and the service is full beyond capacity attracting all the churches in this district... This can only be the Lord's doing," he further declared.

After church, at our village house, I would have a discussion with my wife, Rose (a Rwandan-British whom I married in the UK and who obviously did not know the depth of the preacher's words), and I gave her a background of how 'Mabanta has come a long way out.'

Chapter Three

How Would The World Have Been Without The Church?

One would hardly imagine how our world would have looked like without the Church. And here, I'm not talking about denominations or sects, but the universal Church, the original idea of Church for which Jesus Christ came to this world.

If I would want to imagine, chaos would have been the order of the day without the Church. Even with its existence, there's still chaos. Without it, there would be doom. Even with it, we have witnessed two world wars. Without it, there would be incessant world wars.

The coming of Jesus Christ to the world – an indisputable fact, historians and atheists even attest to – changed the world, changed the course of history for the better. If not, it would be unthinkable that the same Rome under whose powers Pontius Pilate judged and allowed that Christ be crucified, would be the same Rome that today claims to be the seat from where the good news of Jesus Christ is spread around the world.

There definitely would not have been a Muslim religion 600 years after Christ without the Church. History has it that 'Prophet Mohamed' had very early and useful contacts with Christians (one of whom was Waraka ibn Nawfal, a cousin of Mohamed's first wife Khadijah), obviously informing key parts of his message that was similar to the Gospel of Jesus Christ. Mohamed was an Arabian trader who frequently travelled the Syrian trade routes with his uncle Abu Talib and eventually had an encounter with both Judaism and Christianity – not least via the mythical one-night journey to Jerusalem (towards which Muslims used to turn in prayer until it was later changed to Mecca). It is worthy and interesting to note that one of Mohamed's thirteen wives, Safiyya, was Jewish. And perhaps more interesting was what he reportedly told the woman to use as a reply to her Arab co-wives who teased her about her Jewish origins: she should tell them: "Aaron is my father, Moses my uncle, and Mohamed my husband."

It must be stated, however, that most of the large Jewish communities resident at Medina then were opposed to Mohamed for religious and political reasons: they never accepted he was a prophet, as they were "unwilling to admit that a non-Jew could be a prophet"; they disputed his inclusion of Jesus as a prophet (whom they totally rejected), in like manner as Lot (whom they never recognised as a prophet), and Moses (a wholly Jewish prophet); and contended that "some passages in the Qur'an contradicted their ancient scriptures".

But the Medina Jews' opposition was also perceived as political because Mohamed supplanted the Medina Arab leader Abd-Allah ibn Ubayy, whom they were supporting for the position of community arbitrator before it was given to the Muslim leader when he came to seek refuge from Mecca. There would, therefore, eventually be a frosty relationship between Mohamed and the Jews, some of whom he ultimately expelled from Medina. Mohamed accused these Jews of exaggerating the scriptures in their claim to be 'the chosen people of God', adding the enigmatic or 'totally false' charge that the Jews regarded the prophet Ezra as 'the Son of God' without him providing evidence to corroborate the claim. He further charged that the Jews – alongside Christians – had adulterated or altered the scriptures, hence the need for his religion. But all this was regarded as more of a knee-jerk reaction by Mohamed to the provocations he was getting from those he had already acknowledged to be 'the people of the Book' (Quran 29:46).

Being an Ishmaelite (meaning he could claim Abraham's fatherhood), Mohamed's original mission was to turn the idol-worshipping Arabian tribes to worshipping the One true God, who was already being worshipped by 'the people of the Book'. This begs the question of: why are modern-day Islamic fundamentalists like Al-Qaeda, ISIS and Boko Haram targeting western/Christian interests?

By the time of Mohamed, the Roman Empire had already completed its purge of European idol-worshipping when Christianity prevailed! Animists fit the description of 'infidels' or unbelievers. But how can Christians be unbelievers? Today, the Islamic militants' argument is that the West has lost its Christian values to socialite lifestyles. But then I had a rude shock when, accompanying President Ernest Bai Koroma as his Press Secretary to the Egyptian seaside resort of Sharm-Al-Shek, I discovered that sheikhs and other Muslims from around the Arab world would go there to have the good life: dressed in complete Islamic regalia during the day; in jeans and t-shirts at night!

The Israeli/Palestinian conflict or the Arab question is actually more of a politico-geographical struggle than a religious one – which could be the reason why the government of the seat of Islam, Saudi Arabia, Mohamed's birthplace, is a strong ally of the Americans against Islamic militants.

Back to Mohamed's mission history...

By virtue of the Ishmaelites' sour history of their great-great-great grandmother Hagar (the handmaid) being sent away by Abraham, Mohamed knew his people would not accept the biblical storyline or claim God's blessings based on the inheritance of Isaac – the 'child of promise' belatedly born by Sarah to the patriarch at old age. Mohamed, therefore, had to reconnect his people to the blessings through a biological genealogy, apparently tracing it (and rightly so) to God's promise to Abraham when the latter enquired as to what would happen to Ishmael after the birth of Isaac: "And as for Ishmael, I have heard you; I will surely bless him; I will make him fruitful and will greatly increase in numbers. He will be the father of twelve rulers, and I will make him into a great nation." (Genesis 17:20) Mohamed showed acceptability of and respectability for Christianity when persecuted Muslims in Mecca sought refuge (the first 'hijra') in the Christian Kingdom of Ethiopia (then Abyssinia).

To me – and to many others – the Islamic description of Jesus as merely being 'a prophet' and not the Son of God in the Holy Trinity (though He's associated with miracles more than anybody else in the Koran), together with Muslim denial of His death and resurrection (though it believes in His virgin birth, ascension and second coming), could have been due to the influence of Mohamed's 'Jewish in-laws' who held similar views about Christ! The Koran acknowledged the Bible (Torah and Gospels) as having come from the one God, yet it goes ahead to deny the death – the public death on the cross – of Jesus Christ.

And then the logical question arises: 'What is that empty tomb at the 4th-century-built Church of the Holy Sepulchre (also known by its Greek name "Church of the Anastasis", meaning Church of the Resurrection) in Jerusalem that even the Jews/the Israeli government can no longer hide or deny, and is being visited by millions of people from around the world every year as the place where Jesus rose from the dead?' Or to ask a somewhat mundane contemporary question: 'Why did Hollywood star Mel Gibson's 2004 movie "The Passion of the Christ" (portraying the death and resurrection of Jesus) have such huge viewership in many parts of the Arab/Muslim world – with then-Palestinian leader Yasser Arafat calling it "moving and historical," while former Lebanese President Émile Lahoud praised it as "an objective production … that relied on the scriptures of the New Testament"'?

The Islamic narrative challenging the divinity and death of Jesus looks to me like a partly deliberate attempt to assuage the partial connection of the Jews to His killing! A school of thought would contend that, all Mohamed should have done was to have become a Christian like his wife's relative Waraka ibn Nawfal, translated the Bible into Arabic and told his people that the same salvation that was reserved for the Jews was now available to them, irrespective of biological genealogy! That was what happened in Britain, that was what happened in America, and that was what happened at Mabanta!

But then it happened that way, and now we have not just a religious controversy but an intractable war over the geography of Jerusalem. And it's still part of fulfilment of Scripture – with Mohamed claiming to have heard from no less an angel than Gabriel.

Indeed, God's ways and our ways are not the same! It would, therefore, still be logical to believe that Mohamed, an illiterate man, must have been inspired to start a revolution that would see the final destruction of the 360 idols being worshipped at the Kaaba (to become Islam's most sacred site), which the Arabs believed was built by Abraham for Ishmael!

Christian literature writer Anne Cooper in *Ishmael My Brother: A Christian Introduction to Islam* (1995, Tunbridge Wells) contends that perhaps the situation would have been different if the Bible were available in Mohamed's native language at the time, because he seemed "to have gained his knowledge from his acquaintance and association with a decadent form of Christianity… There was no translation of the Bible available in Arabic before AD 737, more than 100 years after his death". What a world of a difference it would have made if Mohamed had read (or heard) Ephesians 3:6 in Arabic: "This mystery is that through the gospel the Gentiles [Arabs and all] are heirs together with Israel, members together of one body, and sharers together in the promise in Christ Jesus." And this was written by Paul, who was at one time arguably 'the most Jewish of Jews'!

Fast-forward to today, through Islam, many people have come to know and accept Jesus Christ as 'God with us'! Many Arabs today proclaim Jesus as Lord; and I find a ready example in a Sierra Leonean evangelical pastor, Rev. Momodu Conteh, once a devout Muslim and trainee imam, who automatically became a Christian when, by his own testimony, Jesus Christ appeared to him on his prayer-mat in the month of Ramadan proclaiming Himself as 'the only Way'! His story is well publicised: https://www.youtube.com/watch?v=4vAxBD5L1CE.

And one of the pleasant surprises I would get during my Vatican visit was seeing an Arab priest reading one of the Bible texts in Arabic, in the presence of the Pope and the world watching! After all, on the day of Pentecost, when Christ's apostles started speaking in different tongues, some of those who heard their message were Arabs (Acts 2:11).

To back that up, one biblical Old Testament story that had always made me have a soft spot for the Ishmaelites (invariably or eventually Arabs/Muslims) was that of Joseph. The Israelite lad was going to be killed by his own brothers over jealousy for his dreams. If those Ishmaelite traders had not appeared on the scene with money to buy Joseph, I wonder what would have happened to him, or the rest of us – never mind they could have done it purely for profit.

God's ways are not our ways!

* * *

If Judaism had continued to exist without the coming of Jesus Christ, there would not have been any security for the Jews against continuous gentile antimony. The Jews have paid too much of a heavy price for continuing to believe they are the only 'favoured ones' or 'chosen people of God' in total disregard of the Christian proclamation of the fulfilment of Scripture in the coming of the Messiah (the Saviour of the whole world), who is Christ Jesus.

The Holocaust is the clearest contemporary example – though indeed throughout their history, Jews have faced persecution either for their faith or for their race or for their land. The Philistines. The terror of the Assyrians. The days of Babylon under Nebuchadnezzar. They were under Roman rule when Christ was born! The siege and destruction of Jerusalem and the Jewish Temple by the Romans a few decades after Christ. The Arab conquest of 631 AD. Even the Egyptian Mamluks had a sway in the area until the Ottoman Empire took control for four hundred years. Did I mention the slavery in Egypt before even becoming a nation?

Eventually, it would take a Christian Britain to conquer the Ottoman Turks in Palestine (Israel having been so named in

131 AD by Roman Emperor Hadrian) during the First World War. The British, thereafter, had a colonial mandate over the area. This was the first major step (though reluctantly from the British who did not want to antagonise the Arabs/Muslims, but definitely for the Americans who coerced the British Government to support the Zionist movement or else would withhold post-war recovery funds) to the re-establishment of the state of Israel in 1948.

And in 2018, it was a Christian America, Israel's closest ally, which was the first to officially recognise Jerusalem as the Jewish capital, and establishing its embassy there! By virtue of what the Jews saw during their exile or Diaspora days in Europe and America, and the intertwined relationship that has evolved therein with Israel, there's hardly any Jew alive who would totally reject (like the ancient Jewish leaders) the Gospel of Jesus Christ – a message originally taken from Jerusalem to these 'foreign' lands by His all-Jewish disciples! The Jews still generally hold on to their Judaism disputing the resurrection (but not the death) and divinity of Jesus Christ, while still awaiting the coming of the Messiah. But their continued survival is tied to America, the country with the highest number of Christians in the world, proclaiming a risen Christ!

Israeli Prime Minister Benjamin Netanyahu, apart from his 'Judeo-Christian heritage' Christmas message of 2017, could not have put it better when addressing evangelical Christians in Washington in July of the same year via video link: "When I say we have no greater friends than Christian supporters of Israel, I know you've always stood with us. You stand with us because you stand with yourselves because we represent that common heritage of freedom that goes back thousands of years. America has no better friend than Israel and Israel has no better friend than America. And Israel has no better friend in America than you."

The Jewish leader (the equivalent of King Herod Antipas who sanctioned Jesus' crucifixion) was speaking to people who believed in 'God the Father, Son, and Holy Spirit;' that is, Americans who believe Jesus is the Messiah, killed by the Jewish leaders of the time but He resurrected and ascended to heaven, and will come again to judge the world! Netanyahu's audience, Christians United for Israel, headed by tele-evangelist Jim Hagee (who would later be the pastor to pray during the formal installation of the American embassy in Jerusalem), would only believe more than ever before that the Lord is on their side!

The point here is that, no one can rationally deny that what we now call civilisation has its roots in the Church of Jesus Christ – western civilisation is a Christian creation. The western world has its foundation and draws its democratic values from the gospels – by virtue of the fact that Christianity ultimately became the state religion of the former Roman Empire, of which Britain was a province. Indian writer Vishal Mangalwadi's *The Book That Made Your World: How the Bible Created the Soul of Western Civilization* could not have put it any better: "In the wake of the Reformation, it was the Bible that reorganized Europe as modern nation-states. Developing vernaculars through Bible translation was only the first step towards linguistic nation-states. The Bible also provided the theological justification for fighting to build independent nation-states...The Bible created the modern world of science and learning because it gave us the Creator's vision of what reality is all about. That is what made the modern West a reading and thinking civilization."

That God is one, that He is our Creator, that all human beings are descendants of Adam and Eve, and that Abraham is the 'father of all nations,' is acknowledged in all the major religions – which all blow away the theory of evolution.

The Genesis story of Adam and Eve is certainly still the most appealing justification for our existence. We exist because we were created or our forbears were created, and we have gone ahead to fill the earth with our kind through centuries of procreation, of movement, of mass migration, of inter-marriages and of multiple races; thereby getting all types of colorations in the process.

Yet, though we all seem to accept that we are from the same ancestry, we are also confounded as to why blacks are blacks, whites are whites, coloureds are coloureds etc etc. So through our natural instincts, we have tried to associate one particular race with a particular characteristic. Yet it has been proven – like in British writer William Golding's *Lord of the Flies* – that humanity, when not civilised, is basically savage. Irrespective of race!

Therefore, the coming of Jesus Christ sealed our humanity. Perhaps there are no sweeter words in all creation than, "For God so loved the world that He Gave His only begotten Son that whosoever believes in Him shall not perish but have everlasting life." (John 3:16) Had the Jews accepted Him as their long-expected 'Messiah', we would have had a different course of history altogether. If Jesus had also been born in any European or Western nation, it would have also been a different scenario. If He were born in Africa, I can't begin to imagine what would have happened – they certainly might have followed the path of Herod the Great by trying to kill Him at birth. But God in His infinite wisdom confounded the world by allowing the greatest 'Man' who ever traversed our world not only to be born in a small Middle Eastern nation but, in fact, to descend from Nazareth where nothing good was expected to come from by the Jews – worst of all born in a manger in the small town of Bethlehem!!! The ways of God are not our ways!!

Obviously, there is no dispute as to whether Jesus Christ came to earth or not. His message, passed on to 12 (well, 11 as Judas fell on the wayside) hapless disciples, with the great commission to reach out to all peoples, has been going round the world – reaching the 'anti-foreign fortress' of my village, Mabanta, through the American Wesleyan Mission which has today been nativised to the Wesleyan Church of Sierra Leone.

* * *

One thing that must also be made absolutely clear is that the Church is not perfect – far from being perfect. Throughout the ages, beginning from Judas (one of Christ's disciples) to today when priests, pastors, reverends, bishops, cardinals and popes have all proven fallible, the Church has shown that we cannot attain perfection on earth. Though the Catholic Church adopted at the 1868 First Vatican Council the dogma of papal infallibility (that the Pope cannot err in his duties), it is worth noting that even Peter himself (the first Pope) was depicted to be fallible when he denied Christ!

Thankfully and graciously, Pope Francis declared in an interview with leftist German newspaper *Die Zeit* on 9 March 2017 that "I am a sinner and am fallible", while talking about 'moments of emptiness' in his life, reproduced by the National Catholic Register online. And then the Pope went on to say: "[Jesus] is the Lord of sinners, not the righteous; also, yes, of the righteous, but He loves you more as sinners. And…no, the crisis is to increase our faith. It [faith] cannot grow without the crisis…and life puts you to the test. Faith is a gift…Faith is not a purchase."

What lovely words from the pontiff! There's no more a need for '95 theses…'

* * *

Leading American evangelical pastors with millions of followers have been found to cheat on their wives for gay men – while they had publicly been anti-gay activists! And the list is long. It is a serious issue that has ignited a lot of debates – both inside and outside the Church.

And then you come to Sierra Leone and find the more bizarre: you hear of a church where the pastors exchange or interchange their wives with no qualms among them, and justifying it with a 'vision'... What! The child sex abuse scandal rocking the Roman Catholic Church has got some rivalry here... Members of the Mormon Church (permitted to marry more than one wife) can also justify themselves... Whenever he hears such stories, my maternal Muslim uncle, Mohamed Tarawalie, who is the village imam of Mabanta, would provoke my Christian aunt Hawa (a new convert from Islam) – both of whom are living in the same family house... I, in turn, will pull his legs with incontrovertible theology when he comes to visit me in the evening, while sitting on my verandah. He would change the topic with laughter, not before saying something nice about 'the people of the Book'...

For such prominent scandals, you want to hate the Church – how many more erring priests are out there leading the flock astray? But then forgiveness comes in, as the Bible teaches you – why or for whom did Christ die, if not for this? Love takes over... You allow the Holy Spirit to take over... We on our own cannot save ourselves... Christ raised the bar so high that you would think it is impossible for a camel to go through the eye of a needle: whoever looks at a woman to lust after her has already committed adultery in his heart. A friend retorted: 'You would have to stop watching television and using WhatsApp.'

Canadian-born America-based Reformed Evangelical theologian and professor of the New Testament, Dr. D. A. Carson, in his 'daily companion' book *For The Love Of God* (1998, Crossway Books/Good News Publishers) put it this way in his September 29 entry: "Even gifted and morally upright believers commonly manifest tragic flaws... But most of the best in Scripture betray flaws of one sort or another – Abraham, Moses, Peter, Thomas, and (not least) David..." He, therefore, contended that the reality must be faced: "Even the finest of our Christian leaders commonly display faults that their closest peers and friends can spot (whether or not the leaders themselves can see them!). This should not surprise us. In this fallen world, it is the way things are, the way things were when the Bible was written." And then he proffered the solution: "We should therefore not be disillusioned when leaders prove flawed. We should support them wherever we can, seek to correct the faults where possible, and leave the rest to God – all the while recognizing the terrible potential for failures and faults in our own lives."

The solution, therefore, is to pray continually to God to 'deliver us from evil' and to 'forgive us our trespasses as we forgive those who trespass against us'...

* * *

And you see charismatic pastors in Africa living the affluent life (with some owning aircrafts) while their followers who bring the offerings and tithes continue to live in abject poverty. When you hear about the wealth of tele-evangelists, you start to wonder why much more has not been done to alleviate poverty and fight disease in the world. Don't they know the story of Jesus and the rich young ruler when the Master told this self-righteous braggart to 'Go sell all you have and give to the poor, and then come and follow Me'? But then I think of myself: there are many poor people around me, have I also done enough? The Church can do more. Does it only have to take the Irish-Scottish musical duo Bob Geldolf and Midge Ure with their Band Aid to prick the conscience of the world with 'Do they know it's Christmas?' Or does it have to take America's United Support of Artists (USA) for Africa with their 'We are the world' to wake us from slumber and then go back to sleep? The preaching is good… But then Jesus fed the five thousand!

The Church is not perfect. We are not perfect.

My father, Rev. John Sheka Tarawalie, who has been a pastor for over four decades and still preaching on the local community radio, is not perfect: one of his usual congregational prayers being, "Lord, if we were perfect, we would not be gathering here today…Thank you for dying for us on the cross…" I can't be perfect… I have those 'journalist' moments… We all have to pursue perfection until it is attained in Heaven.

Invariably, we are still the descendants of Adam, a fallen race, only saved by grace through faith in Jesus Christ as represented by the Church. He paid the ultimate sacrifice on the cross so that the blood of lambs and goats is no longer required for the continual remission of sins until 'the perishable becomes imperishable and the mortal puts on immortality'. It is befitting to quote the King James (British monarch) Bible in its 17th century English: "Know ye not that they which run in a race run all, but one receiveth the prize? So run, that ye may obtain. And every man that striveth for the mastery is temperate in all things. Now they *do it* to obtain a corruptible crown; but we an incorruptible." (1 Corinthians 9:24-25)

The beautiful thing, to me, is that Christians, Jews, and Muslims are all today looking forward, in varied ways though, to the coming (again) of the Messiah – Christ!

Chapter Four

From The Apostles' Christianity To Catholicism

A somehow seemingly little and ineffectual event in Bethlehem of Judea in the first century caused my meeting with Pope Francis in the twenty-first century. What or rather who would have connected us, if not Christ? How would a man from Mabanta have met with the Pope?

The birth of Jesus did not come with pomp. In fact, He was born under Roman rule. Israel, which a few centuries before was God's chosen nation (led by Moses through miraculous events from slavery in Egypt and took over 'the promised land') had been subjugated by a people 'who did not know God'. The tables had turned: the Israelites (Jews), who were once admired and feared around the gentile world, had been abandoned and captured and subjected to foreign rule.

If the world status quo continued unchanged, then it would forever be a cycle of conquerors and conquered – a survival-of-the-fittest jungle life – in which the strongest could overcome the wisest, just as it was through the brawn that Cain slew Abel's brains. The world needed liberation, so that wisdom would reign.

The only hope for the Jews, and indeed for the world, was the coming of the Messiah – the Christ!! He came! But not really the way the world expected. Not the way the Jews expected. The Jewish regent King Herod the Great wanted to kill the new-born babe, having learnt He was 'another king.'

Jesus started His ministry also seemingly ineffectually, choosing a most unlikely assorted group of ordinary men as His disciples. To the chagrin of the Jews, His message challenged the 'hypocrisy' of Judaism instead of the Roman establishment. Accompanied by miracles never yet seen before (like raising the dead, making the blind see, the dumb talk, the lame walk), Jesus turned Jewish tradition on its head and presented a message of direct access to God by ordinary folks. He took a radical departure to liberate the souls of men:

> *"The teachers of the law and the Pharisees sit in Moses' seat. So you must be careful to do everything they tell you... Everything they do is done for people to see: They make their phylacteries wide and the tassels on their garments long; they love the place of honour at banquets and the most important seats in the synagogues; they love to be greeted with respect in the marketplaces and to be called 'Rabbi' by others. But you are not to be called 'Rabbi,' for you have one Teacher, and you are all brothers. And do not call anyone on earth 'father,' for you have one Father, and He is in heaven. Nor are you to be called teachers, for you have one Teacher, the Messiah. The greatest among you will be your servant. For those who exalt themselves will be humbled, and those who humble themselves will be exalted. Woe to*

you, teachers of the law and Pharisees, you hypocrites! You shut the door of the kingdom of heaven in people's faces. You yourselves do not enter, nor will you let those enter who are trying to..." (Excerpts from Matthew 23)

The Jewish authorities obviously hated this and therefore plotted against Him. He was despised, rejected, and killed – hung on a cross on the spurious charge of 'blasphemy' or claiming to be 'king' (a treasonable crime), which was why the Latin initials 'INRI' were placed above His head (meaning Iesus Nazarenvs Rex Ivdaeorvm – Jesus of Nazareth, King of the Jews). But that was how it should be – according to prophesy. And then He rose again and ascended to Heaven – according to Scripture.

The message of love He left with His mostly fishermen disciples (consecrated on the day of Pentecost) has been the most powerful non-violent revolutionary story ever recounted to humanity. He had confounded Jewish law experts when He compressed the innumerable Mosaic laws and commandments into two: "Love the Lord your God with all your heart and with all your soul and with all your mind... and... Love your neighbour as yourself. All the Law and the Prophets depend on these two commandments." (Matthew 22:37-40)

Consequently, Christ's coming into the world empowered the gentiles as much as the Jews – in the affirmation that 'the God of Abraham, Isaac and Jacob' is the one God, and He has become the God of the rest of the world. Jesus came to open the life-gate that all might go in! This was the message that turned the world order around – of the nativity and divinity of Jesus Christ who lived a poorly life, while He owned everything, so that whoever truly believed would be called a child of God.

The message moved from being carried about by ordinary men and women to a colossus of a religious terrestrial authority as encapsulated in the creation of the Roman Catholic Church under the Roman Empire (which at its peak was an area of approximately 5.7 million sq. km with around 120 million people within its borders). With the belief that revelation ended with the death of the apostles, the authority of the Church was transferred or transmitted to their successors, the college of Bishops, with the Pope seen as the direct successor to St. Peter, Christ's appointed foremost disciple.

Rome would surely have been the last place to be the centre for anything that would promote the message of Jesus Christ, the Galilean who was handed over to the Jews (instigated by the Jewish leaders – Pharisees and Sadducees) for execution by the Roman Emperor Tiberius Caesar through Pontius Pilate, then Roman Governor of Jerusalem. Tiberius, though, was reported to have had some liking for Jesus after reading about His activities from the correspondences sent by Pilate – hence the 'washing of hands' from guilt, and giving a much-needed foothold to early Christianity in the empire, especially in Rome. Emperor Tiberius Caesar was so impressed about Jesus (partly because of His landmark declaration to the Jewish authorities to "Render unto Caesar the things that are Caesar's, and to God the things that are God's") that the emperor reportedly suggested that He should be deified among the Roman pantheon – though it did not receive the approval of the Roman senate! It was too late to prevent the death of Christ but it was early rain of favour for the Church to grow. Up to a point…

State-sanctioned persecution of Christians would effectively start under Emperor Nero, who blamed 'the sect' for the great fire of Rome in AD 64 but was allegedly done on the instruction of the emperor himself to make room for him to build a palace, the famous Domus Aurea. It was only after the fire went out of hands and could not be contained for six days that he found scapegoats in the already 'unpopular' Christians, because 'the exclusive sovereignty of Christ clashed with Caesar's claims to his own exclusive sovereignty.'

Christians were accused of disloyalty and treason for refusing to participate in feast days or processions or sacrifices to the Roman pagan gods, while worshiping 'a convicted criminal.' They were accused of incest for meeting at night in private homes, referring to themselves as 'brothers and sisters'; and of cannibalism for eating and drinking 'the blood and body' of Christ. From thence, there would be a systematic persecution of Christians. These persecutions included torching houses, burning Bibles, imprisonment, beheading, stoning to death, and being sent into the public arena to be devoured by lions 'for the amusement of the public.' The apostles Peter and Paul were said to have been among the martyrs. The Roman military conquest to suppress a Jewish rebellion in Israel in 66 AD could have partly been an extension of Nero's anger. His sudden death (he reportedly committed suicide) in 68 AD saw his military commander Vespasian being declared his successor, while the former's son, Titus, expedited the Jesus-predicted physical destruction of Jerusalem and its temple in AD 70 (just 40 years after Christ's death and resurrection). Most historians hold the view that virtually no Christian was killed during the pogrom, having been warned and obeyed to move out of the city before the Roman slaughter – Christian historians say there was some kind of rapture!

Though since Nero there were intermittent persecutions from place to place depending on how the locals or the provincial governors perceived Christians (with some influential softening of persecutions having occurred due to the love affair between a Christian girl Marcia and Emperor Commodus – 182 to 193 AD), the first empire-wide horror was to occur under Emperor Decius who in 250 AD issued an edict for everyone in the empire (except Jews, who were seen as practising the religion of their ancestors and were paying taxes) to perform sacrifices to the Roman gods in the presence of, certified and signed by a Roman magistrate. Yet, the most notable official persecution throughout the empire was initiated by Emperor Diocletan (284-305 AD), implementing what came to be known as 'the Great Persecution.'

Left to choose between their lives and their faith, large numbers of Christians who refused to follow the emperor's edict lost their lives. These included prominent leaders like Pope Fabian (Bishop of Rome), Babylas of Antioch, and Alexander of Jerusalem. Cyprian, Bishop of Carthage, went into hiding during Decius' reign but boldly faced and accepted martyrdom under his successor Emperor Valerian, who also executed Sixtus II (Fabian's successor as Bishop of Rome) together with his seven deacons.

Despite the persecutions, and perhaps because of them, Christianity thrived in the Roman Empire, as more converts were won to the outlawed religion – devoted Christians saw martyrdom as a short route to heaven. There was the ironically humorous tale about a Roman official who had killed so many Christians that, when others turned up professing to be Christians, he drove them away, telling them to go hang themselves instead.

The great turning point (usually referred to as the Triumph of the Church or The Peace of the Church) came when Emperor Constantine ascended the throne – AD 306 to 337. He jointly, with Licinius (emperor of the eastern empire) and Galerius (who was initially a persecution protagonist), signed the edict of toleration in 311 granting Christians the freedom to practise their religion in the empire. Constantine went a step further when two years later he, with Licinius, signed the edict of Milan, adding to religious freedom the return of all confiscated Church property. Though it stopped short of making Christianity the empire religion, it certainly had cleared the way for the Gospel to expand. And Constantine's own personal efforts spoke louder: he lavished the Church with landed property and money, exempted priests from paying taxes, appointed Christians to strategic state positions, built basilicas (including the Old St. Peter's Basilica) and distributed Bibles to the Church. Perhaps more notably, Constantine was credited to have built the Church of the Holy Sepulchre on the twin sites of Christ's crucifixion at Golgotha and His burial/resurrection in Jerusalem. Scholars justifying Constantine's Christianity postulate a few stories: that his mother Helena was a Christian and had converted him in his youth (while some claim he had himself asked her to convert to Christianity); and, perhaps the more decisive one, that during the Battle of the Milvian Bridge (after which he claimed the emperorship) he saw a clear sign from the heavens telling him to adopt the cross against his enemies, to which he commanded his troops to adorn 'the Christian sign' and they emerged victorious. Constantine's unequivocal intertwining of Church and state was demonstrated when he summoned and presided over the Nicaea Council of Church leaders in 325 AD, effectively the first ecumenical council (after the apostles' Council of Jerusalem of 50 AD which decided that non-Jews did not have to follow the Mosaic Law to be Christians) in which the Nicene apostolic creed or declaration of faith in the Trinity was adopted. He is known in Christendom as the 'first Christian Emperor' – having been baptised just before his death.

Since Constantine's demise in 337, the Church grew steadily unperturbed through a string of successive emperors until Julian (361-363). However, already knowing how the Christians could be resilient in persecution, Julian's edicts were more aimed at undermining and incapacitating them by taking away privileges from the Church and proclaiming paganism as the state religion – making him to go down in Church history as 'the last non-Christian ruler' of the Roman Empire.

Julian's successor, Jovian (brought up as a Christian), upon ascending the throne in 363, immediately revoked all the anti-Christian edicts and proscribed paganism, making it treasonable for anyone worshipping ancestral spirits. However, it would have to be Emperor Theodosius (379-392) – jointly with his eastern counterpart Gratian – to officially declare Christianity the state religion of the Roman Empire in the Edict of Thessalonica (380 AD), regarding all others as foolish madmen. Theodosius would however be the last Roman Emperor to rule over both the eastern and western halves of the empire. It is worth quoting the historic edict in full:

> *"EMPERORS GRATIAN, VALENTINIAN AND THEODOSIUS AUGUSTI. EDICT TO THE PEOPLE OF CONSTANTINOPLE*
>
> *It is our desire that all the various nations which are subject to our Clemency and Moderation, should continue to profess that religion which was delivered to the Romans by the divine Apostle Peter, as it has been preserved by faithful tradition, and which is now professed by the Pontiff Damasus and by Peter, Bishop of Alexandria, a man of apostolic holiness. According to the apostolic teaching and the doctrine of the Gospel, let us believe in the one deity of the Father, the Son and the Holy Spirit, in equal majesty and in a holy Trinity. We authorize the followers of this law to assume the title of Catholic Christians; but as for the others, since, in our judgment they are foolish madmen, we decree that they shall be branded with the ignominious name of*

> *heretics, and shall not presume to give to their conventicles the name of churches. They will suffer in the first place the chastisement of the divine condemnation and in the second the punishment of our authority which in accordance with the will of Heaven we shall decide to inflict.*
>
> *GIVEN IN THESSALONICA ON THE THIRD DAY FROM THE CALENDS OF MARCH, DURING THE FIFTH CONSULATE OF GRATIAN AUGUSTUS AND FIRST OF THEODOSIUS AUGUSTUS"*

Slowly but surely, the Church became woven into the state in the Roman Empire: the coronation of the Emperor would in time have to be done by the Pope, with ordinary Romans being simultaneously submissive to the Pope and the Emperor. Eventually, after the fall of the original Roman Empire in the 5th century (with virtually no effect on the status quo of Christianity, as Christians were allowed to practise their religion freely by the new Byzantine rulers), papal authority rose again – perhaps more prominently – with a change in nomenclature to the 'Holy Roman Empire' as Pope Leo III crowned the conquering German king Charlemagne as Emperor of the Romans at the Old St Peter's Basilica in 800 AD! The Church subsequently became powerful enough to rule over Papal States and launch military-style Crusades (with disastrous consequences) against Muslims in 'the Holy Land' of Jerusalem and conquering other territories in the process.

Though the Vatican itself is reluctant to use the 'Roman' part of the title of the Catholic Church – perhaps due to the pejorative 'Romish' origin in the Protestant distinction during the Reformation – there couldn't have been a better way of relaying the message that the mustard seed Jesus of Nazareth planted in the empire has today become a mighty shrub with headquarters in Rome: indeed, re-echoing His own prophetic words, 'the stone that the builders rejected has become the head of the corner'. Effectively, the Popes became the unwitting rulers of an undisputed 'European theocracy' until the Reformation.

The Catholic Church has, through the ages, taken turns in suffering and tumbling (like in the East-West schism that delinked Constantinople from Rome, the Muslim surge, its ceding of most of its then-expansive political and territorial authority, and the great one-man '95-theses-coup' of the Reformation), but to all intents and purposes it has survived. This is clearly seen in its current intertwined 'church and state' status as the Vatican City State and the Holy See simultaneously, recognised under international law. Though it is currently the smallest independent state as per its politico-geographical jurisdiction (with an area of 44 hectares and about 1,000 inhabitants), it has weathered storms with its independent executive, legislative, and judicial functions!

Up until today, there at the Vatican City State (which was established as the final arrangement to reduce the territorial political authority of the Church to its barest minimum while virtually leaving its spiritual powers untouched through the 1929 Lateran Treaty signed between the Church and the Italian Risorgimento, led by Benito Mussolini), the Bishop of Rome is somewhat still convincingly claiming to be the head – or, more appropriately, first head – of Jesus Christ's universal Church. The Roman Catholic Church, with over 1.2 billion followers around the world, confers on the Pope the title of 'Vicar of Christ'. How the tables turned in time! The authority of the Roman-sentenced crucified-but-resurrected Christ has been invested in the successor of Apostle Peter, today sitting in Rome!

Empires have come and gone, but the Church remains. Even the Renaissance, the Age of Enlightenment, and two

World Wars could not decimate it. The message of the Christian Church (Catholic and Protestant) has gone round, or is going round, the world – in view of the fact that there are still countries mainly in the Arab world where Christianity is officially proscribed and defaulters can face the death penalty. And despite the apparent swelling numbers of Muslims today, and the 'sexual revolution' that has swept through the western world, it is a pipe-dream to think that the 'new empire' of Christendom built by the American-led West through the establishment of the United Nations (with headquarters in New York) would fall in the foreseeable future.

Though there is the nuclear brinkmanship with Iran and its 'surrogate Islamic militant organisations', or the tussle with Kim Jong Un over 'peace or no peace' in the Korean peninsula, or the seizure by Russia of the Crimea, or the US' rivalry with China around the world, or the Syrian/Lebanon question, or the killing of Palestinians protesting over the shifting of the Israeli capital to Jerusalem – none of these seemingly has the potential to lead to a third world war. There are now channels of peace-making. People of all nations, irrespective of their religion or politics, sit at table and talk – at the United Nations. It is, therefore, not too dangerous a world after all. And no matter what one says about Renaissance or Enlightenment or Modern Age, the Church or the Judeo-Christian tradition remains a powerful force in the countries that control the affairs of men. Of the five Permanent Members of the Security Council – USA, Britain, Russia, France and China – only the latter has Christianity as a minority religion (but the 67 million Christians there is a huge numerical and spiritual strength). The voice of the Church, alas the voice of the Pope, is well respected by the leaders of those countries.

America, the nation with the highest number of Christians (over two-thirds of a population of about 325 million), has politically leaned towards Protestantism – with recently-demised world-renown evangelical pastor, Billy Graham, having been an 'informal pope' for twelve successive American Presidents starting with Harry Truman in 1950. Today, evangelical Christians are giving the impression that they have never had their own President as in Donald Trump (as they stoutly supported him through the elections and even provided one of their own as Vice President in Mike Pence). Yet the Catholic Church in America is still very powerful. They are not in actual conflict with other Christians. Perhaps Pope Francis would not have preferred Trump as President (with the pontiff's assumed candidate Bernie Sanders not even winning the ticket for the Democratic Party, and the pre-election papal spite for those who wanted to build walls instead of bridges); but then Catholics have only ever produced one American President – John F. Kennedy; and he was assassinated! The Pope is unmistakably still very influential in the American society. The Catholics actually have the largest Christian denominational membership in the USA – even as they obviously murmured why evangelicals voted for Trump with all his 'sins' (not least his self-boasting about grabbing women), while the protestants would just point at the Cardinal Theodore McCarricks of this world in a 'look-at-who's-talking' style! President Trump, after his election, visited Pope Francis in May 2017 at the Vatican. The US President, exuding delight that it was "a great honour" to meet the Pope, further described the half-hour meeting as "great and fantastic", while the Pontiff called it "cordial".

Whether varied or labyrinthine, the mustard seed planted during the Roman Empire has become a shrub where birds from all over are building their nests. It would be argued that the disciples themselves could never have thought of the Church turning out to be a gigantic monolith of the nature and superstructure of the Roman Catholic Church. No ordinary human would have thought of it. Fisherman Peter would not have imagined himself or 'his successor' to be protected by Swiss guards, owning billions of dollars (some put it at between $10 and $15 billion) in terms of wealth and property, living in the most secured 'state' on earth, distinctively dressing like 'the owner' of the world.

Generally, therefore, the world is at peace with itself. And with the technological explosion aided by science and ICTs, never before has the future been brighter to make it a better place. Speaking to young people in London at a town-hall meeting while rapping up his presidency in 2016, former US President Barack Obama said: "You've never had better tools to make a difference. Reject pessimism, cynicism and know that progress is possible. Progress is not inevitable; it requires struggle, discipline and faith."

But Obama (the African-American who more or less was like America's own atonement for its 'sins' to the black race from slavery to the civil rights movement) sounded a note of caution: "Not to say your generation has had it easy, in a time of breathtaking change, from 9/11, 7/7 … and during an age of information and Twitter where there's a steady stream of bad news."

Therefore, we cannot forget that Armageddon is not only a movie! It could be in the distant future; but it is in the Bible too! Pope Francis – seen as one of the most charismatic pontiffs in history – could be praying and acting to delay it.

And God would listen to him – as per Jesus' declaration after Peter's great confession (about the Lord not being a mere prophet but 'the Christ, the Son of the living God'):

> *"Blessed art thou, Simon Bar-Jona. For flesh and blood hast not revealed this to thee, but my Father who is in heaven. And I say to thee, thou art Peter, and upon this rock I will*

> *build my church, and the powers of death [gates of hell] shall not prevail against it. I will give to thee the keys of the kingdom of heaven, and whatsoever thou shalt bind on earth shall be bound in heaven, and whatsoever thou shalt loose on earth shall be loosed in heaven."*

By human design, the Roman Catholic Church took upon itself mundane powers so much so that even its own members like John Calvin referred to the Pope as the 'Antichrist'. The breakaway Reformation dealt Catholicism a heavy blow, but the Roman Catholic Church never fell. It did a counter-Reformation at cleaning its house and it let go of the sale of indulgences in 1567. It is still standing strong and tall today – a great force to reckon with in the affairs of men globally. But its members have realised that it cannot survive all by itself and must now embrace 'the heretics' as being part of the Truth.

Pope Francis is the most symbolic embodiment of this reality – as he reaches out in a spirit of reconciliation to the Protestants, the Eastern Orthodox Church, the Anglican Church, and even to Muslims – creating a platform for dialogue. In a meeting with the leadership of the Lutheran Church of Germany at the Vatican in December 2017, Vatican News reported that Pope Francis welcomingly said, "Through prayer, we are able to see the painful divisions of past centuries in a new light, abandoning our prejudices, purifying our memories and looking to the future with confidence. Through prayer, we are called to recognize the gifts of our different traditions and receive them as our shared Christian heritage."

Chapter Five

From The Reformation To The Mabanta Church

The idea of giving the Church a hierarchical organisational structure was not a bad one at all. Any group of people needs to be shepherded, needs to be led. The Church needed leadership – needed to be led, needs to be led. To be at the top of the affairs of a Church whose membership was growing by leaps and bounds, there had to be authority and a structure.

In biblical times, the apostles had to summon a council in Jerusalem at around 50 AD to address issues of how the Church should be led through a structure. Paul (formerly Saul, who was not an original disciple but became an apostle after a personal encounter with the risen Christ) was accused by Judaic Christians (mainly Pharisees who had converted) of misleading Gentile converts in Antioch (the place where the followers of Jesus were first called Christians) into not abiding by the Law of Moses. The Jewish Christians were saying "Unless you are circumcised according to the custom of Moses, you cannot be saved." Cephas (Peter's other name, meaning 'rock') and James, the head of the Jerusalem church, as leaders, therefore convened a meeting of Church elders and decided that "we should not make it difficult for the Gentiles who are turning to God. Instead we should write to them, telling them to abstain from food polluted by idols, from sexual immorality, from the meat of strangled animals and from blood" (Acts15:19-20). This meeting, in Church history, is regarded as the first ecumenical council – the prototype of all other church meetings down the ages.

With the Church working to fulfil the 'Great Commission' of reaching out to the whole world, it obviously needed continued leadership or direction; and having a Catholic Church – in this sense, a universal Church under one authority –was the most appropriate way to easily convey the authenticity of the Gospel of Jesus Christ.

The Catholic Church, therefore, claimed direct genealogy to Christ Himself, to the message He left with the disciples, anchoring its authority to particularly the Apostle Simon Peter (martyred in Rome). This was why the public arena at the Vatican was called St. Peter's Square, and a church built on the Apostle's grave within the premises of the Vatican. It still claims today to be the 'one true church' – though in its present form, even within itself, it has varied doctrinal sects like Opus Dei, the Jesuits, Mendicant Orders, the enclosed Monastic Orders, and I dare say those who paved my way to visit the Vatican – Love Bridges!

Dignitaries, religious leaders, 'the faithful', tourists who continually flock the Vatican are told the story of how St. Peter's Basilica was the spot denoting where Christ's most trusted disciple (even the one who denied him thrice) was buried. Or re-buried? You would find out if you had time to ask more questions when being taken on a conducted tour.

Therefore, after a failed persecution to eliminate the Church both in Israel and in the Roman Empire as a whole, the establishment crumbled and succumbed to the most anti-violent revolution the world has ever experienced. Truth buried became truth exalted. It gave birth to the universal Church.

* * *

Down the ages, and via the Roman Empire, the Pope became very powerful and eventually superhuman over the affairs of the Church – and even of the state! He did not only have to perform the coronation of the emperor, he became as powerful as, or more powerful than, the latter – a clear example being Emperor Henry IV's humiliation of having to wait in the snow for three days in seeking penitence from Pope Gregory VII.

Papal power perhaps reached its zenith during the time of the Crusades, the first of which was launched by Pope Urban II in 1096. Taken as a campaign to liberate 'the holy land' from Muslims, the successive crusades (leaving trails of destruction and carnage in the process) only gave more powers to the Pontiff, with the acquiescence of the Emperor. A glimpse of such powers could only be seen in Pope Innocent III's 'Papal Decree on the choice of a German King, 1201':

> *"It is the business of the pope to look after the interests of the Roman empire, since the empire derives its origin and its final authority from the papacy; its origin, because it was originally transferred from Greece by and for the sake of the papacy…its final authority, because the emperor is raised to his position by the pope who blesses him, crowns him and invests him with the empire…"*

Writing in 1933, Laurence E. Browne, in his book *The Eclipse of Christianity in Asia* (The University Press), asserted that: "One cannot help regarding the Crusades as the greatest tragedy in the history of Christianity, and the greatest setback to the progress of Christ's kingdom on earth."

The Church had become a superstructure with 'unlimited powers'. Complacency or, rightly so, indulgence eventually crept in. The sale of indulgences, initiated by Pope Leo X in 1515 mainly to get money to rebuild St. Peter's Basilica in Rome, had taken over the preaching of the Gospel. On the back of other internal complaints about papal rule, the sale of indulgences or simply plenary certificates (expressly meaning, people's sins could be forgiven by merely paying a required sum) brought rumblings in the Church. Well-known Catholics like French theologian John Calvin, English Archbishop Thomas Cranmer and Scottish reformer John Knox were all opposed, even if somewhat less antagonistic, to the papal abuse of power.

But it would not be long for someone to be used by the Spirit for 'church revival'. Someone must stand up to the Pope to challenge the greatest authority there was. Someone must stand in the gap for the rest of mankind. The tipping point came when the Pope's salesman in Germany, Johann Tetzel, in 1517 declared that even the sins of the dead would be forgiven if relatives bought the indulgences. According to the book, *Die Reformation in Augenzeugenberichten*, edited by Helmar Junghans, Tetzel told his audience that:

> *"Don't you hear the voices of your dead parents and other relatives crying out, 'Have mercy on us, for we suffer great punishment and pain? From this, you could release us with a few alms . . . We have created you, fed you, cared for you and left you our temporal goods. Why do you treat us so cruelly*

and leave us to suffer in the flames, when it takes only a little to save us?'"

This led to the popular sixteenth-century maxim, "As soon as the coin in the coffer rings, the soul from purgatory springs."

Martin Luther, Professor of Theology and Roman Catholic monk, could bear it no more. He rose to the occasion. On October 31, 1517 he therefore pasted on the door of Wittenburg university cathedral a treatise he titled as the "Disputation on the Power and Efficacy of Indulgences", what has come to be famously known as 'the ninety-five theses'.

Luther did not hate the Catholic Church. He was a child of the Church, its creation. He just found it disagreeable and repugnant that the authority of the Pope was acting contrary to the Gospel. He therefore used a very humble and academic tone to question – not to accuse – papal power on indulgences. He courteously wrote a covering letter to the Archbishop of Mainz, doubting whether the Church was aware how the people were being misled. Luther's main point was that salvation would be attained by faith alone, and not through indulgences. It's worth quoting some of the theses (33 to 54):

- *Men must especially be on guard against those who say that the pope's pardons are that inestimable gift of God by which man is reconciled to him.*
- *For the graces of indulgences are concerned only with the penalties of sacramental satisfaction established by man.*
- *They who teach that contrition is not necessary on the part of those who intend to buy souls out of purgatory or to buy confessional privileges preach unchristian doctrine.*

- *Any truly repentant Christian has a right to full remission of penalty and guilt, even without indulgence letters.*
- *Any true Christian, whether living or dead, participates in all the blessings of Christ and the church; and this is granted him by God, even without indulgence letters.*
- *Nevertheless, papal remission and blessing are by no means to be disregarded, for they are, as I have said (Thesis 6), the proclamation of the divine remission.*
- *It is very difficult, even for the most learned theologians, at one and the same time to commend to the people the bounty of indulgences and the need of true contrition.*
- *A Christian who is truly contrite seeks and loves to pay penalties for his sins; the bounty of indulgences, however, relaxes penalties and causes men to hate them – at least it furnishes occasion for hating them.*
- *Papal indulgences must be preached with caution, lest people erroneously think that they are preferable to other good works of love.*
- *Christians are to be taught that the pope does not intend that the buying of indulgences should in any way be compared with works of mercy.*
- *Christians are to be taught that he who gives to the poor or lends to the needy does a better deed than he who buys indulgences.*
- *Because love grows by works of love, man thereby becomes better. Man does not, however, become better by means of indulgences but is merely freed from penalties.*
- *Christians are to be taught that he who sees a needy man and passes him by, yet gives his money for indulgences, does not buy papal indulgences but God's wrath.*

- *Christians are to be taught that, unless they have more than they need, they must reserve enough for their family needs and by no means squander it on indulgences.*
- *Christians are to be taught that the buying of indulgences is a matter of free choice, not commanded.*
- *Christians are to be taught that the pope, in granting indulgences, needs and thus desires their devout prayers more than their money.*
- *Christians are to be taught that papal indulgences are useful only if they do not put their trust in them, but very harmful if they lose their fear of God because of them.*
- *Christians are to be taught that if the pope knew the exactions of the indulgence preachers, he would rather that the basilica of St. Peter were burned to ashes than built up with the skin, flesh, and bones of his sheep.*
- *Christians are to be taught that the pope would and should wish to give of his own money, even though he had to sell the basilica of St. Peter, to many of those from whom certain hawkers of indulgences cajole money.*
- *It is vain to trust in salvation by indulgence letters, even though the indulgence commissary, or even the pope, were to offer his soul as security.*
- *They are the enemies of Christ and the pope who forbid altogether the preaching of the Word of God in some churches in order that indulgences may be preached in others.*
- *Injury is done to the Word of God when, in the same sermon, an equal or larger amount of time is devoted to indulgences than to the Word.*

This was the start of the Reformation that would change the face of the Catholic Church forever. Protestantism was born.

The papacy did not take kindly to Luther's stance – especially when 'some unknown persons' had printed the theses and circulated them all over Europe. People like Johann Tetzel wrote counter articles, but they only made Luther more famous. Efforts to get him to recant proved futile.

Luther stood up to defend himself in glowing terms when he was accosted for challenging the authority of the Pope. In refusing to recant before the Diet (assembly) of Worms, representing the authority of the 'Holy Roman Empire' in 1521, Luther stated thus:

> *"Since your most serene majesty and your high mightinesses require of me a simple, clear and direct answer, I will give one, and it is this: I cannot submit my faith either to the Pope or to the council, because it is clear as noonday that they have fallen into error and even into glaring inconsistency with themselves. If then I am not convinced by proof from Holy Scripture, or by cogent reasons, if I am not satisfied by the very text I have cited, and if my judgment is not in this way brought into subjection to God's Word, I neither can nor will retract anything, for it cannot be right for a Christian to speak against his country. I stand here and can say no more. God help me. Amen."*

This was an abomination in those days. Luther was described as "an obstinate heretic" in the Edict of Worms issued by the Roman Emperor – because, at that time, the Pope's power was regarded as inviolable, untouchable, and unquestionable. It was absolute. Emperor Charles V and his princes could not get Luther to recant. The time had come for a new twist in God's intervention in history.

A new day had dawned in the world, a new dawn in Christendom. The Protestant part of Christianity had emerged: the establishment of new churches or denominations outside of any authority of the Pope, with the Bible as the direct Word of God to man – to all men. This was how Luther subsequently expounded his core message of 'justification' in the Smalcald Articles:

> *"The first and chief article is this: Jesus Christ, our God and Lord, died for our sins and was raised again for our justification (Romans 3:24-25). He alone is the Lamb of God who takes away the sins of the world (John 1:29), and God has laid on Him the iniquity of us all (Isaiah 53:6). All have sinned and are justified freely, without their own works and merits, by His grace, through the redemption that is in Christ Jesus, in His blood (Romans 3:23–25). This is necessary to believe. This cannot be otherwise acquired or grasped by any work, law or merit. Therefore, it is clear and certain that this faith alone justifies us ... Nothing of this article can be yielded or surrendered, even though heaven and earth and everything else falls (Mark 13:31)."*

Martin Luther's writings, especially the 95 theses, were appealing to the sensibilities of men and women across Europe. He attracted lots of supporters and admirers, eventually leading to the formation of different churches. Today, humanity has lost count of the correct number of churches/denominations in existence – every now and again a new church is being born. Protestants split from the Catholics; and the Protestants have given birth to all kinds of denominations.

One early by-product of the Reformation would be the Church of England, as King Henry VIII renounced papal authority in 1534 to form an Anglican Communion. It would, in turn, give birth to the Methodist Church when Anglican priest John Wesley (and a few others, including his brother

Charles Wesley) in the 18th century introduced firebrand open-air preaching throughout England with a similar message as that of Martin Luther on justification by faith. Wesley's followers would soon after his death make a total break from the Anglican Church, and were initially known in England as the Wesleyan Methodist Church.

The Methodist Church thrived both in Britain and in the American colonies. In the course of the campaign against slavery, the American branch took faster strides in openly denouncing the trade. The zealous campaigners in America further splintered from the mainstream Methodist Church to eventually form the American Wesleyan Mission. After the abolition of slavery, and the subsequent introduction of British colonial rule in Sierra Leone, American Wesleyan missionaries were 'directed by the Spirit' to Sierra Leone's Northern Province, establishing a branch of the American Wesleyan Mission there.

This mission was subsequently localised and known today as the Wesleyan Church of Sierra Leone. It has a local church at Mabanta, my hometown, which largely owes its establishment to the work of my father as founding pastor with over 25 years of continuous labour until he retired. He had started work with a few believers (including his father, my grandfather, whose name I bear) worshipping under mango trees; he succeeded in eventually putting up an impressive edifice where two hundred worshippers (on average) attend every Sunday today.

Martin Luther's actions in the Roman Empire have yielded fruits in Mabanta.

The Gospel of Jesus Christ has meandered its way to us!

Chapter Six

Serra Lyoa

First Founded By Portuguese Explorers – Or Actually By Phoenicians 500 Years Before Christ? Israel's Lost Tribe(s) Found

The majority of the people of Sierra Leone are Muslims (varied sources put it at 75% to 78%). There is an unaccounted-for percentage of Sierra Leoneans who periodically practise what is referred to as traditional religion or are strong adherents to cultural practices – with a lot of syncretism with either Islam or Christianity. Only about 15% to 20% Sierra Leoneans are Christian. But there's no doubt that the minority religion has had greater influence and impact on Sierra Leone as a nation-state, dating back to her founding.

Sierra Leone, like all countries in the world, has always been part of God's creation and certainly within the grand plan of salvation. After all, Christ told His disciples to go and preach the Word to all nations (certainly including Sierra Leone), baptising them 'in the Name of the Father, the Son, and the Holy Spirit'.

When Martin Luther staged his 16th century pro-Gospel protest in the face of the power of the Pope, Sierra Leone was by then being ruled by native kings or chiefs of different tribal kingdoms or chiefdoms. Eventually – however remote the connection at the time – Luther's Reformation would have a direct effect on Sierra Leone.

During the reign of the native kings, there were what historians have referred to as 'pre-colonial contacts with outsiders' particularly with European explorers relating to trade (especially slave-trading, in which the naivety and ignorance of the African rulers were manipulated by the Europeans) and religion; but the single major event that brought Sierra Leone into the community of nations was the campaign for the abolition of the Transatlantic slave trade – and this event would not have taken place without the abolitionists who were, in effect, products of the Reformation.

The whole 'back-to-Africa' or 'Sierra Leone' project was predominantly seen from a biblical lens; and it was most appropriately captured by London-based freed slave Olaudah Equiano (sold into slavery as a child supposedly from Igboland, Nigeria, but who in his will left money for a school to be built in Sierra Leone). In his 1789-published autobiography, 'The Interesting Narrative of the Life of Olaudah Equiano,' he drew parallels between his people (Africans) and the Jews, both groups having had to go through slavery, having similarities in ritual practices and celebrations, and thereby concluding that there could have been some blood relationship between the two races. He even suggested that the Africans must have somehow been descendants of at least one of the lost tribes of Israel. Equiano, married to an English woman, could not be far from the truth.

African-American researcher Brandon Coleman (also known by his African name Yahshurun Obai Agyemang who traced his ancestry to the Temne people of Sierra Leone via DNA tests) in his booklet *The Hebraic Origins of the Temne: According to Biblical and Oral History* stated that, "According to oral traditions, the Temne are from the tribe of Yahudah/ Judah. They left Israel after the destruction of the Temple in Jerusalem in 70 C.E. They then went to Yemen/Ethiopia, to Mali/Western Sudan, then Futa Jallon/Guinea, and later Sierra Leone. What I found in the Bible was very interesting. There is a descendant of Judah with the name Timmannee [1 Chronicles 4:6]" – having already earlier stated that the Temne are also called "Timmannee/Temeni/Temani."

To me, one of the clearest links between the Temne and the Jews is the love for high-street trading. At different scales of course (the one richer, the other poorer), but the passion for monetary gain is not different – it is in the bloodline! On the streets of Freetown, young Temne traders would always be proud to say, wittingly or unwittingly, 'me nar Jew man' (I am a Jew) – meaning a shrewd businessman! A Shylock! Another clear connection between the Jews and the Temnes is male circumcision during childhood. Where would the latter have got this mandatory tradition?

In his sequel, '*The Temne Jews of Sierra Leone, West Africa: The Second Witness*,' Coleman included other tribes in the Jewish connection: "Since my last book, '*The Hebraic Origins of the Temne: According to Biblical and Oral History*,' YAHUAH has used my book in a mighty way. There are Temne people gradually waking up, and returning back to the Torah. Not just the Temnes, but the Limba, Mandingo, Mende, Kono, Krio, Fulas, and other tribes. They are all accepting the fact that they are really Israelites. I think the Torah (instruction) of YAHUAH will be a great way to unite all the tribes when we understand that we have a common ancestry. We all descend from the twelve tribes of Israel. The Temne are from the tribe of Judah and have connections linking them with King David, the great warrior king of Israel."

Isaac Land, in his essay 'On the Foundings of Sierra Leone 1787-1808' (electronically published in December 2013), put it this way: "As Adam Potkay has suggested, the *Interesting Narrative* [by Equiano] mirrors the structure of the Bible, beginning with the simple 'pastoral' peoples of Genesis, suffering under outrage and enslavement, and finally progressing to the forgiving spirit of the New Testament; foregoing the temptation of a bloody revenge for enslavement earns one the right to a New Jerusalem in Africa... The projected settlements in Palestine and West Africa would not be new Englands inscribed on a tabula rasa; rather, they were each a unique remedy for a land that had seen too much history."

Invariably, the evils of the slave trade had been too glaring and were pricking the consciences of some English 'Christian men', who started having qualms with the establishment. Among those men were the biblical scholar Granville Sharp (who started the cause by helping slaves fight legal battles against their masters, culminating to the famous 1772 Somerset judgement of 'any slave that sets foot in England is free') and British MP William Wilberforce, who vehemently condemned the trade and devoted all his adult life in fighting for its abolition – Sharp being the older campaigner.

Even before the formal abolition of the trade, Sharp and Wilberforce (the latter once dubbed 'the Prime Minister of Philanthropy') were already thinking ahead in terms of their compassion for, and mission to alleviate, the plights of abandoned blacks languishing on especially the streets of London, Liverpool, Bristol, and in the American colonies. Working with equally devoted colleagues like Henry Thornton and the Clarkson brothers (Thomas and John, the latter would eventually be the first Governor of the colony and would render a prayer that up until this day resonates with Sierra Leoneans) through what came to be known as the Sierra Leone Company, they therefore fought for the repatriation of the blacks to a chosen appropriate place in Africa. The first batch of the 'Black Poor' (with a considerable number of white wives and girlfriends) arrived in Sierra Leone in 1787, while the first batch of freed slaves from the American colonies, known as the Nova Scotians – having been first relocated to Nova Scotia by the British military in return for siding with Britain during the American war of Independence – arrived in Freetown in 1792.

To these activists, the abolition of the slave trade would not only be an act of compassion for the 'Black Poor' or the freed slaves but a biblical fulfilment and atonement for Britain's sins. Here is how Isaac Land explained it: "If Britain's destiny was to gather up Jewish exiles and bring about the Second Coming, then a parallel suggested itself: British vessels carrying liberated former slaves 'back' to West Africa offered a particularly neat reversal of the barbarities of the Middle Passage…" And then he asserted: "Helping the exiles return to their ancestral point of origin, now supposedly depopulated and unproductive as the result of ancient evils, would also accomplish – in each case – a fitting expiation for Europe's sins."

The Catholic Church was in full support of the slave trade – in fact, the trade was formally authorised by the same Emperor Charles V who excommunicated Martin Luther for his '95 theses.' Amazingly, the same year of 1517 that Luther wrote the theses was the same year that the Emperor authorised slavery! One would then ask whether the evil transaction would have been abolished (or at least at the particular time it was abolished) had there not been a revolution that caused people to think outside of the Vatican's dictates – Protestantism/the Reformation. Not forgetting that the industrial revolution (the invention of machines) was also a factor that contributed in the abolition efforts.

William Wilberforce's Protestant/Anglican devotion to 'real Christianity', with emphasis on Christ's redeeming work for all of humanity, caused him and others to set up a group of parliamentary evangelicals that came to be known as the 'Clapham Sect'. He once wrote in a journal entry that "God Almighty has set before me two great objects, the suppression of the Slave Trade and the Reformation of Manners" and that "So enormous, so dreadful, so irremediable did the [slave] trade's wickedness appear that my own mind was completely made up for abolition. Let the consequences be what they would: I from this time determined that I would never rest until I had effected its abolition."

Having worked with Granville Sharp and others in founding the 'Province of Freedom' (at one time called Granville Town), William Wilberforce became more fired up in Parliament. It's worth quoting a part of one of his speeches in the House of Commons in 1791:

> *"Let us not despair; it is a blessed cause, and success, ere long, will crown our exertions. Already we have gained one victory; we have obtained, for these poor creatures, the recognition of their human nature, which, for a while was most shamefully denied. This is the first fruits of our efforts; let us persevere and our triumph will be complete. Never, never will we desist till we have wiped away this scandal from the Christian name, released ourselves from the load of guilt, under which we at present labour, and extinguished every trace of this bloody traffic, of which our posterity, looking back to the history of these enlightened times, will scarce believe that it has been suffered to exist so long a disgrace and dishonour to this country."*

Their cause won the day when Britain, the then world leader (as America was a budding nation having gained Independence from the British Empire in 1776 but only recognised as such by the British via the Treaty of Paris in 1783), formally enacted the Abolition of the Slave Trade Act in 1807.

As expected, the Catholic Church only (or also) supported abolition after the British law was passed.

* * *

You have to believe this: Because God had pre-ordained it from the very beginning that Sierra Leone would be key to missionary activities, He therefore created a natural harbour in the country. Who else would create a natural harbour? Details of the Freetown harbour had been written since 1462 by arguably the earliest-known European visitor, Pedro da Cintra, a Portuguese quasi-missionary explorer who reportedly described his first visual impressions of the mountains of Freetown from the sea-view as 'Serra Lyoa', meaning 'Lion Mountains'. Sierra Leone's history books have all virtually given da Cintra the credit for founding and naming the country.

However, leading Sierra Leonean historian Prof. C. Magbaily Fyle, who at one time headed the Monuments and Relics Commission, has recently questioned whether da Cintra was the earliest discoverer. He says it is appropriate to only state that the 'Serra Lyoa' name came from 'Portuguese explorers' because "from all accounts, if there is any agreement, it is that we are only sure that the name 'Sierra Leone' comes from early Portuguese voyagers who first reached the shores of the Sierra Leone peninsula." He backs up his argument by stating that "The first Portuguese recorded as having visited the area was Álvaro Fernandes in 1446." Obviously Alvaro visited before da Cintra, but there must have been a strong reason for crediting the latter with the naming!

To me, however, the most astonishing part of my research on this subject is the discovery that the coastal area now forming part of Sierra Leone had been inhabited by natives and was visited by Phoenician/Carthaginian explorers about 500 years before the birth of Christ. The historic Hanno of Carthage, in his recorded voyage, passed the equator to reach Sierra Leone during the first half of the sixth century BCE. Margaret Synge recorded the events (with a map as evidence) in her *A Book of Discovery: The History of the World's Exploration, From the Earliest Times to the Finding of the South Pole* (1912). In some parts quoting directly from the still-existent Phoenician document called 'Hanno's *Periplus*' also known as the 'Coasting Survey of Hanno,' this was how she described Hanno's discovery of Sierra Leone: "...and thence coasted twelve days to the south and again five days to the south, which brought them to Sierra Leone – the Lion Mountain as it was called long years after by the Portuguese. Here Hanno and his party landed, but as night approached they saw flames issuing from the island and heard the sound of flutes and cymbals and drums and the noise of confused shouts. 'Great fear then came upon us; we sailed therefore quickly thence much terrified, and passing on for four days found at night a country full of fire'..."

However, due to centuries of controversial debates by scholars over Hanno's *Periplus,* notable British historian specialising on African history, P.E.H. Hair, in his *The 'Periplus of Hanno' in the History and Historiography of Black Africa* (1987, Cambridge University Press), cautioned on taking the account of Hanno as a veritable fact: "is it wholly fiction? Or, if fact, is it fact fictitiously extended and embellished? Or, a third possibility, is it fact dramatically and perhaps intentionally summarised?" Notwithstanding, Hair (the Cambridge/Oxford scholar who in the 1950s taught history at Fourah Bay College, University of Sierra Leone) conceded that, "the *Periplus* deserves the attention of the African historian". Why shouldn't it then be part of the history or historiography of Sierra Leone in schools – if only for the debate?

Sierra Leone's natural harbour's existence was also reported by the earliest mainstream (as opposed to explorers) missionary, Father Balthasar Barreira, a Portuguese Roman Catholic Jesuit priest who arrived in Sierra Leone in 1605 and made it a point of duty to preach to pagan tribes and baptise native kings. It must however be noted that, at this time, there was already a strong Muslim presence in the hinterland, with the coastal rainforest used as a refuge by people fleeing from 'jihad'. When Barreira ventured to Susu land, he described mission work in the country as "an uphill competition with Islam for the soul of Africa," as he recorded "a number of personal hostile encounters with Muslim clerics". But, contrary to the official position of the Catholic Church, Barreira was "staunchly opposed to the slave trade".

And then there was also the Sierra Leone connection to the 'Amazing Grace' story of John Newton, the slave dealer who was abandoned in the country in 1748 by his sea captain and was rescued by another English captain. Newton was thought to have encountered the Lord through a turbulent storm at sea that left him nearly dead on their way from Sierra Leone. He would later compose the world-famous hymn recounting his Sierra Leone experience: 'I once was lost, but now I'm found…' He eventually became an Anglican clergyman and joined forces with William Wilberforce (who as a schoolboy admired the firebrand preaching of the former) in the campaign to abolish slavery. There is a village near Freetown named after him – Newton.

There was also the 'latest' report by English naturalist Henry Smeathman who had just returned from Sierra Leone on a four-year (1771-1775) sponsored study of the country's 'natural history'. Smeathman, who reportedly married three Sierra Leonean women, would tell Sharp, Wilberforce and other abolitionists that Sierra Leone was the most suitable place for their 'back-to-Africa' project.

Through this combination of factors (historical and natural), Sierra Leone was first chosen as a 'Province of Freedom' by the abolitionists and then subsequently used by the British Government as a naval post to enforce the abolition of slavery, so that the Freetown natural harbour became the port where all slave ships caught in the high seas were brought to berth. As a result, it gave birth to a cosmopolitan country of peoples of all types of tribal backgrounds from the rest of West Africa and even beyond.

This prominent position and function of Sierra Leone in ending the slave trade apparently made it the most qualified candidate for the choice of a British colony in West Africa. Therefore, when Wilberforce could not continue to effectively and independently run the affairs of the Sierra Leone Company together with the Church Missionary Society, it was easy for Britain to declare Freetown a crown colony in 1808. The British Government was at first apparently reluctant to gain territories in Africa, partly owing to the wealth it was already deriving from its Indian colony. However, the evangelical Christian campaigners reminded British politicians of the debt they owed to Africa on account of the slave trade.

Retrospectively, from Britain's King Henry VIII's proclamation of himself as the head of the Church of

England delinking from the authority of the Vatican (which was more or less done to spite Pope Clement VII for not sanctioning Henry's proposed divorce of Queen Catherine, but apparently influenced by Martin Luther's Reformation), to the formation of 'the society for the propagation of the Gospel' by the Church of England, to the extraordinary fact that John Wesley (the 'patron saint' of the Wesleyan Church) wrote his last letter to William Wilberforce (the eventual protagonist for the founding of Freetown) a week before he passed away pleading with the younger man never to give up the fight against slavery, to the birth of the Clapham Sect, and to the records about the natural harbour of Freetown, the train had left the station for the light of the 'Word' that was once an exclusive monopoly of the Pope to reach a once-dark Sierra Leone, which would eventually go to every corner, including the anti-change monolithic village of Mabanta, my hometown.

I would not therefore end this chapter without a part of John Wesley's historic letter to William Wilberforce on the fight against the slave trade:

"Balam, February 24, 1791

Dear Sir:

Unless the divine power has raised you as to be as Athanasius contra mundum, I see not how you can go through your glorious enterprise in opposing that execrable villainy which is the scandal of religion, of England, and of human nature. Unless God has raised you up for this very thing, you will be worn out by the opposition of men and devils. But if God be for you, who can be against you? Are all of them together stronger than God? O be not weary of well doing! Go on, in the name of God and in the power of his might, till even American

> *slavery (the vilest that ever saw the sun) shall vanish away before it.* "

There is a strategic hilly village in Freetown named after Wilberforce, and the country's most reputable military barracks is located there! A key street in central Freetown also bears his name!

Chapter Seven

Britain's 'Athens Of West Africa'

The American Wesleyan Mission In Search Of The 'Country People' Of Northern Sierra Leone

It would be very difficult to imagine that the Gospel of Jesus Christ would have reached the whole world if the Roman Catholic Church had remained as it was before Martin Luther's 95 theses. There was liturgical complacency, with most priests concentrating on the money accrued from the sale of indulgences instead of carrying out 'the Great Commission'.

The Reformation re-ignited and re-energised evangelism with the emergence of several churches or denominations. One such was the Wesleyan Church, which was actually founded as a breakaway advocacy group against the slave trade from within the Methodist Church. The Wesleyan Mission made the decision of having Sierra Leone as the first missionary outpost in Africa, with a focus on evangelising the people in the hinterland, particularly Bombali district in the North. There could have been varied factors that influenced that decision, but it would be summed up as an instruction by the Holy Spirit. This was practically supported by the fact that under British colonial rule, the Western Area and the South of Sierra Leone had been largely evangelised by the Church Missionary Society and other early denominations. Sierra Leone became a trailblazer in the sub-continent. The first university in sub-Saharan Africa, Fourah Bay College, was founded in Freetown and trained the first corps of missionaries, teachers, administrators and other professionals in Anglophone West Africa. This earned it the epithet of 'the Athens of West Africa' – in line with what the Greek City was in Europe. *The History of Christianity: A Lion Handbook* (Lion Publishing, 1977) described early Freetown in glowing terms: "We have seen how [the] 'Clapham Sect' enterprise founded the Sierra Leone colony... It was from these that the first mass movement towards Christianity in modern missionary history took place. Sierra Leone became a self-consciously Christian community, and a literate one... Over the next half century, the tiny Christian population of Sierra Leone produced dozens of ministers, missionaries, catechists and agents for the rest of West Africa, and particularly the Niger territories... The Sierra Leonean was often regarded as a 'black European' – in dress, speech and customs."

Though the Catholic Church was the first to 'open a mission' in Sierra Leone before colonialism, it had closed down following the deaths of some of its missionaries (the last being Fr Manuel Álvares who died and was buried in an unknown grave in the country around 1616/17) and would not resurface until over a hundred years later.

Other parts of the hinterland needed the light too, the Wesleyans believed!

Indeed the Wesleyan Mission's decision was influenced by a Freetown-educated Creole man, John Augustus Abayomi-Cole. He went to America through the Evangelical United Brethren Church, but he eventually joined and was ordained as a clergyman of the American Wesleyan Methodist Church. He was invited to the 1887 Wesleyan General Conference, where he seized the opportunity to plead with the Church to send missionaries to Sierra Leone. This led to the despatch of the first small batch of missionaries, led by Rev. Henry Johnston, in 1889 – making Sierra Leone the first mission field abroad for the Wesleyan Church.

In fulfilment of their quest to reach the unreached, Wesleyan missionaries sailed from America to Sierra Leone, not settling in Freetown but went straight to the north. Apparently, their British counterparts, the Wesleyan Missionary Society (Methodist), were already in Freetown since 1811. It therefore made sense for the new arrivals to find a Gospel-virgin area. They specifically went to Gbanti chiefdom, originally settling at a small village called Kunsho (where the paramount chief resided then). It was this Kunsho seed-planting mission – which would initially have a tragic twist – that grew and spread the gospel to neighbouring villages, including Mabanta, the home of my forefathers.

***

But way before that, in the mid to late 18th century, an unassuming Anglican evangelical called John Wesley had impressed and influenced the global Christian community through his love for Christ and reflecting that love through his love for ordinary people. As a priest in the Church of England (a breakaway denomination from the Pope's Catholic Church), Wesley was not satisfied with the solemnity and coldness that had engulfed the 'British' Church, as it became a social gathering for the middle class with too many liturgical prescriptions. Dilating on Wesley's 24 May 1738 'evangelical conversion' during a service in a London suburb (Aldersgate), author Daniel L. Burnett in his book *In the Shadow of Aldersgate: An Introduction to the Heritage and Faith of the Wesleyan Tradition,* stated: "The significance of [John] Wesley's Aldersgate Experience is monumental ... Without it the names of Wesley and Methodism would likely be nothing more than obscure footnotes in the pages of church history.... Prior to Aldersgate, Wesley was already converted in the 'Catholic' sense of having turned from the world to God. After Aldersgate, he was converted in the 'Protestant' sense of experiencing saving faith."

Just about this time, Britain was in a moral morass. Dr Diane Severance, giving a background of the then status quo in her article, 'Evangelical Revival In England', stated that:

> *"England, at the beginning of the eighteenth century, was in a moral quagmire and a spiritual cesspool. Thomas Carlyle described the country's condition as 'Stomach well alive, soul extinct.' Deism was rampant, and a bland, philosophical morality was standard fare in the churches. Sir William Blackstone visited the church of every major clergyman in London, but 'did not hear a single discourse which had more Christianity in it than the writings of Cicero.' In most sermons he heard, it would have been impossible to tell just from listening whether the preacher was a follower of Confucius, Mohammed, or Christ!*
>
> *Morally, the country was becoming increasingly decadent. Drunkenness was rampant; gambling was so extensive that one historian described England as 'one vast casino.' Newborns were exposed in the streets; 97% of the*

> *infant poor in the workhouses died as children. Bear baiting and cock fighting were accepted sports, and tickets were sold to public executions as to a theater. The slave trade brought material gain to many while further degrading their souls. Bishop Berkeley wrote that morality and religion in Britain had collapsed 'to a degree that was never known in any Christian country'."*

The John Wesley-inspired revival, cutting across denominations, would save the day for Britain; as Wesley was credited for, in the words of then-head of the Church of England Archbishop Randall Davidson in 1928, having "practically changed the outlook and even the character of the English nation."

Wesley emphasised confidence in the Bible, preaching 'repentance, faith and holiness,' and that making the Word of God accessible away from the confines of church-buildings was the only and sure way of offering Christ's salvation to the common people of England. He put his belief into practice through huge humanitarian assistance to the poor, orphans, the unemployed, prisoners and slaves. He then founded the Methodist movement which led to Britain's greatest spiritual revival, and then crossing the Atlantic to the far reaches of its American colonies that would later become the USA. Dr. Severance summed it up this way: "Numerous agencies promoting Christian work arose as a result of the eighteenth century revival in England. Antislavery societies, prison reform groups, and relief agencies for the poor were started. Numerous missionary societies were formed; the Religious Tract Society was organised; and the British Foreign Bible Society was established. Hospitals and schools multiplied. The revival cut across denominational lines and touched every class of society. England itself was transformed by the revival."

It is, therefore, no surprise that such great influence caused the formation of what actually later became the Wesleyan Church – more a North American denomination than a British one, with headquarters in Fishers, Indiana, and founded primarily as a bulwark against the continuation of the slave trade.

Having gained victory via the abolition of the slave trade, Wesleyan missionaries felt further inspired to 'reach the unreached.' Sierra Leone was already known for its geographic and naval role in ending slavery. In addition, even the wealthy British owner of Sierra Leone's notorious slave-post at Bunce Island Richard Oswald and his American agent Henry Laurens played key roles in negotiating America's independence from Britain after the war. Creole man Abayomi-Cole's 1887 admonition to the Wesleyan General Conference, therefore, was just a catalyst in making an obvious choice for evangelism. The decision of the Wesleyans to concentrate their efforts in the north of Sierra Leone must have been the product of intense prayer for direction and careful planning for results. As Freetown was already flooded with many missionary societies, the American Wesleyan missionaries got a vision for upcountry folks who apparently had never had any contact with Christianity – hence the Kunsho mission that led to the Mabanta evangelisation.

The 'wheel of fortune' had been put in motion for Grace to 'found out me'.

Worthy of note is that the Wesleyan Church has gone on to expand in most districts of the north and has planted many churches in the western area, mostly attended by people of northern origins. Its only presence in the south-east is in Kenema – and at a comparatively low scale.

The Wesleyan Church is not as big as the Catholic Church in terms of finances to be able to make a significant nation-wide expansion and presence. They could well have given up on further evangelisation in the South-east mainly because those areas were already thoroughly evangelised by other denominations, not least being among the first outposts of the domineering Catholic Church. The rivalry in the North was enough of a battle to start another battleground. And the Wesleyan Church's origins as a northern-founded mission would obviously not help its cause for obvious ethnocentric reasons. And not many Christians from the North migrate to those areas. The slow expansion of the Kenema exploratory mission bears those marks.

Wesleyan Church leaders have initiated gap-bridging measures like holding conferences for pastors and youths in the South-east, but it is merely that than an effort at evangelising to the inhabitants of those regions. It is at best an effort at opening a communication line with church leaders and Christians in those regions. A way to understand each other.

Chapter Eight

Mabanta Evangelisation

The Church Versus The Poro Society; Plan International's Education Lifeline

I am yet to find a secret society as dreaded and dreadful as the poro. A society some of whose members do not only boast of mystical powers but publicly display such with self-inflicted injuries done with glee in pools of blood, and yet the 'victims' would the next moment look as normal as before, must be out of this world.

To the outsider – as well as to the insider – poro is truly frightening. It is 'a game of brutality' ('angwol anghai ghai'), but it could also possibly be the best social club in the community – one reason why it still attracts new initiates, dry season after dry season.

If there had ever existed a secret society, this was it. This is a secret society whose secrets are even not known by the vast majority of its members. You cannot be a member for ten years and think you've actually been a member. You have really not known anything. This is a society that has layers of secrets.

As an initiate, all you are required to do is to do as others do: if they go to the right, you go to the right; when they go to the left, you go to the left; forward, forward; backward, backward; they turn round, you turn round. Much like the famous saying of 'when in Rome do as the Romans do', when in the poro you do as poro men (popularly known as 'sokos') do. If they dance with one foot, you dance with one foot. If you miss the step, then you'll know about 'angwol anghai ghai' because there is no sentiment or sympathy for even a blood relative – the punishment could be blood-chilling, with the most common form being a rigorous tying of the whole body of any law-breaker irrespective of rank or status.

Poro was a paternalistic secret society to which every mature male was expected or mandated to become a member – except if he belonged to a ruling house and therefore had the discretion of choice; because, according to custom, the Paramount Chief must not be a member of the poro society (a shadowy, if unconnected, reflection of the Western democratic principle of 'separation of powers'). The poro bush was the graduation centre into adulthood, into manhood. (A selected very small number of senior members of the counterpart female Bondo society were regarded as 'poro initiates' after going through some rites. Thenceforth called 'mamborehs', they were still not let into the 'secrets'.) It was the highway through which you would enter into society proper and be regarded as part and parcel of the community as a male member. Membership was generally by consent but forced initiation or 'kidnapping' was also very much used on the flimsiest of justifications like 'looking too much.'

And the latter method was used on me…

In pre-colonial times, poro was also the military wing of the community, being instrumental and forthright in taking part in the continual inter-tribal wars either for territory or for power maximisation or to capture slaves. But the incorporation of the magical or mythical or mystical aspects with the superstitious and presumptive pervading belief in the influence of the 'spirits of the ancestors' to the point of gaining notoriety for having extraordinary powers to cause harm, makes the society more mysterious and actually abhorrent.

It is, however, worth noting that it is not an exclusive secret society to Sierra Leone. It is practised in virtually the whole of West Africa. Apart from the Mende and Temne and Kono of Sierra Leone, the society is also prevalent among the Senufo people found in northern Ivory Coast, southeastern Mali, northwestern Ghana, and western Burkina Faso; the Kpelle people of Liberia, Ivory Coast and Guinea; and the Vai people of Liberia and Sierra Leone. These tribes are, therefore, believed to have had a common source or ancestry!

Nonetheless, if you are ever looking for a people somehow hypocritical about their nativity and culture, check Sierra Leoneans – as far as the poro issue is concerned. Many male elites were and still are members of this secret society; but, of course, due to the British abhorrence of its practices (not least because it was the poro society that was used to fight against the early settlement of freed slaves and the hut tax), it was not incorporated as part of the national cultural practices of Freetown. And ever since, poro has never been part of the cultural groups at official ceremonial activities in Sierra Leone – if anything, poro men would at times gate-crash as self-invitees at ceremonies; and would be quickly hushed away with monetary ablution by officials. When foreign dignitaries visit, all they see are cultural practices of smaller ethnic groups. But the main cultural practice of males of the two main tribes (Temne and Mende) is not on display. The poro is the missing link in the Sierra Leonean cultural story, because native Sierra Leone can't be really native Sierra Leone without it.

The Sierra Leonean nativity is ashamed of itself – somehow rightfully so. Sierra Leone is ashamed or afraid of showing to the world what Sierra Leonean males practise most. They like it. But they hide it. Yet it has very attractive sides arguably worth displaying for the world to behold – if only as a social event.

When you witness the symmetrical rallying display of the 'rakas' (a coterie of specially chosen young men, artfully decorated with carefully dotted white spots on their semi-naked bodies and dressed only to cover their private parts with veils on their heads flowing down the back of their necks, each holding a similarly artfully dotted sword, chanting a long snivel with shrink and shriek voices followed by a similarly melodious chorus from the following crowd of members, with running paces matching their whimpering), then you start to think that whosoever devised the idea must have been very artistically knowledgeable. It is not hard to tell that this was the military wing of the tribe.

Women stand in awe, in admiration – clapping hands in some form of adoration or idolisation, as they would have been taught at the bondo (the counterpart female secret society) on how to do it with symmetry and accuracy.

Similarly, when you witness the night ceremony of 'lenka' (mainly to remember the dead or to declare open the season of initiation) and hear the songs of communal cohesiveness being sung by both men and women in a most peaceful though revelry manner, you notice the ability of man to live life in ignorance.

But the real poro society was much more than that, much deeper, more superstitious. And if I tell you I know anything – though supposedly a member, or more appropriately a one-day 'captive' or kidnapped member – I would just be bluffing. I don't know any secret. I don't know anything. Or they didn't tell me anything – apart from general admonitions of manhood responsibilities, the random giving of poro names to all new initiates, and being taught a few words of a poro language called 'ka rasu' (meaning 'our own') which apparently historically were codes used to identify members during war time etc. They also used bodily marks apparently for the same reasons.

Thankfully, we were never asked to bow to anything or anyone. In that sense, to me, poro is not a religion! And you wouldn't believe they also spoke of 'Kuru masaba' (the 'great God' who created everything and 'baimba Adama ngha Mahawa' – loosely meaning 'forefather Adam and Eve')! It was not therefore as bad as Europe in the Neolithic age where human sacrifice was part of the dial – Britain's 'Lindow Man' (the bog body of a man supposedly killed for 'ritual' purposes and discovered in 1984 in Wilmslow) was even pegged around as late as the Roman period in Anno Domini.

I'm still today as apprehensive of the society as I was before I was taken to that bush for a few hours and back… I had dodged the society through the protection of my father since childhood until I had reached the sixth form. One of the elder relatives decided to 'kidnap' me in the absence of my father. I didn't or couldn't protest, as I was led away 'like a lamb to the slaughter'. The later explanation was this: they had perceived that I was on the verge of leaving the community to further my education, and they believed that if I was not initiated I would never come back, as had happened in the cases of several Mabanta descendants. It would somehow work for me later in life, as I was emboldened to challenge and accuse them, in frank and somewhat friendly discourse, of belonging to the kingdom of darkness, without me having to fear being kidnapped again…

But the mystery of the poro is actually in the mystical powers. Black magic you would want to call it. A man would pierce himself with a knife in any part of his body in full public view – could go as far as cutting off his tongue or pluck out his eye or slice off his private parts and then later get them 'fixed again' – and eventually if he were your neighbour or relative, you would still sit down together and talk normally.

This beggars belief. Very hard to believe by anyone who has never seen it with their own eyes. If the kingdom of darkness has ever got a name, here it is – on full display. Not only the self-harm – they can harm anybody. Whoever refuses to run away or hide when it is required, whoever does not hide when commanded to, whoever peeps while in hiding, whoever insults its members, could be harmed by poro spirits called 'mama sokos' – the threats go on.

Poro was entrenched in community life so much so that members (as a group) were virtually more powerful than the paramount chief, and by extension the government. And for the Temnes, especially Mabanta natives (the most monolithic anti-change ethnic unit), it is not hard to determine that trying to penetrate such an impregnable community for the purpose of converting them to Christianity could be one of the most herculean tasks humanity or Christendom has ever undertaken. "We are Temne Mabanta; that's who we are; we are what we are. We need nothing new. Full stop!" is the common community refrain.

To plant a church in Mabanta would be like entering into another planet, breaking new grounds, making the impossible possible – like going to the moon!

And I descended directly from those forefathers whose duty it was to protect this very society and community from any form of outside infiltration.

* * *

At the forefront of guarding the ancestral spirits as chief priests were my maternal forefathers: those who took care of the shrines and had the oracles of the 'poro mama sokos', the revered ones who could bring curses on anyone who challenged the authorities or tried to bring any foreign elements to dilute the monolithic entity. They were very powerful, the keepers of the shrines, the custodians of the Temne tradition. (My maternal grandfather was called 'Yamba ksainkay' – a revered title in the poro society. I was never meant to meet or see him. I was born when my parents were at the Bible school, and he died before they could return to Mabanta after their first posting to a village called Mabarie. But that's jumping the sequence of events!…).

At the same time, my paternal forefathers were the traditional rulers of the community; they owned the ruling or royal house of the chieftaincy or kingdom of Mabanta, the highest authority, with the responsibility to protect the community and the people's general welfare. They were mandated to ensure continuity, oppose any reforms from outside and protect the community from any foreign intrusion.

Therefore, if the church was coming to Mabanta, its greatest adversaries would be the chiefs and the poro elders. And the Wesleyan Mission took up the challenge, or the Spirit-led lot fell on them to make the breakthrough. It was a tough call. Stories abound about false starts and tough resistances, which sometimes ended in physical fights. But the peaceful persistence of the missionaries, accompanied by their new few Sierra Leonean converts, planted the first seeds.

Interestingly, and miraculously, one of the first family heads to accept Christ and embrace the Wesleyan Church in

Mabanta was my paternal grandfather (whose name I carry – Pa Sheka Tarawalie) at a time when my father was still very young in the late 1930s. My paternal grandfather lived long enough for me to know him – he worked in the Wesleyan secondary school I would later attend and he passed away when I was already at the university and after I had written an academic paper I dedicated to him in my first year!

The conversion of my grandfather (together with his wife my grandmother, Ya Sama who hailed from a famous Islamic-singing family) and a few others meant a new day had dawned in Mabanta, a people once sitting in darkness had seen a great light! But there was a price to pay. They suddenly became the enemies of the community, the traitors, the betrayers of the ancestors. A new fight begun for them. Yet there was no turning back as my grandfather held on tenaciously to the new faith, later assisted by his first son, my father (and by extension my mother), with grandpa's most favourite Christian song in the local language being "Baypi ta Jesus ta diff mi gbo, Kere e bahe ka laftheh sor" (They can go ahead and kill me for Jesus, but I'll never turn back).

One thing was clear, the new converts would not have forsaken all the ancestral spirits if they had not realised that it was futile, that it was a dark alley, it was the work of the devil, a kingdom of darkness. But converting a few people was not enough – could not be the end. The great task of actually building a church both as a body of Christ and as a physical structure lay ahead. It had to take the courage of my grandfather to let go of his eldest son (whom he never sent to school with a purpose to retain him as the next traditional head, but who had made great impression on the missionaries about his spiritual aptitude) to enroll at the vernacular Bible school to be trained as a pastor. Therefore, eventually, my father would be sent by the Wesleyan leadership to Mabanta to evangelise among his own people. He would ultimately move them from worshipping under trees, classrooms, and community centres (structures simultaneously used for worldly activities) to erecting a building exclusively as the Wesleyan Church of Mabanta.

And here – in the efforts to build a church structure at Mabanta – was where my journalism career unwittingly began, I would submit. At a very early age of about nine or ten, I became the letter-writer for my father: writing letters to church leaders, politicians, and other dignitaries to support God's work in the construction of a church building. Week in week out for successive years, I wrote letters dictated by my father in Temne translated by me in English. Each letter would always start with 'I greet you in the Name of our Lord and Saviour Jesus Christ' and ended with 'Yours in Christ, Pastor J.S. Tarawalie'. After writing, I would just read the letter to him aloud in English; and he would respond: "Correct, everything is in." It yielded fruits with appreciable support especially from the politicians during electioneering periods, knowing how influential my father was in the community. A 300-capacity church is standing there today as a testimony.

But it was no mean feat. Spiritual and physical battles would be fought. A land dispute would erupt – the Tarawalie vast lands would be 'trespassed' by impostors leading to a protracted court case that saw the old chieftaincy rivalries re-enacted (one ruling house having won a chieftaincy election over another ruling house, and now the victor wanting to further 'show power' over the defeated 'adversary' by using rival families to try to take away some parts of their land).

My father still vividly remembers the Christian journey of the Tarawalie family starting from the mid 1930s. He owed a lot of gratitude to Rev. Joseph Sedu Mans (a Wesleyan pastor and local interpreter) who had forged a strong relationship with his father Pa Sheka Tarawalie after the latter's first encounter with the missionaries at Kunsho. Rev Sedu Mans, as pastor of Rogbaneh Church where the Mabanta converts were originally attending, would be the great motivator who urged my father (who had displayed a spectacular intellectual, though elementary, understanding especially in the pronunciation of written Temne) to enroll as a student at the Gbendembu Bible School – where I was born together with my younger brother, Hudson (who was subsequently taken by the Lord when I was Press Secretary). Pa Mans would later leave the Wesleyan Church to head eventually the Baptist Convention – but failed in his efforts to go along with my father.

At the Bible School – my father's narration continues – he was loved by the Principal, Rev. Kombo L. Kargbo, for his quick-witted intellect, even surpassing those students who had had some form of previous education. The relationship would grow stronger when Pa Kombo, as he was fondly called, would be doing evangelistic work taking my father along to carry his bag of books (including of course the Bible). They had a Paul-Timothy relationship, my father was always happy to state. It was crowned when Pa Kombo became Pastor and my father Assistant Pastor of Rogbaneh Wesleyan Church. But the relationship became more impactful when Pa Kombo became the District Superintendent (the overall head of the Church who today is known as the National Superintendent).

It was while serving as Assistant Pastor of Rogbaneh Church that my father had a fraternal relationship with the lay-leader Pa Sylvanus Koroma and his wife Ya Alice, the parents of President Ernest Bai Koroma. He became a personal pastor to them, fellowshipping with them at home and in Pa Sylvanus's home village of Yoni, a stronghold of Islam. When eventually my father was transferred from Rogbaneh to Mabanta, the Koroma family provided generous financial assistance to start a new home. I would myself remember Pa Sylvanus very well as a man who loved evangelism. He liked travelling with our family to reach out to neighbouring villages: he liked the praying part, my father would preach, and my siblings and I would be the choristers. We were in school then. He was National Secretary of the Sierra Leone Wesleyan Church (SLWC) – as it was known then.

* * *

When my father arrived as a pastor in Mabanta, there was no particular place of worship as services would be moved from house to house or under trees. Afterwards, through his urgings, a 'pan body' (corrugated iron sheets) structure was erected by the Wesleyan Mission and was used as both a church and a school. When Plan International, a community-improving charity organisation focusing on children's education (without which I might not have been educated), erected a structure for the school away from the church spot, the Christians would use one of the classrooms after the ambitious project to erect a church structure was initiated by my father and the 'pan body' brought down. And when Plan eventually constructed a community centre, the church turned it into its latest place of worship – while the centre was simultaneously being used for mundane activities like a 'disco/night club' by the community in general.

It took many years of persistent labour in one of the poorest communities (obviously with little or nothing for the members to give in terms of financial offerings and tithing) under my father's leadership to build an edifice which is today the village church, with a thriving membership.

Yet the planting of the church didn't mean poro activities were over. They still thrived. Not least because very influential, even educated, people are supportive of it (but most just take it as a social grouping, as they never even go to the bush any longer). Some of my Mabanta brothers, therefore, religiously follow it. Their activities are still very much alive. Otherwise, how would they have eventually captured me and my younger brother? The tenacity of the people to the old ways was unrivalled. Some would be church members for the rainy season; and would go back to their poro in the dry season – even if secretly. But what was clear was that the once impregnable Mabanta had succumbed to the power of the Gospel of Jesus Christ. Grace had overcome by breaking down the walls and reaching out to the lost.

With the help of the Holy Spirit, the highlight of the success of the Mabanta evangelisation was my father's open challenge to the poro society. The story is still being told of how in the late 1970s he attended a poro meeting, rose up and preached in the poro bush, telling all present that the society was abhorrent and sinful. The varied versions of the message (not recorded) would be summarised thus: "The gods of our forefathers are dead. You come to this bush with the pretence of hearing from our forefathers. They can't hear us... There is only one living God who sent His Son Jesus Christ as a sacrifice to save us from our sins. We don't need all these other sacrifices. Come to church and hear the good news." It was a shocker! This was one of their own – or one who used to be one of their own. He knew these traditions very well. He was from the ruling house and had been a part of the secret society since childhood. He mastered its rituals. Today, he was saying it was all foolishness.

There was a big schism in the village: while most of those who heard him repented and became Christians, there were even some elder churchgoers who felt so insulted by the denunciation that they left the church. One of the poro men, Pa Beareh Kanu, would eventually become one of my father's closest allies, and he would rise to the position of lay-leader of the church; but he refused to take a 'Christian' name. One of those who left the church, Pa Saysay (aka Say) Kargbo, a maternal uncle of my mother, is today the village 'headman' or 'town chief' – inevitably having to work with the Mabanta ruling house, of which my father is the head. Pa Kargbo attended the church service of the crowning of my mother as 'Wesleyan Woman of the Year, Makeni District' in 2015.

In one of his sermons welcoming the poro converts, Reverend John Sheka Tarawalie criticised those who felt insulted and left: that 'the dogs have gone back to their vomit.' One of my father's greatest allies who became a big boost to the Mabanta evangelisation was a blind gospel singer, Pa Ansumana Kanu. He was not born blind. He was also a strong poro man but fell terribly ill and was virtually given up for dead. Intense prayers were offered on his behalf. He recovered, but lost his sight. He however testified of the power of God and gave his life to Christ, churning out melodious songs about salvation in his native Temne language. His fame grew throughout the region, as his services were hired by other churches and even other denominations, especially at funerals. When I was in the sixth form and Pa Ansumana needed to undergo some abdominal surgical operation, my parents asked me to accompany him to the highly-equipped 1967-founded St John of God Catholic-run Mabessaneh Hospital at Lunsar (65-odd kilometres from Makeni on the Freetown highway), where my aunt Marie (my mother's only sister – a Muslim by adopted upbringing and by marriage) was settled with her family. She dutifully and constantly provided food for us throughout the three-week stay at the hospital. My primary twin-role was to act as an interpreter between

Pa Ansumana and the mostly foreign medical personnel, and to guide him on how and when to take medication. I learnt a lot of folklore from him at that time, as he was a human encyclopedia of Mabanta history. He later passed away when I would have become Press Secretary to the President. The vacuum he left in Temne gospel singing is still gaping.

My father officially retired in 1998. And then became one of the most celebrated radio preachers through the local community station, Radio Mankneh, built just in front of our village home (a house now befitting royalty). My immediate elder sister, Alice, is a founding and longest-serving staff of the station. It must be noted that our dad's radio evangelism dated back to his pastoral hey days in the 1970s and 80s when his sermons were transmitted via the 1951-founded Christian radio station, ELWA (Eternal Love Winning Africa), based in Liberia and broadcasting to the whole of West Africa.

As emeritus pastor, my father still preaches in the church at special occasions. He continues to provide strategic support to any pastor posted (I think six now since he retired), with a permanent seat for him in the pulpit area of the church.

It could not have been anybody else to be used by God to get the Word established at Mabanta. He was a 'pope' for Mabanta.

* * *

The Mabanta Wesleyan Church is today an 'A' station to which many pastors would be glad to be posted – the hierarchical alphabetical rating having been earned by its financial and membership strength. And virtually all those in the church no longer publicly associate with the poro society – though they inevitably continue to live, at times in the same houses, with poro relatives and neighbours who are still very much in the majority. The fact that church numbers are increasing means the light of the Gospel is penetrating.

The influence of the poro has been seriously weakened by the mass attention being paid to education, as parents are now more than ever before sending their children to school in great numbers – sometimes using me and the few other success stories as examples worthy of emulation.

When I became a government functionary, I made enormous personal and official contributions in the building and capacitating of my village alma-mater Wesleyan primary school, not only in infrastructure and furniture but even bringing my white British friend from Manchester David Oglaza in addition to my Rwandan-British-Sierra Leonean wife to further inspire the kids. I would participate in their athletics sports meet, and would give speeches of encouragement for them to endure. I worked hard with the headmaster, making representations at the Ministry of Education, in ensuring that the school became independent from the Makama Wesleyan primary school – a status it had found itself in since formation in the 1970s.

When I started pouring personal resources for the further beautification of the church, some poro men grumbled that they were not getting anything from me. I told them they were welcomed to join the Mabanta Farmers Development Association, which I had formed with village elders to cultivate our vast ancestral lands. It was open to everybody, not just Christians. And I aptly added: “I’m not a politician. I’m a missionary.” This word was taken to the district highest authorities of the then-ruling party who became very angry with me. I was happy.

The Word had reached the politicians, many of whom were also poro men!

Chapter Nine

Wesleyan And Catholic Rivalry In Bombali

Rev Usman Fornah, Bishop George Biguzzi, Fr Joe Turay, Rev. John Sheka Tarawalie, Pres. Ernest Koroma As Love Bridges; UNIMAK, 'Building A Civilisation Of Love'

Today, the graves are there at Kunsho where the first American missionaries sent by the Wesleyan Mission to evangelise in Sierra Leone made the ultimate sacrifice and were buried. They came. They evangelised. They died. They had planted the seed. It was a supreme sacrifice – as others still followed, despite the initial tragic setbacks.

Although the common killer of white men at the time was malaria (the notoriety reached a level of labeling Sierra Leone as 'the white man's grave'), there were several other conspiracy theories surrounding the missionaries' demise in 'the heart of darkness.'

One strand of the accompanying explanation was that a strange illness struck the missionaries after they ate some fish given to them by natives. Some locals believed it was witchcraft played on the missionaries to get rid of the Gospel that had come to dilute the culture – you wouldn't be surprised if the hired mercenaries came from Mabanta, or at least some assistance came from there: so long as it was to resist change or to eradicate the agents of change.

One would not be sure whether the people of Kunsho had heard the tragic story of Umuofia in Nigerian writer Chinua Achebe's *Things Fall Apart* wherein 'the white man's religion' (is it really the white man's religion?) caused the disintegration of a once solidified African society. A famous quote of that book stated thus: "The white man is very clever. He came quietly and peaceably with his religion. We were amused at his foolishness and allowed him to stay. Now he has won our brothers, and our clan can no longer act like one. He has put a knife on the things that held us together and we have fallen apart." If, or as, Achebe's novel was reflecting a reality of things that happened in Ibo Nigeria, it's almost certain that the story would have easily spread through the trade routes that interconnected West Africa during the ancient empires and during colonialism. If the Kunsho people had heard such stories and then saw some ill-fated white missionaries sneaking their way into their community, they would obviously be apprehensive and find ways of preventing a recurrence of 'things falling apart' in their community.

But that's mere speculation. The Kunsho people might or might not have heard of Okonkwo's Umoufia. And, if I can be personal, being an indigene of nearby Mabanta, I know the Kunsho people to be very affable and amiable human beings (traits I would assume they inherited from their forefathers). And I also know them to be – just like my Mabanta people –

strict adherents to their customs and traditions. They might not have had any role in the mystery of the early missionary story, but those graves which are frequently being visited by generations of American missionaries will continue to produce different strands of narratives and emotions.

Six American souls – young and old – died in the 'heart of darkness' and were buried there; five others managed to 'escape' but died immediately after returning to America. It is hard to pinpoint a particular reason why the deceased were not taken away to be buried in America. Perhaps it was to tell the locals that they as missionaries had come to stay until the Gospel was accepted, no matter what (dead or alive). Or it would have been too cumbersome for the bodies to be flown back to the US, taking into consideration the colonial terrain at the time. It could also have been that there was not enough money from the coffers of the mission to immediately take them (as there were obviously no funeral home services at the time). No matter the reason, those graves have continued to be testimonies of selfless sacrifice.

Gracefully, the official Wesleyan position has been that the missionaries died of 'blackwater fever'.

Indeed, as the Bible states, there is no greater love than a man to lay down his life for his friends! And the successor American missionaries who followed after this debacle did the incredible – legend has it that they actually came with their own coffins, ready to die just to ensure that the Gospel was rooted in Bombali! And a more profound way of making the point stick was when one of those missionaries, John Wesley Taylor, married a local Kunsho woman, Ya Mam! That relationship gave birth to a succession of missionaries whose descendants are still very much present with us and making meaningful contributions in the affairs of the Wesleyan Church.

Therefore, as the missionary work continued beyond Kunsho to other parts of Bombali district, Wesleyan missionaries claimed Christian ownership or perhaps assumed a special spiritual bond with the land. The Church grew, and most towns and villages in the area were reached, forming small groups of believers, drawing leaders from among them, emphasising the importance of education – setting up churches and schools here and there, even if as 'pan bodies' or private houses. The important ingredients – the people – were available. Make use of whatever else was available.

One by one, many local people became Christians, and agreed to send their children to school. My grandfather accepted the Christian faith in one of those Wesleyan outdoor services, sent his boy kids to school – except the eldest, my father, whom he would not let go because he had to be prepared to take care of the land and farms and swamps. He could not be sent to school. He had to be with his father in the farm. And his son accepted, and supported his younger brothers who had been sent to school.

But God's ways are not our ways. The one who never went to school would become a pastor – a Reverend!

* * *

While the Wesleyan Church was struggling to have an infrastructural stronghold (it is still unimaginable to me why the Americans of all people were not showing generosity in terms of visible material establishments – yet their defence of targeting to win the soul and not the body is also convincing), the Roman Catholic Church's Xaverian missionaries led by Monsignor Augustus Azzolini appeared on the scene in 1950. Massive buildings were erected, little 'basilicas' built, schools, and hospitals, different types of gifts all poured in, of course attracting crowds to the new 'father/mother' missionaries – and among those crowds were some Wesleyans.

The Wesleyan Mission would definitely not take kindly to her members being taken away by the Catholic Church. It was a rivalry that did not miss the agenda of some Wesleyan preachers, including my father, exposing what they believed were the grey areas of the Catholic Church.

The Wesleyans believed the Catholic Church had dismissed or diminished the use of the Bible as 'the Word of God' through their adoption of certain catechisms. So the Roman Catholic Church was not perceived as a Bible-believing church. Wesleyans also criticised the Catholics for their veneration of Mary, the mother of Jesus, especially when they used her as an intercessor to 'pray for us sinners'. Wesleyans also believed that one of the prayers of the Catholic Church, 'world without end', was a Christian misnomer as the Bible clearly taught that this world would come to an end. The Wesleyans were further infuriated by the Catholics' use of the crucifix (a symbol/figure of the crucified Christ on a cross), as the former believed that the risen Christ should be celebrated with a plain cross – to show that He is no longer hung or dead, but resurrected!

The Wesleyans were angry and grumbled that the use of material wealth to attract membership was not a good way to evangelise and win souls; they believed that the 'too short' liturgical worship services being conducted by the Catholics were not enough to bring illiterate country people to a full knowledge of the Gospel of Jesus Christ.

The Catholics' response would be more infrastructural development or general material windfall – feeding the poor, helping the blind, and providing for orphans and widows – like saying, 'look at my faith by my works'. They paid school fees for children, adopted some, even took some to Rome, etc.

The threat to the Wesleyan congregations was real, was sustained. Wesleyans were very reluctant to associate with Catholicism in any form – and would demonstrate this by refusing to send their children to catholic schools. The rivalry, or even animosity, did not abate – until it was changed by the 'hand of God' through the war, ironically, in the 1990s.

Frequent open-air inter-denominational prayer services against the war were held at Makeni's Wusum Stadium. Though the Catholic Church was not part of the Council of Churches of Sierra Leone, an invitation extended to them by then pastor of Rogbaneh Wesleyan Church Rev Usman Fornah to pray for the country was honoured by then-Bishop George Bigguzzi, a happy-go-lucky Italian. Gradually, some realisation of the need for each other emerged. What divided them was smaller than what united them – they were all Christians, they believed in the Trinity of One God in three Persons – the Father, the Son, and the Holy Spirit; and they believed that Jesus Christ was the Son of God born by the virgin Mary, that He was killed and was buried and rose again in three days, that He ascended into Heaven and would come again to judge the living and the dead.

Wesleyans and Catholics overlooked the differences with the acceptance that they were all carrying the same core message, as they could now sing together at inter-denominational services at Wusum Stadium: 'Brothers we are treading where the saints have trod – we are not divided, all one body we, one in hope and doctrine, one in charity..... Onward Christian soldiers marching as to war, with the cross of Jesus going on before.'

However, the real foundation of the Wesleyan-Catholic 'communion' in Makeni was solidified after the rebels invaded and took over the city in late 1999. While all Catholic priests fled – including Bishop Bigguzzi – the Wesleyan

Church's Usman Fornah stayed behind. After hiding in the bush for a few days, he came out and was at first manhandled by the ruthless rebels. However, he continued in prayer and ministration and gained favour before the rebel commando called 'Superman' to the extent of saving the lives of seven secondary school boys who were going to be executed if he had not intervened.

Rev Fornah's fame grew in the city and he offered to be preaching to the Catholic congregation, in the absence of their priests, at their 'Our Lady of Fatima' cathedral early every Sunday before going to his own Rogbaneh Wesleyan Church. The great barrier between the two churches had been broken. In reciprocal gratitude, when Bishop Biguzzi returned to Makeni after the war and discovered what the Wesleyan pastor had done, the Catholic missionary attended service at the Wesleyan Church to say thanks. Beyond that, he took Rev Fornah on a pilgrimage to the Vatican and met with Pope John Paul II. Biguzzi also took Fornah to some catholic churches in Rome for the Wesleyan preacher to deliver sermons.

On the heels of these groundbreaking events, an original member of the Rogbaneh Wesleyan Church would eventually become President of Sierra Leone. President Ernest Koroma, whose parents were devout Wesleyans, would continue to bridge the gap between Wesleyans and Catholics in Bombali. Though he did not attend the Catholic-established St. Francis Secondary School, apparently due to the aforementioned earlier antagonism, his first job after graduating from the university was teaching at this Catholic secondary school.

As President, he would forge a relationship that would forever change the religious status quo of Bombali District. That he could facilitate the acquisition of hundreds of acres of his parental lands by the Diocese of Makeni for the building of a catholic institution, the University of Makeni (UNIMAK – the first in the region), was more than building a bridge. The land-owning families received handsome payments. He went further to personally construct an edifice for the Chancellor and staff of the same university for use as offices at his home village of Yoni. He also constructed and donated some living quarters for university staff. He influenced some Chinese company to build classrooms for the university at the same location. The then-Bishop of Makeni, George Bigguzzi, had unfettered access to the President in getting things done for the implementation of the UNIMAK project. It would be hard to imagine the UNIMAK idea bearing fruit without Koroma's inputs! First started as a vocational institute in 2005, it got fast-tracked and accredited as a University under Koroma in 2009. UNIMAK has today put Makeni on the educational map, as it attracts students of all faiths from all over Sierra Leone and even beyond, and also has lecturers from as far as Italy.

Furthermore, former President Koroma would attend Catholic services at 'Our Lady' cathedral unencumbered. One of his closest friends was businessman Vincent Kanu (late), who was not only a Catholic but actually reputed to be the first registered pupil of St Francis Secondary School and was adopted and raised by the Xaverian missionaries as a seminarian. When a Makeni street was named after him as a retired President, he ensured another was named after his late friend.

The Wesleyan-Catholic relationship in Makeni blossomed so much that when the thorny issue of Bishop Aruna's rejection by the local Catholic laity arose, the scenario was compared to a previous standoff at Rogbaneh Wesleyan Church where controversy over the choice of a pastor caused its temporary closure. There were threads of evidence connecting local

Wesleyans working in concert with the Catholics to ensure they prevented the nominee of Pope Benedict from taking over the Makeni Diocese as Bishop. And when successor Pope Francis backed down on the choice of Bishop Aruna for the Diocese, Wesleyans joined Catholics in the triumphant celebrations – all in the belief that the method used in proclaiming Aruna as Bishop was flawed and dictatorial.

One person that's worth mentioning in all this is Fr. Joe Turay, UNIMAK's first and current Principal who acted as a thread connecting the others. A native of Kambia (a district bordering with Bombali), Turay attended St Francis Secondary School and became one of the enlightened and educated local priests with university education. He was very much a 'disciple' of the first Catholic Bishop Azzolini and continued in the same vein with Biguzzi. He was well known and well liked in the Makeni Diocese and could possibly have been a welcome choice as successor to Biguzzi – though he was not one of the candidates. Invariably, he became very much the 'foot soldier' of the university project and eventually became instrumental in filling the vacuum in the confusion that erupted after the departure of Bishop Biguzzi and the controversial appointment of Bishop Aruna. Turay's focus was not the priesthood but the implementation of the UNIMAK idea. He developed a strong relationship with President Koroma and maintained the international contacts necessary for the establishment of the university. He therefore mobilised and marshaled all the requisite resources, human and material, for the establishment of the university. No wonder, when it was completed, he became the natural leader to head the institution. With its motto 'Building a Civilisation of Love', UNIMAK, under Fr Joe Turay, became so quickly one of 'the most progressive universities' not only nationally but internationally – with a wide-ranging curriculum, collaborating with highly-rated western universities, and attracting European lecturers. Prof. Fr. Joseph Turay's passion in propagating the university as open to all and sundry irrespective of religious beliefs has greatly helped in further mending fences between Catholics and Wesleyans in the region. The ever-increasing number of students coming from the western area and the south-east to acquire education in a northern university indeed is a testimony to a pursuit of UNIMAK's motto guided by wise leadership.

And then the last, but not the least – to use a common refrain – is Rev. John Sheka Tarawalie. It has nothing to do with the fact that he is my father. He, on his own merit and by the grace of God, played a major part in sowing religious tolerance in Makeni or Bombali as a whole through his messages via Radio Mankneh. Having gone through the war, many perceptions changed – even those towards Catholics and Muslims. And when Radio Mankneh had to be relocated after the war from Mankneh to Mabanta, next-door to our home, there was no greater opportunity for my father to continue preaching in retirement. My elder sister, Alice's being a founding staff could only make things better. Sunday after Sunday our dad's messages were the breakfast for many in Bomabli: Christians (all denominations), Muslims (Sunni or Shia or in-between) and apparently the general public got addicted to these Temne messages. He preached in the native language, soaked in traditional stories. Everybody was interested. While preaching Jesus Christ, crucified and resurrected, in a most Wesleyan protestant way, he would always bring along the undeniable relationship (as it plays out from its Abrahamic origins to John Wesley) with Catholics and Muslims. He uses a cajoling method of effortless beckoning to the saving grace of Christ. There is no force. It's just story-telling: telling a real-life story amid competing stories, without outrightly condemning the others. He believes that Jesus wants everybody in. Tell them the wonderful story, and the Spirit will do the rest, he believes. The relevance of the radio can never be more profound than on a people listening to the message of salvation in their own native language. For someone to make Christ a Temne (in like manner as many made Him white or English), relaying Him raw in your own mother-tongue, as God's blank cheque of love handed over to the whole of mankind, is sovereign realism. I feel the Gospel nativised when I listen to him too: Christ personified, Christ personalised, God with us. Whenever I visited Makeni, people would come to relay to me their appreciation: Wesleyans as well as Catholics as well as Muslims.

Of course, my dad got the radio evangelism training from the Gbendembu Bible School under American Wesleyan Missionary Alton Shea, Director of the recording studio at the time. The messages were recorded in Temne and sent to Radio ELWA (Eternal Love Winning Africa) in Liberia for broadcast to the whole of West Africa on shortwave. Even when my dad was already at Mabanta, I remembered this tall Fula missionary recording assistant, Abdulai Sheriff (whose dad was an Alhaji), always looking for my dad to record his Temne messages. The 1989 civil war in Liberia consumed ELWA. Abdulai Sheriff disappeared from the scene. Radio Mankneh, then located at the village after which it was named, Mankneh, was already filling the gap for ELWA when the war reached in Makeni in the late 90s and consumed it as well. After the war, the station resurfaced at Mabanta with the same name – Radio Mankneh. And Rev. John Sheka Tarawalie would sit in its studios on Sunday morning and do a live broadcast, preaching the Gospel as a love bridge in Bombali.

Notwithstanding, it has to be stated that the rivalry has not totally disappeared. There are still the doctrinal debates.

The little suspicions and recriminations are still there as humans. That often comes out strongly during inter-school competitions or comparisons of academic capacity even with later generations.

And I would be a classic example of how it played out, because I had my schooling in both worlds.

Chapter Ten

Why I Would Not Attend St. Francis 'Catholic' School – But I Eventually Did

The Birch Memorial Wesleyan Foundation

When the Catholics built their schools, they did it with pomp, pageantry, and academic fanfare: solid buildings, latest educational materials like scientific laboratories, books, pens, pencils, even uniforms, and attracting the best teachers with better pay, thereby producing more successful students.

St. Francis Secondary School, founded by Catholic Xaverian Fathers, was nicknamed the 'Oxford of the North', making Makeni (the headquarters of Bombali and the Northern Province) a magnet that drew students from far and wide. Despite the Wesleyan mission having been in the area since the nineteenth century, it would be the Catholics to first open a secondary school there in 1958 (it would be ten years later that Birch Memorial was founded by Wesleyans). Every bright male student in the community was expected to attend St. Francis. I was a bright student (I can say with all humility). But I would not attend St Francis – in one major sense; but I would attend it in another sense.

My father became a Pastor of the Wesleyan Church – almost by default. A man whose father did not allow him to go to school, trained as a farmer and became a palm-wine tapper was the most unlikely candidate to become a Reverend or anything that had to do with spreading the Word of God as a preacher. But then Peter – the most trusted disciple of Jesus Christ – was a mere fisherman! The Pope's patron saint was just a fisherman! No one would think of a modern pope being an unschooled fisherman. But here was the first pope being just that. And here was another who was a palm-wine tapper. A pope is a pastor. And my father is a pastor. He is, therefore, a pope in his own right when it comes to the affairs of the church of Mabanta. Only by Grace would that be.

* * *

The Rev. John Sheka Tarawalie had found favour before God and before man when he kept attending the village gathering of believers with his converted father. Joseph Sedu Mans (later to become Reverend), the missionaries' native interpreter and local preacher, found a special knack in my father and through continued engagements discovered a depth of knowledge ready to be utilised in a most special way. Pa Mans told my illiterate dad that it was possible for him to actually read and write; that if he was willing, then there was a fountain through the vernacular Bible School the missionaries had opened at Gbendembu.

Past age 30, my father would for the first time enter a classroom – now having been released by his father because the younger ones had finished school and were now working; and he had already gained enough knowledge of the traditions and history of the family and the community anyway. The right time had come for the one who would not be sent to school to go to school.

I was born there at the Gbendembu Bible School, some 20-odd miles away from Mabanta. Here, my father and mother learnt the vernacular alphabet and mastered it, and could eventually read and write in their native Temne language. Then my father crossed the boundaries and was now able to also read and interpret the English Bible into Temne. Yes, in English. Wonders would never end! With God, all things are possible! And all this within three years. A man like that would – should – forever be grateful to God and to the Wesleyan Church. He would always appreciate the value of education. He would, therefore, send all his children to school.

As a young graduate pastor, he was sent to two stations before he was transferred to his home village. The Mabanta converts were struggling and frequently in need of stability, because the age-old stubborn and recalcitrant nature of the 'Temne Mabanta' was still very much ingrained in the people. It seemed nothing good would ever come from Mabanta. Only one of their own would perhaps turn the tide – the Wesleyan authorities believed; and who else would be a better ambassador of the Gospel to Mabanta than the former palm-wine tapper from the famous Tarawalie ruling house who would now return to his home as a pastor.

Both church services and school lessons were being conducted in private houses. But it did not seem to matter; as long as the pastor and the teachers were available to do the work. In the Wesleyan tradition, the pastor automatically became the school chaplain. I, therefore, naturally had to attend the Wesleyan Primary School of Mabanta with all my siblings. And with the rapid double promotions I secured, I skipped three years and entered secondary school at the same time as two of my uncles and my eldest sister, leaving my immediate elder sister in primary school. I passed the-then 'selective entrance' examination (now called National Primary School Examination) with flying colours.

That meant I was bright. But I did not – could not – apply to enter the school where all the bright students were expected and accepted. I could not attend St. Francis. Because it is a Catholic school!

My father obviously had a strong emotional attachment – in addition to the spiritual – to the Wesleyan Church. If it were you, dear reader, you would likely do the same. The denominational rivalry aside, it would have appeared as a display of ingratitude if his son were to leave out the Wesleyan secondary school for a Catholic school. The man who had preached about the oddities of Catholic Christianity would not now turn round and eat his words by sending his son to a Catholic school. He did not even have enough money, as in those days pastors were a very poor group of shepherds with negligible salaries and underprivileged congregations. So if he would have to require or expect assistance through the Wesleyan network he had already established, the natural path would be by sending his kids to the Wesleyan secondary school – where in fact my grandfather (Pa Sheka Tarawalie), due to the same emotional attachment, was working as a security.

There was no school more appropriate in my circumstances, no school better equipped to continue to shape me in the Wesleyan faith and tradition that I had been born and brought up in, than Birch Memorial Secondary School, named after an early American Wesleyan missionary (Marion Birch). I have no regrets for that decision of my father! What I learnt at Birch Memorial I wouldn't have learnt at St Francis: the Wesleyan chaplains/pastors who conducted daily morning devotions did a good job; the curriculum there would not have been much different from that of St Francis (though as I indicated earlier the latter obviously had better teachers and a more conducive learning environment). Being so young and tiny, entering secondary school at age ten, it was also reassuring to continue to be in the same school with my eldest sister, Rebecca. It wouldn't have happened at St. Francis, because it was an all-boys school from Form 1 to 5.

I would again stress that it was not officially compulsory or mandatory for the child of a Wesleyan Pastor to attend a Wesleyan school. But, as that was the trend of showing affinity to the Wesleyan mission, my father ensured it happened in our own case – that me and my siblings should attend Wesleyan primary and secondary schools. In retrospect, I could now see how that decision gave him access to us in school. For example, I would be in the middle of a class, and the teacher would just be called outside, and he would come in again to call me outside only to discover that my father was there to see me – with some lunch money. So nice of him. It would not have happened at St. Francis. He could not have had the access. The teacher-pastor relationship within Wesleyan circles was strong.

My father would in the end allow me to attend St. Francis to do my sixth form primarily because Birch Memorial's academia stopped at the fifth form. Using the Catholic school as a passageway to the university was easily justifiable. I was already too Wesleyan to stray into Catholicism. Or was I? Would the natural journalist in me – that instinctive nature of curiosity and crosschecking – not make me wonder and wander?

* * *

It was not because I attended St. Francis that I got to meet Pope Francis; but the coincidence is worth mentioning, even as it rhymes: a former student of St. Francis meeting Pope Francis! If it were purely a matter of human design in sequential catholic terms – left at the discretion of the Catholics in Sierra Leone – it would have been a Catholic or at least someone who attended a Catholic school in full that would be chosen to meet the earthly universal head of their Church.

But the circumstances were different, the divine nature was different. His ways and our ways are not the same.

Chapter Eleven

'Corpus Christi,' A Schoolboy Tale

How Wesleyanism And Catholicism Crossed Paths In Me

Doing my secondary education at the Wesleyan-run Birch Memorial was worth it – not least because it brought joy and satisfaction to my father and grandfather (who manifested his love by working as a security at the school) and the rest of the family, including my mother (the silent and enduring bedrock in the family's missionary journey). Birch gave me a foothold in the Wesleyan Church, and accorded me the opportunity of first contact with virtually all the major church people that I would have to network with later in life – some of my teachers went on to become leaders of the Church. Birch was to me as the eye was to the body. It was an eye-opener. And the curriculum was not too different from those in other schools – though there were variations in terms of facilities, as St. Francis was more equipped. I got to know this better through one of the uncles I sat the entrance exams with, Robert (now a policeman). While my eldest sister and I went to Birch, he had chosen St. Francis. I would gain a lot from reading his notes – he might have gained from mine too. All schools took the same external examinations.

Doing my sixth form at St. Francis was, therefore, an icing on the cake, and it was a superb top-up that would also prove invaluable in terms of social and educational networking at the time and later in life. Doing a year or two in any educational institution made one as *bona fide* an alumnus as anyone else who would have done five or six or more years in that same institution. Every student had their own admission number, which would never be taken away by another. So I was as much a student of St. Francis as of Birch. But, of course, not everybody would subscribe to that notion. There were always those who held the view that the sixth-form experience was too short to be regarded as a full-blooded 'Franciscan'. And they did have a point! You met with people at a somewhat mature or advanced stage, and would do less intimate or naughty things together as those you started with from the cradle.

But I would not be bothered by any distinction or difference between old and new. Mine was an opportunity to explore further educational pursuits – and I was determined to maximise that. It was not how long, but how much, you would absorb and how much you were transformed by what was made available in school. And before long, certainly with active performance in class, I would soon become as popular as those who started Form 1 at St. Francis.

Makeni was a small close-knit community and I was already known at Birch as 'the Mabanta boy' with a knack for education. I didn't need to go overboard to establish myself at St. Francis. The camaraderie with other students improved, and we all sang the same school song with glee and passion (there was no school song for Birch in our days!): "Always remember we are friends together... Boys of St. Francis School, keep the banner high!" I felt greatly inspired and motivated by the huge educational resources available – a totally different scenario from Birch where even the library was a mere room. At St. Francis, it was what it was, a library – a hall full of shelves filled with books. My appetite for reading had found a Xaverian grocery.

Perhaps the most glaring and important point to note about the difference in resource provision in the two schools was that the Catholics had direct links with the headquarters in Rome, with white 'fathers' and 'brothers' from Italy serving in the school. As late as our own time in the late eighties, one of them PT Coffey was the Principal. At Birch, school affairs were merely left to be managed by the locals, and not much of an American missionary presence was felt – they did not even act as chaplains (albeit once on a while, the proverbial once in a blue moon, some exuberant missionaries would come on visitation to give a talk or sing a song during assembly). Birch Memorial, having been named after an American Wesleyan missionary, would have had a befitting honour to have been hosting missionary chaplains. But no, the school administration was entirely left in the hands of the locals – meaning the needs of the school, including resource provision, were not particularly on the agenda of the missionaries.

So I got integrated at St. Francis. It was an easy thing to do because Makeni was a community where everybody virtually knew everybody else – especially with so much inter-school interaction and intra-family connections. I was soon to be introduced and inducted to some streetwise activities. Yes, this was a boys' school (not Birch with boys and girls where my sisters were present – my immediate elder sister, Alice, entered the secondary school when I was already in the third form);

and boys must be boys (St. Francis only accepted a minuscule number of girls in the sixth form – having its counterpart Catholic girls school, St. Joseph's Convent). I would get to know the 'boys forest home'; and had to put up with some bullying here and there – the big boys calling the shots for the small boys. And I was in the latter category, of those at the receiving end of the game. What saved me was the fact that I came there as a sixth-former and could not be treated as a raw 'fresher'. With what I saw, I would subsequently wonder whether I would have survived or endured or gone on to concentrate on my studies if I had started my secondary education at St. Francis. Big boys bullying, taunting, threatening, calling you names – all in the name of a boys' game! Would I have gone through it? Thank God my parents made the decision to send me first to Birch!

Not that there were no uncomfortable moments at Birch. They did not just amount to bullying, the St Francis way. At Birch, it was more of the classmate rivalry from older, bigger boys. A kind of competition in intelligence – as to who was cleverer. But it could be reduced to the physical if one became too clever. One such competitor was Elvis Hallowell, whose father was the Principal (the feared and fearsome disciplinarian, J.E. Hallowell). So much was expected of Elvis owing to his father's position. He was very clever but at the same time outgoing, and perhaps playful. He saw me and another friend, Hassan Koroma, as his most potent competitors in class. He would not restrain a knock on anyone's head and get punished for it when he got outsmarted – he used to call me a *'fityai borbor'* (a disrespectful boy). He particularly hated my habit of asking questions at the tail end of lessons, thereby keeping the teachers much longer in explanation. But we grew above it as time went on and became very close, together with Hassan forming an intellectual triangle, especially during sessions of the literary and debating society. The presence in class of my eldest sister, Rebecca (who would turn out to be a police officer), was also a cushion – she was always ready to confront other students in defence of me (and I would never stop paying back for this).

Elvis Hallowell would later in life become so African-oriented that he officially inverted his names and took the poro name of Gbanabom as his forename. He would subsequently tell me he reached the decision while sojourning in America, where many people rejected his Elvis name-claim for not having any resemblance with Elvis Presley! Elvis is a white man's name! Gbanabom Hallowell would, during the administration of President Koroma, be appointed as Director General of the Sierra Leone Broadcasting Corporation, the state radio and television broadcaster, while I was the Deputy Minister in the Ministry of Information and Communications which officially supervised the broadcaster. Career-wise, Elvis – sorry, Gbanabom – established himself as a poet and has published so many, low-key though.

But, back to St Francis, there was the good side of integration – there would always be the good side. Or perhaps the better side. Integrating into St Francis meant participating in the various aspects of the school's life, one of which was lunch-time mass at the school chapel. At first I was naturally reluctant to attend – taking into consideration the Wesleyan vehemence to Catholic worship. But there came the day when a few of my classmates got the better of me and convinced me to attend. My first ever experience of attending a Catholic service! And it turned out to be a most memorable one.

The white 'brother' priest wore a long white robe with accompanying abracadabra and a long rosary hanging down his neck. The chapel was very small to accommodate just about forty or so students at a time; but it was very neat and well organised inside. Candles were lit, and some smoke was coming from a small pot by the pulpit. As we were on the aisle and about to take our seats, my colleagues bowed and performed the sign of the cross. I followed suit and did the sign. (What was I doing? A Wesleyan pastor's son, now emulating Catholics?) . We sat on the middle pews; and very short monotonous prayers, mimicked from a local prayer book and catechism, were recited. There was no message as such. After a few more readings, the priest called for a partaking in the 'holy communion'.

Communion service in the Wesleyan Church – or more appropriately in the Mabanta Church – was a rare occurrence. I could only remember having previously participated in it twice in my whole Christian experience – and it was actually conducted by the District Superintendent assisted by my father as the local preacher. Therefore, to come to know that Eucharist at the St. Francis chapel was a frequent or normal activity that did not need a special service fascinated me – and attracted me.

When the priest called for the faithful to partake in the drinking of the blood and eating of the body of Christ, I did not have any hesitation to line up with my colleagues to receive 'the bread and the wine' – after all, we were all Christians; and all of us were hungry anyway. But I realised that my friends were looking at me with some skeptical and suspicious eyes in some sort of disbelief and consternation. Yet I thought they were admiring my quick integration and breaking of barriers. Alas, it was for something else.

The moment the service was over, and we went out of the chapel, they all started laughing at me. Only then did they explain that the 'holy communion' should only be taken at the chapel by those who had been baptised as Catholics, and not by a protestant Wesleyan like me. I tried to blame them for not telling me earlier – or why they had always insisted on taking me there anyway. They would not listen to me again. It was so hilarious. And since that day – and for some of them till this day – they gave and started calling me the nickname of 'Corpus Christi', meaning the 'body of Christ'. I would however, for obvious reasons, never again attend lunch-time mass throughout my stay at St. Francis Secondary School.

But I would bizarrely go on to attend mass at a main Catholic Church – the St. Francis Xavier Church itself. If there's any literal meaning to the saying "the Holy Spirit led me to this church", that was it. For it was not something that I planned; neither was I invited to any special service, nor did I tell my parents what I was doing. But on that 'God-morning' of a Sunday, I dressed up and just went away. Was I trying to find meaning to the chapel service? Was I looking for a comparison? Was I just being a teenage rebel? Any of these could be true.

I found myself inside St. Francis Xavier Church along Azzolini Highway (arguably the most important motorway in Makeni, named after the first Catholic Bishop Augustus Azzolini – connecting the city to the Capital Freetown on one end and the 'diamond' city of Kono on the other). A couple of my friends saw me; but I was not bothered. Just like the school chapel service, every activity in the church was very stoical, solemn and somber – a complete contrast to the dancing and loud singing in the Wesleyan Church with all the emotions expressed even during prayer. Here, at St. Francis Xavier Church, the emotions were suppressed and man became a stoic. No wonder it's called 'mass,' I consoled myself.

It would certainly always be hard for the Catholic Church to attract ordinary illiterate people. Those who joined would more likely than not have been initially attracted by the material provisions that came along with Catholicism instead of to actually follow Jesus Christ – but thereafter some had gone on to establish their faith. Most Catholics were literate. The Catholic Church was too liturgical, with lots of prepared readings in English: there was no way a man like my father (with his illiterate background) would have become a Pastor, let alone a Reverend, in the Roman Catholic Church. Then how would the Mabanta people have known Christ in their native language?

If the German monk Martin Luther had not sparked the Protestant movement, one would wonder how many Africans would have really come in contact with the Gospel and accepted the Lordship of Jesus Christ. The Catholic way of worship was certainly out of tune with the nature of the native African. To worship God just as you are is to know God. To worship God in your natural genetic being is the best way to get closer to Him. Until recent modifications that have seen some evangelical-style worship partially introduced in some Catholic churches in Sierra Leone, the appeal of the Roman Catholic Church or its impact in terms of spirituality was very minimal. Many would say they were Catholic Christians but were actually not – there were those who might have just attended a Catholic primary or secondary school but had never since gone to church again, while still claimed to be Catholic.

It was clear I didn't belong here; I didn't want to belong here. I couldn't fit in. I was not meant to belong here. I was a total stranger. But I could sense some kinship feeling: that I could be a part of it, that I was a part of it. Somehow. Therefore, catechism in hand, when it came to reading out the Apostles' Creed (which I knew was a summary of all what I had learnt in the Wesleyan Church), I did not hesitate to confidently and loudly chant along:

"I believe in God, the Father Almighty, Creator of Heaven and earth;

and in Jesus Christ, His only Son Our Lord,

Who was conceived by the Holy Spirit, born of the Virgin Mary, suffered under Pontius Pilate, was crucified, died, and was buried.

He descended into Hell; the third day He rose again from the dead;

He ascended into Heaven, and sitteth at the right hand of God, the Father Almighty; from thence He shall come to judge the living and the dead.

I believe in the Holy Spirit, the holy Catholic Church, the communion of saints, the forgiveness of sins, the resurrection of the body and life everlasting.

Amen."

However, when it came to the 'holy communion' time, I had already learnt my lesson at the school chapel. I stood still, while others processed. I could see two of my friends giggling when they passed by to kneel before the priest for the bread and wine. I was now making a point. I could not reverse the event at the school chapel, but I was not prepared to be a Catholic. I was perhaps saying by my action 'I could attend a Catholic Church but I would remain a Wesleyan Christian.'

The good thing – if it's good – about the Catholic mass was its brevity. Therefore, I was able to return to Mabanta and again attend the Wesleyan service – for at least another two hours! It was a good and memorable Sunday for me! Never had I done that before – and I've not done it since – attending two church services on the same Sunday! It was a foreshadow of what to come: that Wesleyans can commune with Catholics; that the Pope could no longer see every protestant as a Martin Luther;

that a future Pope would meet with a Wesleyan Christian from Mabanta – that Christ reigns in all and over all.

In order not to unnecessarily put any of my friends in the spotlight (perhaps they never disclosed anything to their families), I would prefer not to mention who really did what with me at St Francis. Among my closest pals at the time were Michael Kizito Kargbo (now a senior public servant after a stint as a university academic), Hassan J. Koroma (with whom I came from Birch and has been based in the USA for decades, now being a pastor), Salifu Obasanjo Kamara (who incredibly ended up in the medical profession), Dowzy Tunkara (I lost track of him), Bob R. Kanu (now based in Canada), Lawrence Kai (somewhere in Europe, we bumped into each other at some point in London), Samuel Tarawalie (working for the Office of National Security, and a Wesleyan) and Ibrahim Jallomy Jalloh (worked for Catholic Relief Services and CARITAS for years, now mostly operates as a journalist; he calls himself a 'liberal Muslim', most of us call him a 'Catholic by proxy'). And I'm tempted to name two of our female classmates: Sattia N. Koroma (now Tarawalie by marriage, based in USA) and Salamatu Kamara (saw her once or twice about ten years ago).

It was a moment to behold!

Chapter Twelve

From Grass To Grace

Grafted Into The Family Of The Wesleyan Church Leader; From Fourah Bay College To Concord Times To The Torchlight To Prison

> *"Now, therefore, you are no longer strangers and foreigners, but fellow citizens with the saints and members of the household of God, having been built on the foundation of the apostles and prophets, Jesus Christ Himself being the chief cornerstone, in whom the whole building, being fitted together, grows into a holy temple in the Lord, in whom you also are being built together for a dwelling place of God in the Spirit." (Ephesians 2:19-22)*

The so-called witches who, I was later told, confessed to having tried to 'eat' me while I was a baby but had a change of mind (when one of them intervened on the basis of my parents being 'good neighbours'), must have by now given up. The other witches who made confessions in my teenage years in my presence (of having been unable to 'steal' my pen while they had 'stolen' all the other village pupils' pens – which eventually made me the first ever native-born locally-brought-up son of Mabanta to be admitted in a university), might well have given up on me in terms of trying to use superstitious means to prevent my progress in life.

But one strong natural hurdle remained: poverty.

Not that we were poor in terms of genealogical inheritance: no one came from a ruling or royal family and was poor. After all, we inherited vast lands of thousands of acres spanning several villages in our chiefdom. But these were family possessions. Therefore, although my dad had become the head of the family ruling house during the twilight years and after the passing away of his dad (by virtue of the patrilineal inheritance system of transferring authority to the eldest son), there were several other members of the extended family who would certainly not entertain the idea of selling such lands for the education of one child. They had not done it before; they would not do it now. They could not sell the land to build a house; how would they have sold it for my pursuit of education, with the uncertainty of whether it would be of benefit to the family?

The once-famous Tarawalie ruling house of Mabanta had crumbled to smithereens. Ever since the passing away of the paramount chief installed by that house in 1945 (and the subsequent defeat suffered by his son who was also put forward by the family to succeed his father in 1972), the family's reputation suffered a battering – not least because the chief palace practically fell apart and remained a mound. The family made the mistake of giving the 'crown' to a member from the maternal line whose children (including the son who was defeated) had abandoned the family and deserted the village. This was how members of the Tarawalie family became a homeless marauding group without a house to point at as their own – descendants of a revered ruling house now scattered in various houses in the village as tenants.

My parents had made a major breakthrough by becoming pastors (my mother also had a bit of the pastoral training, as the missionaries gave even the wives an opportunity to study and therefore she could also read the Temne Bible – of course not as well as her husband. So either because of her having been also trained as a semi-pastor or because she was married to a pastor or for both, my mother eventually came to be known, up to this day, as 'Marie Pastor' in the community, as a way of differentiating her from all the other Maries in the village – in the same way as my dad was known as 'John Pastor'). They had certainly broken down the walls of primitivism for the light of salvation and civilisation. They had become rich in spirit and natural thinking, which was why they had put us (their children) in school and endured difficult times – including debts and hard labour – to ensure we were educated. I had, through the grace of God, wholeheartedly grabbed the opportunity and had scaled the heights to be the first pupil of the Wesleyan Primary School of Mabanta to gain admission at Fourah Bay College, a most famous university in Sierra Leone and beyond.

But poverty still stood in the way. And the witches did not need their 'supernatural' powers to know this. It was glaring. Barefaced! I was born in poverty; but in dignity. A bit like being born in a manger; while actually in royalty. Born practically in the hands of white American missionaries (supposedly from the richest country), yet that's not reflected in our family's physical circumstances – at that time.

In terms of actual earnings, Wesleyan pastors were on the list of the least paid. The salaries they received were ridiculous; the clothes they wore were the remnants of the American missionaries' charity, with coats of all sizes hanging loose or tightly gripping their hungry-looking bodily frames. A pastor's home could go for a whole day without the fireside being lit to cook enough food for the whole family. If it were left on my father's earnings alone, we would not have continued with our education because his salary was not even enough to pay the tuition fees of one child. Later-generation American Wesleyan missionary Paul Shea – having had a first-hand experience of what pastors went through in Sierra Leone in the 1970s – would confirm this decades later. In response to an enquiry email of mine in 2006 (as explained in the 'acknowledgements'), even though we had never met (I was very young when he was serving) but knowing now that I was a son of 'those pastors', he stated that: "You have a rich heritage even though the finances on this earth were poor." Indeed, we were poor. And at that time, the 'rich heritage' was still a 'promised land' – not yet realised, not fully grasped.

Therefore, in the meantime, my parents were able to utilise the family land for agricultural purposes. Though it could not be sold, our vast land inheritance was available for cultivation. And mother – a dutiful woman whose tenacity, resilience, obedience and hard-work (who diligently instilled in us 'dignity in poverty' instead of stealing or begging) were unparalleled – made good use of it to sell all types of garden products to get us afloat. But her gardening could only yield as much as to sustain the family during our primary and secondary school days – not to absorb the burden of paying for university and its attendant upkeep expenditure.

The first cushioning intervention had come from above when a charitable international non-governmental organisation, Plan International, came to our chiefdom with the purpose of promoting education by building schools and paying fees for kids. The beautiful part of it was that each child had what they called 'foster parents' in the West who directly shouldered their schooling responsibilities. I loved to exchange letters with my foster parent explaining progress of my schooling. She was female, and I regret not having any of her letters anymore after the war; but I think her name was Christine. She would write to tell me about her country America and about her family (and I enjoyed reading these letters to my parents). But Plan officials strictly warned us never to beg for anything in our replies (in fact, we never had the addresses of our foster parents; we wrote the letters and handed them over to the Plan officials who then posted them on our behalf – likewise the letters we received were without the addresses of the foster parents. I am still to understand the rationale. Oh how I would love to reconnect with my foster parent today, to thank her for her generosity, to tell her how her good deeds helped to make me who I am today – if she is still alive!). Therefore, in terms of getting the necessary educational kick-start in life, it was Plan that saved the day. It was Plan that rescued my education at that point. It was the plan of God!

Plan International provided resources for our primary school to be moved from the corrugated-iron-sheets structure, which was at the same time the church premises, to its current site with a concrete building; Plan paid all our fees, and also provided school materials for us.

But the policy of Plan International at the time was only to support students through primary and secondary school; but not at university.

A new stumbling block to my further pursuit of academia had arisen.

It stirred the family a bit. My father was ruffled, as he made frantic moves to contact wealthy acquaintances: the Member of Parliament of the area at the time, a wealthy relative whose father was given the chieftaincy by the family from the maternal side and who also was put up as a candidate and lost the chieftaincy elections, other prominent relatives; but there was no major headway apart from promises. These were trying times. It was a time for prayer for God's further intervention.

When we went to church on a Sunday and started singing 'Mang Israel ang dayr ang wurr ka ratar' (When Israel out of bondage came), it was not as if we were singing of a distant Israel. We had been brought up to believe that we were the new Israel. Our family saw itself as the new Abrahamic seed – however far-fetched that could have appeared to others. To connect with Christ was not only to become a descendant of Abraham, but a son of God! That was how our grandfather, Pa Sheka, who had mastered the Temne Bible but was embroiled in a bitter land dispute with neighbouring land-owners (apparently backed by the then reigning paramount chief due to chieftaincy rivalry), saw it. That was also how my father who had become a pastor and was continually supportive of his dad took it. Though we were a ruling house that had a very powerful and famous paramount chief, but had now become so poverty-stricken that we did not have a house of our own (except the 'mud-blocked' parsonage), we never gave up on our faith. We were with the firm belief that the Lord was with us and would come to the rescue to roll the sea in front of us away and revive us again.

And He spectacularly rolled it away! It came in a most pleasant way – obviously in consonance with what the Lord actually wanted me to be – and I couldn't have asked for anything better.

* * *

Each year, according to discipleship tradition, Wesleyan pastors were called to a general conference by the Church leadership. And it happened that this particular year the conference was held in Makeni, at the new conference centre that was inherited from Fugerol, a road construction company. This was in 1990, which I would call the year of the great turn-around, the year I was lifted from the miry clay and set upon a rock to stand. We had been praying for this mountain to be moved a thousand times, but the answer from God could not have been more flattering. The proverbial last card – the winning card. There was no better way of showing that the answer came directly from Him.

When things were heading to nowhere in terms of getting the sponsorship to the university, I was already preparing myself for job-seeking, even if it was teaching, in order to remain within academia and at the same time gather resources to enter university the coming year, as this particular year seemed to have hit the rocks. I told my parents not to worry as I appreciated their efforts. But God had a better plan – which He rolled out at the Wesleyan annual conference at Mankneh in Makeni.

If you ever heard of God changing one's circumstances in the twinkling of an eye, if you ever heard of a rags-to-riches story, a 'Cinderella' or 'Slumdog Millionaire' tale; then here's another one – and I am the protagonist. The twinkling of an eye started with the twinkling of a move by my father. He had asked me to come with him to the conference centre on the second day of proceedings. It was not unusual as he used to take me – at times with my brother – to previous Church programmes including conferences if they were held in the Makeni vicinity. I knew he had discussed it with my mother as she found nice clothes for me to wear and she took a thorough meticulous look at me to make sure I was kempt enough.

It had happened that the Wesleyan Church of Sierra Leone had undergone undoubtedly its greatest leadership transformation in terms of giving it a truly national character and prominence when it elected a new leader in the person of Rev. Dr. Yaidy Martin Kroma (commonly known as Pa YM). Before him, the head of the Church had the title of 'District Superintendent.' This was because the Sierra Leone Wesleyan Church (SLWC) was officially a district of the American Wesleyan Mission (AWM) with resident American missionaries very much in charge of administration. When Pa Kroma took over, coming with a wealth of experience from Liberia where he had lived for decades and became successful, one of his first reforms was to change his title from 'District Superintendent' to 'National Superintendent' and the name of the church from 'Sierra Leone Wesleyan Church' to 'Wesleyan Church of Sierra Leone'. Independence. The Americans would now be 'Global Partners'.

The purpose of my father taking me to this conference at this particular time was for me to meet the new head of Church. He had already spoken to him about me. It was a very informal encounter in a formal setting. There was a morning session where prayers, exhortations, felicitations and 'singspiration' were performed and thereafter it was break-time.

Pa Y.M. Kroma was a natural, down-to-earth, person-to-person leader, as I would come to know him. During the break, he took time to have pep talks with the pastors. The aura of his magnanimity stood out in the fact that he came to the Church with personal wealth, being the owner of a business chain called 'Koni Enterprises'. He was on his own merit a very powerful, highly connected and influential personality, having had a stint in Sierra Leone's early politics before 'escaping' to Liberia where he again created strong political ties with the ruling class there (the reason his surname was spelt the Liberian way) and was only forced to return home to Sierra Leone after his political godfather President William Tolbert was overthrown and assassinated in a bloody coup.

Pa Kroma, as he was fondly called by many, had his fleet of vehicles, and didn't need one from the Church like his predecessors. He even refused to take a salary – his private business was enough to take care of his family's needs. He brought a new flare of authority in the Church, with administrative acumen, by creating new departments manned by young energetic men and women, raising the Church's profile nationally and internationally as he had a powerful networking relationship with the missionaries in America. With all this, Pa YM was still a very down-to-earth man who had time to chat with half-literate and poverty-stricken pastors during break.

He was in a dark suit, white shirt and a red tie to match; and I could vividly remember my dad bidding his time to catch his eye, clutching my hand and looking for the opportunity. And when it did come, it was Pa YM himself who called on my dad. "Yes, John, how are things going?" And I could feel my dad's hand pressing mine harder, drawing me nearer, and responding, "Thank God, sir… I have just brought my son I told you about yesterday," pushing me to the front for him to see me.

"You mean this is the boy?" Pa YM asked in surprise, looking at my little physical frame, a village teenager, and continuing, "He's the one that has gained admission at the university? What a smart boy!!" I knew immediately that he liked me, and his subsequent actions confirmed that. He immediately told my dad that indeed he would take me in to reside at his house in Freetown, and directed my dad to take me to his wife, who was simply called 'Mammy YM' and was in the kitchen leading the cooking for the conference. It was pre-ordained, I would wholeheartedly acknowledge on reflection, as the wife's own reaction was more poignant after seeing me: "It's good to have a child that makes his parents proud. We will take him in. Let him come to Freetown next week."

Wow. That was it. My life had changed in the twinkling of an eye. The doubts, the obstacles, the barriers to my further pursuit of education had just been broken down and the door to greater opportunities had just been opened wide. To merely say my circumstances had changed would be an understatement. It was a very radical change vis-à-vis when I took into consideration the roof-leaking 'dorty-block' house of a parsonage I grew up in and the mini palace I was transferred to in the Lumley aristocratic suburb of Freetown. Pa YM's house was one of the most magnificent and resplendent mansions in Freetown with 24-hours electricity supply via a private generator plant and all the goodies that went along with that.

It was so easy to become integrated into my new family: if the parents had liked me, their children fell in love with me. All of them became fond of me, as per the way I spoke (especially the Temne language, alongside with its traditional stories) and the way I did things with natural honesty and diligence (never losing a single cent when given the task of running one of the family shops, doing bank transactions without a hitch, my devotion to Church work and participation during morning prayer etc etc). I became particularly, of course naturally, attached to the Kromas' youngest son, Benjamin (Benji), as we were in the same age bracket. But that did not mean I was not also in bond with the others – boys and girls. However, soon, I would find myself being used as an example of seriousness as against my buddy (Benji) who was having great challenges in his educational pursuits. Not surprising – a young boy, surrounded by opulence: no time for school books! Automatically, and naturally, he and I bonded; and we got engaged in many youthful escapades – especially with cars at night… I'll rather stop there… He eventually went on to thrive in the US anyway!

As a family, we became a close-knit group. Morning prayer at those early stages of my coming was a must for all, reading the Bible, discussing with exhortations and singing on a daily basis. There was no discrimination as to the food we ate, we went to church together in the same vehicles, and I was soon to be incorporated into the Kissy Dockyard Wesleyan Church choir, of which Mammy YM was the choir leader (and I, having been a chorister and even youth president of the Mabanta Wesleyan Church, didn't find it hard to jell into the new setting). To complete the jigsaw of integration, confidence in me grew so rapidly that, as I had a few more months before university would open, I was given one of the Koni enterprises shops on Mill Street in the east of Freetown to run. Certainly, this was an example of someone gaining favour before God and before men.

I lived with this family for six years, and I could not have asked for a better pedestal for exposure to the wider world through education – with one of the Kroma kids, Lacee, being a student at FBC at the same time an extra advantage for me (she used to cook a lot!). My record as an exceptional student at FBC both in class and on campus in general still rings a bell – as lecturers used me as an example of brilliance and my colleague students admired my journalistic prowess. The Students' Union government gave me a special award as 'The Most Objective Journalist' on campus, and I eventually graduated with one of the most enviable degrees – BA Honours in English Language & Literature, having had to be one of seven students out of hundreds to be invited to the Honours class in the first place. The Kroma influence and amenities played a great part.

My benefactor became more interested in my affairs simply because he was a man who naturally liked progressive and education-loving people. I became like a special assistant to him, writing letters and other documents whenever he asked me to, and travelling with him to important Wesleyan conferences around the country. The attachment became so strong that when the pa started fresh political escapades by moving around the country with President Momoh after the former was appointed Chairman of NPA, my value increased literally. The pa would come home and update me on his activities.

We have a family joke that has stuck through the years about one of these updates going bad after I had mistakenly taken fuel in the pa's car meant for the generator and filled it into the tank of the mammy's car instead. It was a genuine mistake on my part. But the pa was not happy about this, and he made it clear. He was updating us as a family as he showed pictures of a ceremony at his hometown of Kambia attended by the President wherein he (Pa YM) was carried aloft by supporters for all to see. His emphasis was that he stole the show. And then he turned to me, "Sheka, do you get the humour?" Excited as I was, I responded "Yes pa, I got the humour." We all started laughing. But not knowing that the issue of the fuel was still bothering him, his immediate reply was, "But Sheka, who told you to take my fuel and pour it in the mammy's car?" All of us just burst out laughing the more! To this day, we share that joke!

* * *

A memorable national action I took, through Pa YM's concurrence, was during the NPRC junta that overthrew President Momoh, as some politicians using the media wanted him to be arrested and were writing all types of articles against him as an 'APC apparatchik' or a 'Momoh lackey' because he was Board Chairman of the National Power Authority. I realised he was very confused and tormented, he was looking for support, and he was even contemplating on going back to Liberia if it came to the worst. I prayed over it and received an answer through an article I wrote in his defence. When I showed him the piece, I could see how his face brightened and glowed and showed radiance of relief. After reading all of it, he embraced me and then asked that I went with him to the office to improve it with more facts. And then instead of merely an article meant for the press, he said I should do it in a letter-form addressed to the Head of State then, Capt Valentine Strasser, copying all Secretaries of State (as the military government called their Ministers), all diplomatic missions, and the press itself.

The letter brought out the truth about YM Kroma's life, how he was not a 'yes man' APC member, but was one of those who stood up against Siaka Stevens when he became 'dictatorial' by forming a breakaway group called the UDP. How he fled to Liberia following the persecution that resulted from that action. How he had stopped politicking since his return and was now the head of the Wesleyan Church making great contributions to national development, and that the position of Chairman NPA was actually apolitical – and the ceremony during which he 'stole the show' was traditional rather than political. Strasser's response of calling Pa Kroma to State House to assure him of his safety was most welcome news to the family. You would imagine the love for me becoming more buoyant and exceptional. It's regrettable that letter was lost during the war.

It must be stated that the impact of a letter bearing my name was felt nationally on the heels of me having been the first to actually fire a very critical shot at the NPRC military regime with an incisive article I had titled 'Captain Strasser is not our redeemer' just few days after the coup. This was my first ever article published in a national newspaper and it caused a general furore that unwittingly brought me into the national and perhaps the international spotlight.

* * *

The overthrow of Joseph Momoh's APC by the NPRC was a most dramatic and unexpected event that changed Sierra Leone's socio-political landscape forever. The APC 'one party' regime had apparently appeared as if it was going to live up to its motto of 'live forever' even when the administration had obviously become hopeless in addressing the needs of the citizens including security, and strangled by IMF 'conditions'. A war which started as banditry, as propagated by the regime propagandists, roused a poorly-equipped army from its sleepiness in ceremonial duties of march-passing to its natural function of defending the nation. Caught unawares would be an understatement. The war became the window used by disgruntled soldiers to topple the regime of JS Momoh, bringing in Valentine Strasser. President Momoh ran away to Guinea, and most former government functionaries were arrested and locked up in Pademba Road maximum prison, the most prominent prisoner being the once ubiquitous and fearsome Inspector General of Police James Bambay Kamara.

Ever since I entered the university, I had established myself as a writer/campus journalist from the very first year. It was a distinctive vocation that endeared me to various sectors of the university, ranging from the college administration to lecturers to student clubs and the students union government (which would eventually give me 'The Most Objective Journalist' award). Week in week out I would write articles on both campus and national issues. The coming of the NPRC would not deter me.

Due to the entrenched nature of the one-party government, the APC seemed impregnable; and for the enlightened, it was weird for a one-party government that had already started reforms by initiating a democratic process with many registered political parties, to be overthrown. The international community was wary. The khaki boys needed legitimacy; whoever among them brought up the idea of going to FBC to seek it from the students did them a lot of good. And it was just coincidental (or is it?) that the ground was fertile for that, as the students union government at the time was controlled by 'anti-APC' students, making it easy for the military to be given a platform to speak to the general body of students. And it worked; as we all virtually instinctively marched down from Mount Aureol, dancing with the soldiers, followed by civilians on the streets, to the Siaka Stevens national stadium. We were all dipped and steeped into the euphoria of the moment, singing insulting songs against the APC politicians, and praising the military boys as our heroes and their new leader Captain Valentine Strasser as 'our redeemer'.

A week later, the journalist in me, the real me, woke up and I wrote an article titled 'Captain Strasser is not our redeemer', as usual for the campus press. I thought it was an ordinary article; most who read it thought otherwise – that it was extraordinary. The usual accolades I received from colleagues reached fever-pitch, in admiration of the article, as I reflected in it that the exuberance and overzealousness for the NPRC junta was clothed in over-ambition and could actually be counterproductive – that if a man had shot a crocodile that was trying to prey on another man, the rescue mission would only be complete when the drowning man would have been brought out of the water to the shore. Shooting the crocodile was good enough, but not good enough for the drowning man as yet. I argued that the unreserved praises and jubilation were actually premature and could also only lead the new leaders into complacency in thinking that the one act of overthrowing an apparently hated regime was enough. The people had obviously given legitimacy to the unconstitutional act, but Sierra Leone urgently needed to be rescued socio-economically, not just politically. Political rescue without economic rescue was ephemeral. Our economy was held hostage by a Middle-Eastern Indo-Lebanese cartel, with the governing class doing nothing about it but instead patronising them amidst general poverty and malaise for the majority of native Sierra Leoneans. Captain Strasser would only become a redeemer if he would actually overturn the status quo in terms of the general welfare of the ordinary man.

The article was the talk of the campus and our Political Science Lecturer Dr. Habib Sesay had to stop lectures to give me an opportunity to talk about it in class. But a senior student had another idea: Ibrahim Sobonikeh Sesay (who had all along been known as an 'APC student leader') did not only praise the article, he said it was too good to be left for campus eyes only. He encouraged me to take it to a national newspaper.

I had somebody to consult: Lansana Gberie – his peers preferred to call him Lans Gberie. By the primordial standards of Sierra Leone's ethnocentric socio-political make-up, we should not be friends. But what a university education does, or is supposed to do, is to break the yoke of primitivism in making sense of the universe. University education, during the acquisition of which we meet people outside our 'normal environment', should make our basic instincts or baser elements not totally irrelevant but only relevant in a wider perspective of understanding the wholesomeness of humanity and the universe. Lans was from Bo, southern Sierra Leone; I was from Makeni, northern Sierra Leone. He was Mende; *mineng me Themne*. The traditional parallel lines that should never meet. He was a Catholic; you now know who I am.

When I entered Fourah Bay College and joined the 'bus tick' or 'chuks press' media frenzy on campus, one man who admired my writing skills and nudged me on was Lans. I naturally became attached to him because I met him in the profession there – he was two years ahead. He was also a very fine and prolific writer. We belonged to the same 'socio-political camp' in campus politics. Whenever I took on established campus writers and prevailed in argument and ideas, Gberie would always commend me. And some of these guys I battled with were his schoolmates from Bo.

Lans and I developed a friendship that became better when we worked together at *Concord Times* newspaper after graduation – we would proffer different opinions on particular topics in the same newspaper, at times in the same edition; but we still got along perfectly. Notwithstanding, such a man would not be one of those to follow me in my patriotic adventurism and zealousness of leaving *Concord Times* to open *The Torchlight*. During the military interregnum, Lans and I had differing views on solutions to the critical national challenges then, and we had a long and open-hearted discussion about it in Banjul, The Gambia, after the reinstatement of President Kabbah. We ended up understanding each other – again. When I returned from Banjul and worked with the Truth and Reconciliation Commission (TRC), Lans, then already based in Canada, came at some point and we together visited and witnessed some of the 'reconciliation' sessions in Kono. Lans and I collaborated on research work while I worked at the David-Tam-Baryoh-founded Centre for Media Education & Technology (C-MET) – I remember we interviewed the ubiquitous civil-defence-chief-turned-Minister-of-Internal-Affairs Sam Hinga Norman before he was arrested by the Special Court for war crimes. Lans made a two-day personal visit to me in Manchester during my sojourn in England (at the time, I was already working for the Citizens Advice Bureau, where I took him). We would over the years meet several times in London, even as he attended my engagement party in London. When I was appointed into Government by President Koroma, Lans and I continued the relationship. He would come to my house and we would hang out most times he visited Sierra Leone as colleague journalists, discussing the issues away. When I was Deputy Minister of Information & Communications and he was in Ethiopia working with the AU, I stopped by and spent a night on a trip to Rwanda.

We had our political differences but we never allowed them to becloud our sense of patriotism. Our informal rule was to play the ball and not aim at the man. We would argue over issues, sometimes sharply; but that was it. At times we did it through articles: when he was the apparent or suspected writer of articles discrediting the government in *Africa Confidential* (he never admitted being the very influential magazine's correspondent to me, tongue in cheek), I used to respond with the same vituperative ferocity as Deputy Minister of Information & Co-Government Spokesman. One such response from me that vividly stood out was titled '*Africa Confidential's* Campaign Of Calumny Against Sierra Leone.' Things would subside from their side until after the President deemed it fit to transfer me to the Ministry of Internal Affairs. I would later get Lans to try to understand President Koroma by making them meet in person. He understood – but only for a while. When the politicking season was on the horizon, the campaign, with not much of the calumny, resumed. He and I would later meet in New York over drinks to discuss issues bordering on academia and politics. Sierra Leone was always bigger than us.

Lans was recently appointed by President Julius Maada Bio as Ambassador to Switzerland. I would suppose, apart from the Bo connection, their relationship took firm roots when Bio, as then military Head of State, had, in collaboration with the Ivorian authorities, organised direct peace talks with rebel leader Foday Sankoh in Abidjan, and Lans witnessed the historic event as a representative of the Inter Press Service. But above all, he is qualified for the job. I am happy for him – just as he was happy for me when I served in the preceding Government.

It is worthy to note that, days before his appointment, we had a long chat on nationalism, patriotism and the like – as usual – and he was weighing in on the necessity to serve in government. I would suppose my assurances to him that it was a venture worth taking, using my personal experience as an example, as service to country by way of paying back, added to his resolve. It was during that conversation, talking about my pending publication of this book, that he enquired about my 'war-time diary' (an actual diary I kept when I was in hiding during the latter part of the war), which I used to serialise in *The Torchlight*. I told him it would be the next book… The tenacity of our friendship has outlasted turbulent political waters.

So – back to the main story on FBC journalism – it was Lans (having actually been one of the first persons that lauded the article the morning I pasted it, he being an early reader of campus articles) whom I consulted on the issue of whether to take the article against the NPRC (of which current President Bio was one of the leaders) to a national newspaper. "Why not? You can see how it has already ignited debates on campus," he pushed me. He suggested the *New Shaft*, operated by the late crusading Franklyn Bunting Davies. I took it to five newspapers, but only the *New Breed* edited then by George Khoryama (an internationally-exposed veteran journalist) published it. At the time, the *New Breed* was arguably the most widely-read newspaper in Sierra Leone. And it did the trick of shooting me into prominence when the article was published. I broke the glass ceiling!

The regime was irked, and soldiers came looking for me on campus. I made an escape through the 'canal' (a walking pathway down the hill) when I got the news through students' information networks. The matter was later resolved when I re-appeared after about two weeks of absence from campus and tempers had calmed down – as even the NPRC boys themselves could not believe I was the author when they saw my 'little body frame'. They ended up admiring me. And to this day Captain Strasser is an acquaintance (he and I appeared on a radio programme in the 2012 elections in support of the re-election of President Koroma of the APC as against the SLPP's Maada Bio, who was Strasser's Deputy in the NPRC but would eventually organise a palace coup against his boss… And the same Maada Bio is now a civilian President… Life is a cycle).

* * *

Therefore, going back to the Kroma family story, it was the journalistic clout gotten from that article which made the letter I wrote in defence of my benefactor, Rev. Y.M.Kroma, to be taken more seriously. My name was no longer strange to the leadership of the NPRC. Pa Kroma could not believe when Strasser called him to State House to assure him protection. My personal relationship with my benefactor grew stronger and stronger – I became like a son and a confidante.

But the story with a fairy-tale beginning would end in tragedy, a heartrending tragedy. Pa Y.M. died in the process – rather, he was killed by rebels during the civil war. What started with a roller-coaster high ended in a deep pit. Let me narrate that part quickly and briefly.

Having graduated from the university with an honours degree in English language and Literature, many doors were open for me in terms of employment – in the public service, in the private sector, even in the Wesleyan Church itself as it was headed by Pa Kroma; but I had made up my mind that the journalism I had started with would be my path of reaching out to the world. Pa YM had no qualms with that. And when I decided to leave *Concord Times* newspaper (which – as I will narrate in detail in a subsequent chapter – I had been working for since my second year at the university) to set up *The Torchlight*, Pa YM was very supportive both morally and financially, as he brought in his then-political ally John Karefa-Smart to contribute to the project (I also sought support from elsewhere including a big fan of mine who was ECOWAS Executive Secretary Dr Abass Bundu and outgone President Koroma, who would later actually be the main support for the continued existence of the paper).

At the time I made that decision, Pa YM had already become a full-blown politician, having benefited from the transition from military to civilian rule as a Member of Parliament representing Kambia for the John Karefa Smart-led UNPP. However, this was one thorny issue in the YM Kroma family, as Mammy YM was totally opposed to any involvement in politics, preferring to totally remain in the Church. She harangued and dissociated herself from it, never attending a single political meeting, and stamping her foot that not one meeting should be held in the house. Her reason was simple: "I've seen enough of the bad side of politics both in Sierra Leone and in Liberia." Apparently, they had agreed or as she put it 'vowed' after the Liberian debacle never to dabble into politics again. But the pa said times had changed. And I was in the middle of it as a Christian journalist – a profession she liked me doing as well. She liked my writings! And I would like to add that my journalistic passion was honed in the Kroma family home where I started a domestic news-sheet for family members only! Mammy YM loved it. The pa also loved it. But it faced its own trials. That's where I'll stop as far as the family newspaper was concerned.

Despite the apparent support *The Torchlight* received from the political class (well, a potpourri of opposition support), I made it very clear that it would maintain an independent status with the country's interests placed above political and personal interests. It wouldn't take long for the test to come. The writings in *The Torchlight* were incisive and thought-provoking as I assembled a radical firebrand group of young journalists with a patriotic fervour. The baptism of fire came when we published a front page story titled 'Tejan Kabbah Bribes MPs'. Pa YM was very angry with me for the publication. I came home in the morning to find out I no longer had a room in the house and my belongings had been thrown out.

However, in sharp contrast, Mammy YM was very sympathetic to me, giving me words of encouragement to stand by what I believed in – to stand up and stand out and live my dreams, through Christ. This was not a surprise because – as I stated earlier – she had always been fiercely against her husband going back into politics, and would only want to remain and was satisfied with being the wife of the National Superintendent of the Wesleyan Church of Sierra Leone – not the wife of a politician, even if he were president. This was a tough position, and the fall-out was visible. She refused to participate in any political activity, whether it had to do directly with her husband or politics in general. She was always about church choir, church women's conferences, crusades, and church, church, church. Therefore her advice to me – just as she had been doing about my education since I lived with them – was invaluable. Her admonition to be my own man stuck. And I regarded it as coming from a mother – like from my own biological mother. Because, in actual fact, in one of her admonitions in the past, she confidently told me that I had now become like her biological son with all the diligence and honesty I had demonstrated in her home. "To be regarded as a son does not have to be biological; an adopted son can be like a biological son or even more if he behaves in a proper and respectful manner. And you have more than satisfied me," she had said. I would have to shed tears about two decades later when I would have become Press Secretary to the President and decided to visit her in her location in Florida USA and she would remind me of those words.

* * *

But back to my journalistic encounter with Parliament and the fall-out with Pa YM. Late afternoon of the day of the publication, I received a letter from the Clerk of Parliament summoning me to 'the well' on a charge of 'contempt of Parliament'. In that Parliament, of course, was the Hon. Y.M. Kroma; and it would be the moment to meet him face-to-face since the publication and since my eviction.

My parliamentary summons stirred the nation; and while I became a villain to some, I was a hero to many. I appeared confidently in a long-flowing African dress, knowing full well the support I had from the press gallery and some sections of the public. You should have heard the gasps and seen the grinning countenances of parliamentarians when I was ushered into Parliament in ceremonious style by the sergeant-at-arms in like manner as the President, except for the purpose and the absence of a signatory tune. The Speaker of Parliament, SMF Kutubu, in a husky voice was yelling: "Sergeant-at-arms, where is Mr. Sheka Tarawalie?" The sergeant-at-arms, a tall and imposing figure, responded: "He is right behind me, Mr. Speaker', but only when he moved aside did the Speaker see a Mahatma-Ghandi-looking small figure in front of him; thereby exclaiming: "Is this really Mr. Sheka Tarawalie, the man who is making us not to sleep? Is this he who has been causing so much controversy?" – thereby generating murmurings and laughter from both MPs and the general audience.

MP after MP from both sides of the aisle, including the opposition UNPP's John Karefa Smart who accused me of hijacking a newspaper that was supposed to be a mouthpiece of his party, lambasted me. To his credit and respect, Pa Kroma did not say anything; but in one of my attempts to have eye contacts with several MPs in the hall, he and I looked at each other for a long while without knowing how to interpret it.

In my response, I stood by the story, refusing to reveal my source. I said I was just doing my professional and constitutional duty with no malicious intent against anyone, that I held the House of Representatives itself in high esteem, and that MPs should look at the merits of the story vis-à-vis the country's democracy. But if, in the process, I had hurt them – I submitted – I was sorry about that. I stopped short of apologising for the publication. This merely brought more anger and outrage from the MPs, with some shouting "You cannot preach to us" "You are not more patriotic than us" "Look at this small boy." In the end, the Speaker said I had not shown any remorse, though nobody denied the story or tried to explain why MPs accepted a so-called loan from the government-owned Sierra Leone Commercial Bank. The secret deal was hatched at night with President Kabbah just after the MPs had embarrassed him by rejecting his nominee for the Ministry of Works & Housing. According to our sources, the 'loan' was given on condition that the MPs should go soft with other nominees;

and no collateral was pegged on the said loan. To this day, as I write, those loans have never been repaid, with most of those MPs now dead (including Speaker Kutubu himself)!

During the parliamentary proceedings, what surprised or amazed many, including even government sympathisers, was the clear fact that the decision to jail me had already been taken before I was heard. We had already received the news the night before, and I was prepared for it; but the Speaker exposed himself when he took out a well-prepared type-written verdict that he read out pronouncing a guilty sentence on me and sending me down to the Pademba Road maximum prison for one month with no alternative fine or any room for an appeal. From press man to prisoner; from penman to prison. Life's twists and turns on course.

When the Speaker was reading the verdict, I was looking straight into his face without blinking. When he pronounced my sentence, I turned to the side of the opposition and had a long look at John Karefa Smart and Pa YM, and the rest of the opposition MPs with a feeling that they had sold out. The trumpeted democracy was for sale. It had been sold for a personal loan to purchase Mercedes Benz cars for the private use of MPs. I could see the joy in their faces, their taunting eyes, eyes of satisfaction, that something great had been achieved – with the hitting of their desks in approval of the Speaker's decision. But if they expected me to be downcast, they were mistaken. I paid them back with a smile. So I was really smiling broadly as the sergeant-at-arms escorted me back, now a bit roughly, out of the hall only to be taken straight into a police car which was actually the presidential vehicle that escorted President Kabbah's convoy every day to work. That was how high the matter was taken.

This was a most unprecedented action in the history of journalism in Sierra Leone. Not that there had not been astute legendary Sierra Leonean journalists before: there was the anti-colonial and post-colonial crusader I.T.A. Wallace-Johnson (well known in Nigeria and Ghana as much as in his home-country) who was thrown into prison several times by both the British colonial authorities and our immediate post-Independence leaders; there was also firebrand Ibrahim Bash-Taqi, for whom the notorious 1965 Public Order Act was enacted by Albert Margai of the SLPP (but every other government has left it there to this day I'm writing) and he ended up being executed during the APC's Siaka Stevens; and there were the *Tablet* boys (Pius Foray, Hindolo Trye, I.B. Kargbo, Frank Kposowa, Wilfred Leeroy Kabs-Kanu, Cleo Hanciles etc) who stood up against the one-party rule of Siaka Stevens and got proscribed; Sarif Easmon, Sam Metzger, Sam Short, Saaba Tumoe, Paul Kamara, Olu Gordon, Franklyn Bunting-Davies, Lansana Fofana, Julius Spencer, Abdulai Bayraytay, Sorie Fofana, Chernor Ojuku Sesay, Umaru Fofana, Sylvester Rogers, Jonathan Leigh, David Tam-Baryoh, Philip Neville, plus many others including reporters, all of whom at one time or another suffered persecution and/or incarceration for their journalism under previous regimes (others like Paul Mansaray and Conrad Roy were killed by rebels or died in prison, as it were) – thereby making it the most unattractive profession for those who wanted to have peace in life.

But under the SLPP of President Kabbah, I was the first victim – as mine was a first to have been summoned to Parliament as a journalist and be sent straight to prison. The matter, happening just few months after a transition from a military junta to a civilian government, consequently attracted the attention of international press-freedom organisations like Reporters Without Borders (with its more popular French acronym, RSF) and the Committee to Protect Journalists (CPJ), which actually wrote a letter to President Ahmad Tejan

Kabbah condemning my incarceration through "conviction without trial".

I will not be the last. Ibrahim Seaga Shaw, Charles Abayomi Roberts, Gibril Gbanabom Koroma and Max Jimmy all of *Expo Times*, Hilton Fyle of *123 Newspaper*, Edison Yonghai of *The Point* would either be summoned or 'sentenced' by Parliament or/and be detained at the CID – though none more than just days, the government having already felt the weight of international press-freedom organisations in my instance. Actually, going to jail in your twenties – or at any age whatsoever – for not committing a crime (and when you sincerely believe you are doing a service to your country) is a most unfathomable scenario! A court trial would have – perhaps – made little sense. But I accepted the situation.

(There would perhaps not be a more poignant occasion of reversal of fortunes than when, a little over a decade later, I would appear in the same Parliament for approval as Deputy Minister. Just one or two of the members of the Kutubu-led Parliament were now remaining as I faced Speaker Abel Stronge. And now, that my same issue was brought up by some Members of Parliament as a patriotic stance deserving of my endorsement. They unanimously approved me! Politics, at times, makes me laugh). That was some digression or running ahead of the story....

On the way to prison, I was sandwiched in the back seat by two police officers, one on my left and another on my right. Another was seated in front; and the driver was also a police officer. All of them were older men. I had a brief chat with them as they drove me with breakneck speed with siren to prison. Whether they were acting or genuinely tried to console me, they were very courteous and one was saying something like 'That's how your namesake Siaka Stevens started'. I took courage in that. They handed me over to the prison officers, who took my details and my personal belongings including my clothes and gave me a prisoner uniform.

You would have to indulge me, dear reader, to make the point that I never had any prior plan to denigrate parliamentarians. I did not denigrate them. As a person, I would have refused to publish the story knowing it was going to affect my benefactor; but as a professional working with an editorial team that had decided in favour of publication, I could not have prevailed on the basis of me being the editor when in actual fact I knew it was a fact. Taking that course would have undermined the independence of the paper. I would have sold out. And my colleagues would have lost faith in me. But by taking the prison flak, we were collectively making a point that we were standing up for Sierra Leone. And my team continued to write very fiery articles while I was incarcerated, tormenting the government, causing the police to invite the Acting Editor (Tatafway Tumoe, one of those who followed me from *Concord Times*, but unfortunately would pass away when I would have become Deputy Minister several years later and I had to bear the burden of reading Scripture and doing a tribute at his funeral) to CID headquarters and threatening to send him to prison like me. Tumoe also wrote a very popular, revolutionary column which he had started at *Concord Times* and carried over to *The Torchlight* too. He titled it 'The Heart of the Matter' – named after English author Graham Greene's award-winning 1948 novel, whose plot was set in colonial Sierra Leone when he was a British intelligence officer during the Second World War. Tataf (as we fondly called my then-Deputy Editor) was always fond of the fact that 'the Catholic novelist' and former journalist himself wrote *The Heart of the Matter* (or its first draft) at central Freetown's once-famous City Hotel (turned to rubble during the civil war). At times when we wanted to look for 'the muse', we would go hang out at "the Bedford Hotel on Bond Street". It had, at one time or another, hosted prominent world leaders like France's Charles de Gaulle during World War II itself and a-then-35-year-old Queen Elizabeth II during her 1961 visit – accompanied by the Duke of Edinburgh, using the same old transatlantic sea-route with the royal yacht *Britannia* berthing in the waters of the self-same natural harbour, this instant a quay named after her – for post-Independence celebrations (though she still remained Head of State until 1971).

Perhaps nothing made the establishment feel guiltier than when my colleagues continually left out a blank page in every edition of the paper with regards my famous 'From The Black Tank' column, with the words *"This space is empty because the writer is in jail!"* . It was the idea of my colleagues. The police wanted them to stop it; but how could they! Until I came out amid fanfare after a month, rallying with cars around the city – sending a message to the authorities that the ideological struggle had only begun.

* * *

In a nutshell, that was how I fell out with the man who was virtually a father to me. I came out of prison to a new address, of course. I made efforts to patch up things with him, in trying to prove to him I was just pursuing a genuine and sincere cause with no personal malice. I met him a couple of times in his private office and we continued attending the same Kissy Dockyard Wesleyan Church (though he had become an infrequent attendee). We would meet in public gatherings in his capacity as a politician and me as a journalist.

But destiny had put a wedge between us, because the ideological divide widened when I continued my anti-establishment (what others called anti-SLPP) stance, and he was drifted away to abandon the UNPP to cross-carpet to the SLPP. President Kabbah eventually appointed him as Resident Minister North. He held this position until he was reportedly killed by RUF rebels when they entered Freetown in January 1999.

By that time, so much had happened in the political status quo, as the SLPP was overthrown a few months after my imprisonment, heralding the ill-fated and internationally denounced AFRC military regime. I was obviously associated with the regime with the wrong feeling that I knew about the coup beforehand due to my critical articles against the overthrown government. The military junta was roundly condemned for being just that – and matters were worsened by the invitation of the rebels to join the government as a way of ending the war. However, the rebels' presence in the cities was menacing to most civilians and their violence-prone activities would only harden the international resolve to reverse the coup. Notwithstanding, our newspaper took the stance of an anti-military intervention by Nigerian-led forces, as ironically the 'big brother' nation was under the tight grip of General Sanni Abacha's military junta. We called for a peaceful resolution of the conflict, even as we revealed that an estimated fifty thousand people would perish, according to military sources, in the event of a military intervention.

That did not go down well with the ousted Kabbah regime. Therefore, when the interventionists at last succeeded in removing the junta through sanctions – backed by a military blockade of land, air and sea borders, with jet fighters constantly bombing mainly military but sometimes civilian targets – and an actual infantry combatant operation, my life was in clear danger. My name was on a death list that was being read out on radio. At a time when jungle justice was the order of the day – burning 'collaborators' alive by hanging tyres on them, pouring petrol and jeering them to death – I had to run for my dear life to hide in Mabanta, my home-village (if there's need for a reminder). It was during that period (that is, the second inning of the SLPP government of President Kabbah) that Pa Kroma made the final turn-around and got the ministerial appointment.

Though I was already in hiding in Mabanta, when the news of the killing of Pa Kroma came through the radio, I wept profusely as if I had lost my biological father. I had not had time to cry over my circumstances; but I cried for a man from whom I had learnt and benefited so much. I was grateful to him. I would not forget his great contribution to my education and my life in general. He was a good man.

When I would eventually come out of hiding after the cataclysmic events that forced peaceful negotiations and the signing of the Lomé Peace Accord in July 1999, I reconnected with the YM Kroma family, given a room again in the house – underlining the chord of love that existed between us – before moving out on my own to stand alone. It's worthy to note that they all along knew I was in hiding in Makeni, and at one time I sent a note to elder daughter Martina through a Wesleyan Church delegation led by the man who succeeded Pa YM as National Superintendent, Rev. S.D. Kanu. I had merely recounted Scripture: "In this world you would have tribulation; but be of good cheer, I have overcome the world."

I would later travel to the UK, where I sought political asylum and got married there. I only returned when called upon by President Ernest Bai Koroma to serve as his Press Secretary after the APC had defeated the SLPP in 2007. I eventually used one of my trips to the US as Press Secretary to visit Mammy YM who had since relocated to one of her daughters, Elleen, in Florida. It was one of the most memorable moments in my life, a great re-union of life-enduring impact. She surprised even her own children when she took to the kitchen to prepare cassava leaves for me – something they said she had not done in virtually all the years she had been there. And she and I were up till about 2am (US time) talking, chatting, reflecting: she was proud of me, she took me as her own son, she prayed for me, gave me pieces of advice, and blessed me. What I gave her was between us, and would remain so. However, I did not know it was a valedictory meeting – that when I was leaving Florida, I was actually saying goodbye to her for the last time on earth. Just about a month after my return, she passed away peacefully.

When her memorial service was held at the Kissy Dockyard Wesleyan Church, I was the one chosen by the family to give tribute on behalf of the children. That explained the bond. And I made it clear that she was like Sarah, the mother of all nations, as she did not discriminate between her biological and adopted children. The bond between me and the Kroma family was clearly divine-ordained, and it has continued with the Kroma children to this day. They are my brothers and sisters – without any doubt – especially Martina, who by virtue of our mutual likeness for academia, got hooked to each other to the point that a potential suitor got jealous of our relationship.

It has to be a jealousy of a lifetime!

Chapter Thirteen

Sierra Leone Today

Christian State, Muslim Country, Secular Nation; No Local Support For Extremism; The Evangelist Ajisafe/Mufti Menk Affair

It would be harsh and wrong to depict Mabanta as the only or one of very few impregnable strongholds that resisted the Gospel. Evangelisation had started in Sierra Leone since the 19th century and, to this day, it is still questionable whether the Christian population is even fully twenty percent. In reality, the whole of Sierra Leone was impregnable, refusing and resisting change – a classic example being the early resistance to the colony's establishment and protectorate incorporation by the natives.

Perhaps what only isolated or distinguished Mabanta was its resistance in totality. Other areas of Sierra Leone had already welcomed some kind of change through their general acceptance of Islam since the early 18th century. The first major converts were Temnes, as the Fulani/Madingo conversion came from Guinea, the northern borders of present-day Sierra

Leone. There was already a strong Muslim presence in Susu parts since the 17th century or thereabout – as reported by catholic priest Balthasar Barreira who left the country in 1610.

But Mabanta was too rooted in the primitive 'religion' and resisted Islam (which could be easily syncretised to accommodate native customs, like marrying more than one wife) – the Mohammedan religion, therefore, made minimal impact as it could hardly be noticed in the township. Only itinerant visitors practised it, with virtually no local converts. The only time it registered influence in the village was in the 1930s to 1940s during the reign of Paramount Chief Massa Yeli Kabba (who was chosen by our family from the matrilineal side because there was no eligible male from the legitimate patrilineal line; and he had come with the religion from his paternal home of Buya Romende, some 50-odd miles away). He built a small mosque in the royal compound at Mabanta, went to Mecca and became an 'alhaji' – but still with a small number of converts, mainly jesters. However, the situation worsened for Islam in Mabanta when the chieftaincy ended in fiasco with revelations of witchcraft bedeviling the administration. The chief himself was accused of being a participant, and members of the poro society (traditionally acting as a check in the balance of power – because the paramount chief was not a member) declared him unfit to rule, while composing a song questioning the validity of him ever going to Mecca. He and his immediate family had to disappear from the scene and went back to their paternal home. It only strengthened the Mabanta people's resolve to stay where they were in the resistance movement.

Therefore, when Christianity came along with the British founding of 'the province of freedom,' it was clear the 'new religion' would be up against strong opposition from Islam – or rather would have to live with it. Isaac Land, in his essay,

'On the foundings of Sierra Leone 1787-1808,' first revealed how religiously non-denominational the new settlers were: "Meanwhile, in the *UNESCO General History of Africa*, the Ghana-based scholar A. A. Boahen argued that nineteenth-century Freetown offered a liberated space where Africans could control their own Christian churches and the diverse residents, whether migrant, indigenous, or recaptive, could forge their own syncretic culture that was neither entirely European, nor American, nor African."

And perhaps more reflective of the country's 'Christian state, Muslim country, secular nation' origin is Land's narration about the early days of the 'province of freedom': "From the viewpoint of the new settlement's African neighbours, however, Freetown would remain a peripheral development in an increasingly Islamic region – one of the first messages it received from a local ruler was a piece of Arabic calligraphy reproducing a passage from the Koran – and one ruler of a local polity, Naimbana, left himself plenty of room to maneuver by educating 'one son locally as a Muslim, sending a second abroad to France, and a third, John Frederic, to London'(Northrup: 51). "

The rest of Sierra Leone, in many instances, resisted the 'white man's religion' but accepted the educational opportunities that came with it. Therefore, some Muslims and even traditionalists sent their children to school. Mabanta was not bothered. While my hometown stood still and stuck in primitivism, other parts of the country were marching towards westernisation. Notwithstanding, the crusading criss-crossing evangelisation by Christian missionaries has still left a majority of Sierra Leoneans Muslim, even if some by name only.

Yet, despite this status quo, Sierra Leone has never experienced any major religious conflict or even inflammatory tensions. There could be arguments or debates or even quarrels here and there about which religion is good or bad, or that a certain church is complaining about a certain mosque and vice versa, but you would never hear of all-out long-drawn animosity between Christians and Muslims. Even the infamous civil war did not take any religious dimension.

Perhaps the nearest the country came to the brink of a Christianity/Islam turbulence was immediately after the visit of Zimbabwe-based Islamic scholar Mufti Ismail Menk in September 2017. For the first time under the auspices of Islam, Menk attracted thousands of people to the national stadium, which normally was the domain of Christian 'crusades'. Nigerian evangelist and founder of Sanctuary Praise Church, Victor Ajisafe, did not take kindly to this; and in a message (which went viral on social media within minutes) delivered in his church, he denounced the Muslim cleric as 'an angel of darkness' in relation to the latter equating Islam to Christianity and limiting Jesus to a mere 'prophet' status. The evangelist went to town on Islam.

There was uproar from the Muslim community – with some saying the Nigerian pastor (married to a Sierra Leonean lady) wanted to ignite 'another Boko Haram' in Sierra Leone. The government had to arrest the evangelist and keep him in custody for several days "for his own safety" – and would only be released after issuing a written and video-relayed verbal apology. The scenario became more interesting in considering that Rev. Ajisafe's evangelical non-denominational church was officially opened by then-President Ernest Bai Koroma (a Wesleyan Christian), who subsequently authorised the visit of Mufti Menk (meeting him at State House) and accorded him all the honour of a state visit. Invariably, the way both Christians and Muslims jointly condemned the pastor's 'hate speech' meant the religious-tolerant foundation had not been eroded by the episode. While his church members massaged the incidence as a requisite persecution for a true disciple of Christ, Ajisafe had since resumed his fiery preaching and the 'let my gate be opened' monthly crusades, with teeming numbers.

* * *

In Sierra Leone, Christians marry Muslims, Muslims marry Christians, and each would continue to follow their religion without any rancour. You would find a family or household where the father would be Muslim, the mother Christian, and the kids divided by their own choice – some to the mother, some to the dad – and they are still all comfortable with that.

Therefore, while the world is full of fear of extremists and terrorists under an Islamic banner – and the universal apprehension of Muslims rising to unprecedented levels, causing the President of the USA Donald Trump to slam a temporary ban on people from selected Muslim-majority countries from entering the world's most attractive country – Sierra Leone is at peace with itself, religiously speaking. We are not to be bothered by *Charlie Hebdo* controversies, not about the Israeli/Palestinian conflict, not about the Middle East in general – not even when 'our good friend' Muammar Gaddafi was slaughtered in 2011. There may be shudders or apprehensions in some people, but not to the extent of going to the extreme to hurt anyone in reaction. There would always be individuals deeply committed to their beliefs on either side of the religious divide – but it has never led to extremism in Sierra Leone. There has, however, been a couple of foreign-bred Sierra Leoneans associated with terrorism – a UK-based Sierra Leonean boy killed in Syria as a volunteer terrorist and another arrested in the US for supporting ISIS online. But that has not been reflected in the country!

Even with the very strong historical and cultural ties between Sierra Leone and Nigeria, there are virtually no Sierra Leonean Muslim sympathisers for 'Boko Haram', the anti-West nihilistic entity that has been causing mayhem in northern Nigeria in the name of Islam and Sharia Law. Sierra Leonean Muslim clerics and imams describe Islam as 'a religion of peace' and, therefore, denounce all forms of violence – even if others say it would be the way to 'paradise'. To the local clerics, anyone who kills in the name of their religion, even while shouting 'Allahu akbar' (Muslims' most popular religious refrain) in the process, is not a true or real Muslim.

Kevin A. O'Brien and Ismail Rashid made this point succinct in their 22 May 2013 journal-published article titled 'Islamist Militancy in Sierra Leone': "There is some evidence that prolonged economic impoverishment and foreign religious influences, especially from Saudi Arabia and Iran, have led to a reinvigoration of Islam in post-war Sierra Leone. Though this reinvigoration has resulted in the visibility of more purist strains of the religion, there are no indications that the Sierra Leonean Muslim groups are actively participating in any worldwide jihadist network or will engage in large-scale religiously-inspired extremism and violence. The recent history of the country indicates that attempts to mobilise religious sympathies for political ends in Sierra Leone have been short-lived and largely unsuccessful..." Even the short-lived Gaddaffi influence which saw the Libyan dictator being pronounced an honorary Member of the Sierra Leone Parliament – even with him having built a magnificent mosque named after him, and dishing out material support to both the governments of Presidents Kabbah and Koroma (the Libyan leader visiting Sierra Leone during both tenures) – did not provoke militancy from Sierra Leonean Muslims when he was slain through an apparently West-inspired insurrection in Libya – not least because Gaddaffi was previously associated with sponsorship of the rebel war.

The only apparent link Sierra Leone has with terrorism is connected with some resident Lebanese who in their support for surrogate groups like Hezbollah have been found with Sierra Leonean passports, arms and ammunition, plus allegations of financial support to terrorist networks. After a large cache of terrorism-associated arms were found by police in Nigeria, the Lagos-based *Vanguard* newspaper of 4 June 2013 had the headline 'Hezbollah Weapons warehouse Belongs to Sierra Leonean' – when it was actually a naturalised Lebanese with a Sierra Leonean passport.

In Sierra Leone, Muslims go to church; Christians go to mosques, especially on occasions like weddings, funerals, and thanksgiving services. There are even those who do make it a routine practice to go to mosque on Friday and to church on Sunday with no qualms whatsoever.

This religious serenity amidst a world embroiled in a 'war on terror' impelled the United Nations in 2013 to describe Sierra Leone as 'the most religious tolerant nation in the world' following the visit of the Special Rapporteur on Freedom of Religion or Belief, Heiner Bielefeldt, from 30 June to 5 July of that year. Part of the executive summary of his report submitted to the General Assembly on 23 December 2013 read: "The Special Rapporteur appreciates the admirable culture of inter- and intra-religious open-heartedness cherished in families, neighbourhoods, schools and public life in Sierra Leone. People from the country's two main religions – Islam and Christianity – live together in peace and harmony and this tolerant attitude generally extends to adherents of traditional African spirituality. The same amicable spirit guides the relationships between different branches within Islam – Sunnis,

Shias, Ahmadis – as well as the different denominations within Christianity – Anglicans, Catholics, Evangelicals and others. Interreligious marriages and conversions in various directions are widespread and generally receive approval from families and communities. The Inter-Religious Council of Sierra Leone has played a pivotal role in the ongoing process of rebuilding the nation…"

There is, therefore, no doubt about Sierra Leone's unique religious status. Otherwise, which other nation in this world has a 75 per cent Muslim population but has ever only seen one Muslim Head of State out of six, and still there has not been any religious brouhaha? They are satisfied with the status quo, and the trend is bound to continue in the foreseeable future.

The reason for this could be traced to the manner by which Islam entered and spread in West Africa via the ancient empires of West Africa. The religion had come from North Africa through trade routes – though not totally without conquest. When trade was booming through the empires, Islam became a traders' religion. One only needed to know a few Quranic verses to be regarded as a Muslim and would, therefore, go about doing their business around the empire with a few Arabic words in their mouths.

The Mandingos and the Fulas, the craftiest of men in transactions, were the main carriers of the Muslim religion in this part of the world. And no businessman wanted war – at least not where he operated from. Consequently, in the course of their business dealings, they tried to convert the locals. They found trading skills in the Sierra Leonean Temne people and got most of them to accept the new religion. They traded with each other and accepted Islam primarily (but arguably) because it was very accommodating to their traditional beliefs – a blending of the two beliefs was widespread. They were businessmen. They were bothered with profit-making. Not with extremism.

That blended tradition was handed down to coming generations. Therefore, when Europeans (mainly British) and Americans later came with Christianity and western education through colonisation, there was virtually no stiff resistance from the Muslims – except if one associated Islam with Bai Bureh, who actually did not fight a religious war but only initiated a resistance against an imposed hut tax. The protagonists of both the early resistance to the colony formation and the hut tax war were, it must be said, more of poro guerrilla fighters than religious zealots.

Arguably, the greatest ingredient in Sierra Leone's religious tolerance was the acceptance of British/Christian colonial education by Muslims. The fact that the freed slaves who were as black as the natives were part of the colonial set-up must have greatly helped matters. The similarity of colour would make it easier for integration once language had been mastered – not surprising the British introduced and cherished an 'indirect rule' system. As a consequence, Muslim parents sent their children to school, despite still practising their religion at home. Unwittingly, they were opening their children up to access to the Gospel, especially those who attended mission schools. In these schools, Bible Knowledge was a subject in the curriculum; and Christian prayers were said during the assembly by all students irrespective of background. And in the purely Christian (as opposed to government-owned) schools, particularly the Catholic-run ones, there were chapels for prayer during lunch time – and the Roman Catholic 'brothers/sisters' and 'fathers/mothers' (missionaries) would show so much love and compassion in the form of material gifts to even attract Muslim boys and girls to church. With the Muslims' 'day of worship' (Friday) being a school day, it meant Muslim boys and girls attending school were missing out on one of the most important rites of their parents' religion. They grew up knowing so much about Christianity while still nominally maintaining, as per parental inheritance, that they were Muslims – even though they might know very little about Islam. Some were forced to take koranic lessons in the evening and during the holidays. But one thing that put many off was the high-handedness of the koranic teachers who apparently delighted themselves in merciless flogging for the slightest of mistakes in pronunciation of an Arabic word. The children, therefore, found solace in Western education. Their disposition became that of Muslim by name but Christian by orientation; hence the nickname 'Chris-Mus'.

It is worthy to note, however, that the original foundation of this religious tolerance was also based on the initial British colonial policy which was averse to Christianisation of Muslim areas. In his book, *Unveiling Modernity in Twentieth-Century West African Islamic Reforms*, historian Ousman Murzik Kobo, of Ohio State University (USA), revealed the fact: "As early as the 1820s, British administrators in the colony of Sierra Leone, Britain's oldest West African colony, had adopted Arabic as the official language of correspondence with indigenous rulers... Because they needed Muslim intermediaries in colonial administration, the British encouraged the study of Arabic and discouraged the establishment of mission schools in predominantly Muslim areas of the interior..." This policy was apparently preventive, as the British feared any incitement of a Muslim rebellion. And they would find a willing and inspirational ally in Caribbean-born Edward Blyden, who in 1870 initiated the teaching of Arabic at Fourah Bay College, the first university in sub-Saharan Africa founded in 1827 as an Anglican missionary institution by the Church Missionary Society.

However, even with the opening of 'Muslim' schools which incorporated an English curriculum (different from the ad hoc karamoko-lashing madrasas), many Muslims still found the Christian or government schools patterned after British tradition preferable – even with their Monday-to-Friday calendar week. This was mainly because these schools were more famous and more well-equipped, invariably resulting to best-pupil performance. The gap would narrow down as the years went by. It has to be said that the non-extremist and flexible nature of the Christian schools also prepared the way for the peaceful co-existence and integration. Muslim boys and girls went on to become head-boys and head-girls of these Christian schools. Even those who did not reach that apex continued to have links with their former schools, participating in the 'old boy/old girl' networks, still actively contributing to the name-promotion and development of their alma mater.

Inevitably, even though it was more of a Muslim country by virtue of population density, it needed not be engraved in stone that Sierra Leone was virtually a Christian state. The British colonial establishment and general governance structure was in an Anglo-Christian fashion – with the Queen of England, the titular head of the Anglican Church, being the Head of State. Despite attempts at encouraging Arabic teaching, English was the official language. Government business was conducted from Monday to Friday, after the Anglo-Christian tradition, and Governor-Generals were inaugurated at the Anglican Church. The first Governor, John Clarkson, offered a Christian prayer for the colony that resonated with every facet of society – and it is still adored even today by Christians and Muslims alike. The Sierra Leone media landscape was patterned after the British press. It would have to be after Independence that Muslim prayers were largely incorporated alongside Christian prayers at official public ceremonies and activities.

* * *

Almost everybody in Sierra Leone says they believe in God. And Sierra Leone would continue to be at peace with itself religion-wise in the foreseeable future. Terrorists, sub-regional or international, would find it almost impossible to ever attract local Sierra Leonean Muslims – even with a promise of wealth and a phantom paradise. They are not the type. Sierra Leoneans by nature love their lives (perhaps we have the lowest rate of suicides in the world), no matter how terrible the circumstances we find ourselves in: *'we lef we case to God'*. Sierra Leoneans love peace – that's one reason why historians would one day come to the conclusion that there would have never been a war in Sierra Leone without the initiation and active participation of foreign mercenaries, especially Liberians who formed its rank and file at the beginning. No wonder former Liberian President and warlord Charles Taylor was actually indicted and incarcerated by the Special Court not for the pogrom in his country but for the Sierra Leone war!

The arguments between Christians and Muslims have mainly been theological or philosophical, without being physical. Many Muslims, in rebuffing Christian evangelisation, would put up a defence of worshipping 'the same God'. They would cite the imitative nature or similarity of the Quran to the Bible in terms of the storyline from Adam to the prophets and even to Christ Jesus. But there were fundamental differences for which most or all Christians would never accept the notion of 'same God.' It is all anchored on the divinity of Jesus Christ as the begotten Son of God who died and rose again from the dead, nullifying the need for animal sacrifice because He has become a sacrifice once and for all. The Muslims would want to limit Christ to 'another prophet': though they accept the virgin birth, they deny that He was crucified. But these differences are not taken to the extreme (except, perhaps, for the aforementioned Ajisafe-Menk affair). And for that, we have witnessed many peaceful conversions from Muslim to Christian – and vice versa, though the latter hardly happened.

A great bastion that has held the religious tolerance together in Sierra Leone is the Inter-Religious Council which comprises of virtually all the Christian and Muslim denominations, and none is bothered whether it is headed by any of them. They have come together in times of great crises like the war and Ebola to act as the moral voice of the nation.

The tolerance is so effortlessly embraced that Sunday is now accepted nationally as a day of rest, where no work is done. The regulation was first enforced during the fight against the Ebola outbreak, but it has endured. This makes more sense in terms of impact when it is considered that more than 90 per cent of traders are Muslims but are all complying to the regulation without any complaint.

In my own desire to unravel this unique nature of the Sierra Leonean religious tolerance, I found an analogy in Scripture (Isaiah11:6-9):

"The wolf shall dwell with the lamb,
and the leopard shall lie down with the young goat,
and the calf and the lion and the fattened calf together;
and a little child shall lead them.
The cow and the bear shall graze;
their young shall lie down together;
and the lion shall eat straw like the ox.
The nursing child shall play over the hole of the cobra,
and the weaned child shall put his hand on the adder's den.
They shall not hurt or destroy
in all my holy mountain;

for the earth shall be full of the knowledge of the Lord
as the waters cover the sea."

I can't beat or bypass *The Economist* of 31 May 2014 in summarising the situation in an article aptly titled 'Religion In Sierra Leone: All Things Happily For All Men.' The London-based world-renown newspaper reported thus: "Sierra Leone straddles Africa's religious equator, where the Muslim north meets the Christian south. Other countries in the region are experiencing religious violence, with Islamist militants creating mayhem in the Central African Republic, Mali and Nigeria. But in Sierra Leone the president, Ernest Bai Koroma, a Christian, was elected by voters who are roughly 70 per cent Muslim. His vice-president is a Muslim. Marriage across sectarian lines is common, as are conversions. Neither religion played a part in the county's civil war in the 1990s. 'We all believe in one God,' says Wurie Bah, a Muslim from Freetown. 'If my friends invite me to church, of course I will go'."

What is clear is that Sierra Leone is a secular nation where the sentimental aspects of religion are totally separated from the state. The laws and court system are secularised. Therefore, Christians, Muslims and animists would all meet in secular occasions and have a good time together. If they are watching their football matches or enjoying themselves in parties or socialising on the beach and night-clubs or are participating in their cultural societies or during wedding ceremonies or funerals, you would hardly tell who is who.

Sierra Leoneans are peaceful. Sierra Leone is at peace with itself either as a Muslim country or as a Christian state or as a secular nation.

Chapter Fourteen

Why A Pope Has Never Visited Sierra Leone

Can It Happen Under First Catholic President Julius Maada Bio? Church Politics And The Makeni Diocese Rebellion Against The Pope

The visit of the Pope – or a Pope, any Pope – to any country is an extraordinary affair. Even America that bragged of being the most powerful nation on earth came to a halt in reverence of Pope Francis when he visited President Barack Obama in 2015. The 'Vicar of Christ' was in town; therefore even the President of the United States of America was humbled and diminished.

Very few nations would not look forward to a visit by the Pope. He's a living example of 'the rock of ages': thrones and kings have perished, kingdoms and empires have risen and waned, but the 'Holy See' has remained as the longest-serving entity with enduring diplomatic relations. The papacy has survived through the ages, even after it had come close to extinction, having had to cede most of its authority and territory. But even the remarkable success in negotiating the establishment of the Vatican, an independent state within the state of Italy whose capital is Rome (the biblical Rome), remains a wonder that cannot be overlooked by the world. The words of the Pope still act as a moral guide even to world leaders – a planned American bombing of Syria in 2013 was reportedly not carried out when it was criticised by the Vatican! The word of Pope Francis got the communist anti-American Cuba to release hundreds of prisoners when the American government had failed to get the Castro government to do that!

Many people believe that a visit by the Pope to their country would come with many blessings, both collectively and individually – and such a belief is definitely not limited to only Catholics but to other Christians, Muslims and non-religious people. The Catholic Church is an undying dinosaur ('gates of hell can never against the Church prevail'). It is the richest Church on earth (pundits put it at between $10 and $15 billion). Some of the riches were gotten through sometimes very controversial circumstances, such as during the bloodletting Crusades and the role played during – and the acquiescence to – the Transatlantic slave trade. Thankfully, Pope Francis is on record to have rejected 'blood money' for "hearts that are open to the mercy of God". The Roman Catholic Church being the richest Christian denomination, the biggest non-governmental charity worldwide, and having the combined authority of Church and state, its leader must certainly be someone who magnetises the world. He is virtually the most powerful figure on earth.

When Alie Wasco (I'll tell you more about him soon) and I met Pope Francis at the Vatican and posted pictures of the encounter to a friend in Uganda through WhatsApp (with a pending papal trip to the East African country a week after our visit), the response was, "You are blessed. Look at my people busy washing the streets of Kampala waiting to receive him here." That's how much a Pope's visit would excite a people. But that's taking the story too far too soon.

* * *

By virtue of Sierra Leone's long Christian history, dating way back to pre-colonial times when an itinerant priest (Father Berreira) evangelised to chiefs and natives in the seventeenth century, one would wonder why no Catholic Pope has ever visited the country. With the long Catholic tradition, which resumed at full-scale during the colonial period after a pre-colonial interval, one would have thought the Catholic Church of Sierra Leone should have by now been able to attract a Pope's visit. They are still waiting – and counting the years.

The closest a Pope has come to Sierra Leone was in 1992 when it was announced and even published in newspapers that Pope John Paul II, the longest-serving pontiff in modern times, would visit Freetown. But the visit was cancelled at the last minute – some sources informally citing the intensification of the then-rebel war as a reason for the cancellation. The Roman Catholic Church has, however, never given any official reason that I know of. It becomes more interesting to note that it was on the same cancelled trip that the Pope visited neigbouring Guinea, Senegal and The Gambia, which have far fewer Christians than Sierra Leone (Guinea and The Gambia having approximately 8% each and Senegal about 4%).

And perhaps the Pope that would have found it most appropriate to visit Sierra Leone should have been John Paul's successor, Pope Benedict XVI. But a rejection of his appointee as Bishop of Makeni in a lethal succession battle saw the local laity belittling the powers of the pontiff. If Bishop Aruna, Pope Benedict's choice to succeed Bishop George Biguzzi, were allowed to take up leadership of the Diocese of Makeni, there was every likelihood that an invitation to visit would have been given due pontifical consideration.

But local dynamics, some say church politics, took precedence over papal reverence – causing the members of the Makeni Diocese to assert that, at this time on this particular issue, the Pope was not speaking on behalf of God; that the 'head of the Church' was wrong, and that in actual fact God did not want the Pope's appointee to become the Bishop of Makeni. And the Makeni Catholic Church members would go all out, against all the odds, and even using physical action to barricade the diocese, to prevent the Pope's appointee from assuming office over the Makeni Diocese.

The whole episode unfolded with little thought from even the initiators that it would make such impact on the tapestry of Church administration to the extent that some believed the inability of Pope Benedict to have his way in the Makeni church could be one factor that influenced his decision to also do the unthinkable – to resign as Pope after only eight years in office, the first time such a thing would happen in about 600 years. Don't think this was too far-fetched – of course, in addition to the more immediate and more publicised 'Vatileaks' scandal of Pope Benedict's butler leaking to the press confidential Vatican documents about internal power struggle (alleging that gay bishops were exerting "inappropriate influence" in the affairs of the Church)! The official reason given was that Joseph Ratzinger's physical and mental powers were declining – but he is still active today in 2018, making a few public appearances, and has gone on to have a book ('Faith And Politics' [2018]) published in his name, with a foreword by his successor.

* * *

It all started with the somewhat innocent retirement of Italian-born George Biguzzi, the long-serving Bishop of Makeni (1987 – 2011). It's worth noting that since its establishment, the Diocese of Makeni had always had a 'white' Bishop – Biguzzi was actually the second. His predecessor, the Diocese's first Bishop Augustus Azzolini (who arrived in Makeni in 1952 as founding leader before being ordained as Bishop in 1962, and retiring in 1986), was a most popular figure who has remained a legend of the city, with the gateway highway of Makeni named after him. Even though he died in retirement in Italy, his wish to be buried in the city was honoured: "And they will tell you, Muslims and Christians alike, that Azzolini was the first Catholic Bishop of Makeni, that he loved the country very much, and that his body is buried in front of the Catholic Cathedral", to quote a 2015 write-up by fellow Xaverian Fr. Luigi Brioni.

By 2012, the Makeni Catholic Church had come a long way and should be able to have a local priest as bishop (as it was the only Sierra Leonean Catholic diocese that had never got a native Sierra Leonean as Bishop). It was, therefore, the hope of many locals that Biguzzi's successor would be a Sierra Leonean – it was in fact clear that it was the common agreement by all, as all the candidates proposed for succession were Sierra Leoneans. The stage was set for the first black bishop of Makeni. It appeared. But not to be – as yet. Still waiting!

The choice of Bishop Aruna, despite clear warnings from the laity, put spanners in the works. The people of Makeni – a congregation of mostly the most stubborn tribesmen, despite their religion – saw this as papal arrogance. They refused to accept the choice regardless the announcement was the Pope's decision. They organised public demonstrations, preventing 'Holy See' messengers from having their way, threatening to break all hell loose if Bishop Aruna ever stepped his foot in Makeni as Bishop.

The Vatican did not have any Swiss guards in Sierra Leone to enforce its decisions; it would not call on state security to enforce the Pope's orders. Either the people would yield or Bishop Aruna would not become Bishop of Makeni. The Temne people, with their resilient and resistance character, would definitely not yield.

Many believed the Pope was misinformed about the local dynamics (church politics) and made a decision that prompted a reaction most unheard-of in papal authority – only short of the magnitude of Martin Luther's 'insubordination'! The Makeni Catholics had hoped and prayed that a priest from their local diocese would be chosen as bishop – but for Pope Benedict to have bypassed the four or five 'eligible' Makeni priests (reportedly presented by outgoing Bishop Biguzzi) for a priest from another part of the country, from another diocese, was considered as contempt and was treated with contempt. The contention of the laity was that the Makeni Diocese, despite being the largest geographical entity of the Catholic Church in Sierra Leone, did not have any representative as Bishop in the Conference of Sierra Leone Bishops. "The heart of the matter is that the Makeni diocese also wanted to be part of the universal Church at the level of the episcopacy where key decisions about the appointments of Bishops, heads of institutions and the general welfare of the Church are made," a Makeni priest told me.

But, to others, it was beyond that. Perhaps, just perhaps, a priest from the Western Area would have been accepted – perhaps they would have yielded after a few solicitations. But Sierra Leone's historical ethnocentric (northwest versus southeast) rivalry in politics also apparently had something to do with this Church politics – particularly the Temne versus the Mende, dating back to pre-colonial days, coming down the ages in different forms. The choice or 'imposition' of Bishop Aruna (a Mende man from the south-east) to become Bishop of Makeni, a Temne-dominated diocese, was obviously a most repugnant action to the locals – to the laity of Makeni. And they decided to bind it on earth. And it was bound in heaven. Martin Luther reincarnated in Makeni in the form of the laity challenging the authority of the Pope – and they prevailed!

The Makeni people were not, however, the first to challenge the choice of a bishop under Pope Benedict. In December 2009, 131 priests (about 80%) of San Sebastian in Spain signed a letter rejecting the papal 'imposition' of Bishop José Ignacio Munilla in their Diocese – and their action was labeled as "politically motivated". Earlier that year, Austrian bishops rejected the Pope's choice of Bishop Gerhard Maria Wagner as auxiliary Bishop of Linz.

And the Makeni Diocese would not be the last in opposing Pope Benedict's bishopric choice either. In January 2013, a similar occurrence took place in the Diocese of Ahiara Mbaise in Imo State, Nigeria, where the appointment of Monsignor Peter Okpalaeke from Anambra State sparked protests and denunciations. The protesters, as if borrowing a leaf from Makeni (barricading the gate to the big cathedral, displaying rejection placards), stated that "till date, no priests or bishops from Owerri Province have been assigned as bishops, whether auxiliaries or substantive, in Onitsha," and that "We believe we have credible priests who can be made bishop, instead of imposing someone who does not understand the culture of the people and we have an obligation to reject anything that imperils the faith of our people." And Pope Benedict resigned in February that year!

* * *

A school of thought held the view that the whole process of installing Aruna as Bishop of Makeni was not well thought-out and not well-timed. There was an apparent rush from the Sierra Leonean heads of the Catholic Church. They did the announcement in Freetown instead of going to Makeni, which evidently raised suspicion and only hardened the resolve of the laity against the Church's national authority. And to have made that announcement in 2012, an election year in Sierra Leone, with the then-ruling APC being a northern-studded party, whereas Bishop Aruna hailed from the south-east, was poor timing. Pro-SLPP (then opposition) newspaper *Global Times* didn't leave a stone unturned in casting blame. With an unequivocal headline 'Catholic Church Now Politicised In Sierra Leone', the paper was clear about the apparent intertwined Church-and-state politics: "There is a growing view among Southeasterners that the absolute rejection of Bishop Henry Aruna by the priests, men, women and laity in Makeni the home town of President Ernest Bai Koroma is being politically motivated. The fact that President Koroma who is himself a Wesleyan Christian and Father of the nation had at no time denounced the action of the Catholic Community in the North clearly underscores the point of political motivation…" The former President's own reaction was that he would never meddle into church politics – Wesleyan or Catholic.

Another school of thought believed the whole shenanigans were the handiwork of the out-gone Bishop Bigguzzi who some Catholic analysts described as a 'professional in chicanery'. It was alleged that he did not actually want to leave Sierra Leone (having just established the University of Makeni, of which he was to be Chancellor), and he therefore played church politics and got things mixed up – that he secretly supported or at least sympathised with the Makeni locals, while officially supporting the Pope's choice of Aruna – in the hope that he would have benefited from the confusion by an extension of his term. If Biguzzi felt slighted by Pope Benedict, he was only being human. One would only hope this school of thought was wrong! And the Makeni priests believed it was a wrong school of thought, which was "making insinuations against Bishop George Bigguzzi out of malice". They apparently alluded that the out-gone Bishop would have loved a local Bishop for the Makeni Diocese to be a representative at the Episcopal conference, but that he was not the kind of man to stand in the way of a papal decision. "He was not in any way prolonging his stay or episcopacy. If there is somebody we owe a lot to as a church and as a nation, it is Bishop George, a simple and holy man," one priest asserted in absolute terms. Bigguzzi, having retired to his native Italy, now carries the title of Bishop Emeritus of the Makeni Diocese – and is also the current patron of UNIMAK.

Invariably, when Pope Benedict suddenly resigned and was succeeded by Pope Francis, there was a lot of jubilation in Makeni. They believed Bishop Aruna's greatest pillar had gone. After he was rejected as Bishop of Makeni, the Church re-assigned him to the Vatican; and there was always the lingering fear of the unknown as to what would be the next step of Pope Benedict, who also seemed unprepared to budge by not announcing a replacement. But Benedict's resignation opened a window of opportunity for the Makeni laity to have their way.

The succeeding pontiff, Pope Francis, met their aspirations – albeit partially – by withdrawing the bishopric of Bishop Aruna for the Makeni Diocese and sending him to his Kenema native land in the east instead. But Makeni lost out in wanting to have their own native priest as Bishop (that part was bound on earth but not bound in heaven – God always overrules for the Church's good). Another Italian was appointed to act as Bishop – the 'white Bishop' tradition continued for Makeni, even as the Bishops of the Dioceses of Kenema and Bo and Freetown were all Sierra Leoneans. And that was one of the fiercest contentions of the Makeni laity – that why was it that all the bishops in those other Dioceses were from the South-east and the West , while the North had never got any bishop either in Makeni or in any other diocese? Notwithstanding, it has to be stated that Catholicism has had a longer and stronger foothold in the South-east than in the North – with the first indigenous bishop, Joseph Henry Ganda, installed in Kenema in February 1971 after he was appointed by Pope Paul VI in November 1970! Makeni wanted their own Bishop.

Yet still, a counter school of thought has argued that the priests of Makeni were 'too worldly' and had too many skeletons in their cupboards – with each allegedly having fathered at least one child, totally against the oath of celibacy and therefore not good examples for the flock. This echoed the spirit of the official position of the Vatican: "In his decision [to choose Bishop Aruna] the Holy Father has painstakingly and carefully taken into consideration all of the human, spiritual, and pastoral qualities that make up a good Priest and, most especially, a good Bishop." Yet the accused priests argued that their own deeds were merely the known, while the other priests who were in charge of local dioceses could be worse but had merely kept their closets locked (They should have known that only those who are caught are punished!). And they also posited that, at the international level, priests and bishops who had been enmeshed in the child abuse sex scandal had not suffered such fates of stagnation as were being meted out on them in Makeni.

Be that as it may, with such schisms in the Sierra Leone Catholic Church, Pope Francis would certainly not put Sierra Leone on the itinerary of his first visit to Africa – even if a school bearing his name, St. Francis, was the 'Oxford of the North.' In November 2015 (just a week after our meeting with him) Pope Francis' first visit to Africa was in Kenya, Uganda, and the Central African Republic. The hope of having a papal visit was still deluding Sierra Leone!

And in order for me not to appear too critical or harsh or condescending to the Catholic Church about that ugly occurrence, I find it necessary to state that a similar schism had occurred in the Wesleyan Church of Rogbaneh, in the same Makeni. This church was by and large 'the mother church' of the Wesleyan Church in Sierra Leone, by virtue of it eventually hosting the headquarters of the mission and was the preferred local church for the American missionaries who resided at headquarters. That Wesleyan rupture also erupted over the controversial choice of a pastor by the national church leadership as against the wishes of the majority of the local congregation. The resistance it ignited, accompanied by public demonstrations, caused the authorities to close the church for several months until the impasse was resolved by bringing a compromise pastor. Could the Catholics have borrowed a leaf from the Wesleyan experience? Especially with cross-denominational membership? Apparently!

Admittedly, all sides – from the Vatican, down – made some mistakes. Pope Francis' decision cooled tensions, and there has been closer collaboration with the other dioceses since the arrival of Natale Paganelli at the Makeni Diocese. Moving forward, they say.

* * *

All in all, a Pope has still not visited Sierra Leone. The people are still hoping. That hope got some faith injected in it when Sierra Leoneans woke up to the news in November 2015 that Alie Wasco and I had met with Pope Francis at the Vatican – splashed on the front and inside pages of several local newspapers, and having wider coverage on social media after I broke the news with pictures on WhatsApp and Facebook.

Some exuberant commentators said this must be the beginning of a new chapter in Sierra Leone's papal relations; and that if we could meet the Pope at the Vatican, we should be influential enough to get him or rather be able to use the same network that facilitated such a meeting to influence him to come to Sierra Leone. It was, to me, a possibility if the Sierra Leone Catholic Church would put its past behind it and mend fences as a united force. But even at that, it should not be taken for granted. Every meeting with the Pope is a divine arrangement, many Catholics believe. Even with peace within the Sierra Leone Catholic Church, even with continued peace in Sierra Leone as a nation, it would have to be God who would decide when the Pope would come. That is a Catholic belief.

Two years after our visit would be the time President Koroma himself, together with a delegation of some former contenders for the presidential candidature of his party (with elections looming), would meet Pope Francis – making him the first Sierra Leonean Head of State to have gone that far on Vatican relations. The onus of 'bringing' the Pope to Sierra Leone immediately shifted from us to him or to his party – having taken along his handpicked successor, then-Foreign Minister Samura Kamara, who didn't eventually succeed him.

Still, the faith remained that only God would bring the Pope to Sierra Leone. With the vacillations and constellations, the question that lingered still was: why would the war have intensified just as Pope John Paul would have visited? And two months after the cancellation of the papal visit, the civilian government was overthrown by the military.

* * *

Sierra Leone is still waiting for the coming of the Pope. When? Nobody knows. Waiting for Godot? Perhaps not. Perhaps there is a silver lining on the horizon, as we now have a professed Catholic as Head of State of Sierra Leone in the personality of President Julius Maada Bio who definitely has a good relationship with Bishop Aruna, the man who spent a considerable time at the Vatican after the Makeni Diocese rejected him. And Bio is a South-easterner like Bishop Aruna.

The SLPP's Bio (married to a Muslim) displayed a great deal of his Catholicism when he submitted to his local Catholic church's post-elections mediation efforts of bridging the gap between him and the defeated candidate of the then-ruling APC, Samura Kamara, who is a member of the same St. Luke's Catholic Church at Wilberforce village, a suburb of Freetown. Bio himself came in contact with Catholicism in early childhood as he attended the Roman Catholic Primary School in his home village of Tihun, Bonthe District, southern Sierra Leone. President Bio could not grant me an interview for this book; but when I sent him a copy of this chapter, he added the following in his own handwriting (verbatim): "And also later attended the Holy Family Primary School in Pujehun" – in the same geographic region.

Pope Francis could possibly be interested in coming to Sierra Leone to kill two birds with one stone: celebrate or recognise the first Sierra Leonean Catholic President; and settle the Makeni Diocese Bishopric palaver once and for all, because Fr. Natale Paganelli who is currently overseeing its affairs is not really a Bishop but an 'Apostolic Administrator with Episcopal character'!

And the Pope's coming to Sierra Leone has become more plausible when, just a couple of months into Bio's presidency, the Bishops of Sierra Leone and Liberia extended an invitation to the pontiff during an 'ad limina' meeting at the Vatican on 11 June 2018. Freetown Archdiocese head Archbishop Edward Tamba Charles came away feeling optimistic, stating that the meeting of 'a brother with his brothers' could see St Peter incarnate visiting his ecumenical district.

But perhaps the last say on the Sierra Leone side would not rest with the Archbishop, but with the political leaders. Conceivably, it's more a responsibility of President Bio. Hand in hand with religious fervour, the Pope – simultaneously being a political leader – also looks at socio-political circumstances like good governance, peace, and human rights in deciding where and when to visit!

When the Catholic Bishops of Sierra Leone formally met President Bio on Monday 6th August 2018 to congratulate him, they gave him a template of what was expected of him as one of their own. "On several occasions, you have assured us that you shall remain steadfast in upholding your Catholic faith. We encourage you to bring the values of the Gospel and the social teachings of the Church to bear on the execution of your duties," a statement read by the Most Reverend Charles A.M. Campbell, President of the Catholic Bishops, admonished. "We pray that you will take up the challenge to re-imagine leadership, patriotism, sustainable development, good governance, civic responsibility, transparency and accountability… Our Holy Father, Pope Francis, has said that corruption infects the world like a cancer, and that the Church must combat it by working together with society, infusing it with mercy," the statement said.

In other words, if these things happen under President Bio, they could well pave the way for the coming of the Pope to Sierra Leone! But things didn't look good immediately after, when the State House Communications Unit only reported on the issue of 'the fight against corruption' while leaving out the other aspects mentioned by the Bishops. Coming at a time when the Government had set up commissions of inquiry on members of the previous administration, the Opposition harped on a 'witch-hunt' motive. Only the release of the Bishops' full statement calmed tempers. The coming of the Pope, therefore, remains a wait-and-see affair even under a Catholic President.

Chapter Fifteen

Pope Francis

The People's Pastor Has Eventually Emerged

> *"Annuntio vobis gaudium magnum: Habemus Papam!*
> *Eminentissimum ac reverendissimum Dominum,*
> *Dominum Georgium Marium Sanctæ Romanæ Ecclesiæ Cardinalem Bergoglio,*
> *qui sibi nomen imposuit Franciscum"*

This was how the man whose function it was to announce the name of a new Pope, the Cardinal Protodeacon, in this case Frenchman Jean-Louis Pierre Tauran (who died on 5 July 2018 at 75), announced to the world the choice of Cardinal Jorge Mario Bergoglio of Argentina as the successor to German Pope Benedict XVI at 19:06 local time on Wednesday 13 March 2013 in Rome. Translated in English, the Latin quotation above reads: "I announce to you a great joy; we have a Pope; the most eminent and reverend lord, Lord Jorge Mario, Cardinal of the Holy Roman Church, Bergoglio, who takes to himself the name Francis."

The world – and tens of thousands of people in St. Peter's Square at the Vatican – had been waiting with baited breath since the papal conclave convened on 12 March and for hours on end on 13 March for this 'Habemus Papam' ('We have a Pope'). And when – as age-old pontifical tradition dictated –the white smoke finally plumed from the chimneys of the Sistine Chapel of the Vatican and was followed by the pronouncement of Bergoglio's name as the new Pope, Church historians and scholars knew a major change had occurred in the doctrinal direction of the Roman Catholic Church. To those who knew the new Pope's background, very few were surprised that he took the title of 'Francis' in remembrance of the 'poor man' saint, Francis of Assisi.

* * *

The parents of Jorge Mario Bergoglio – Mario Jose Bergoglio and Regina Mario Bergoglio (née Sivori) – of course, never knew they were giving birth to a Pope. When the future Pope was growing up in Argentina and became a janitor and nightclub bouncer, the world must have embraced him as one of its own – as certainly the nocturnal duty was not an appropriate initial route on the path to the Vatican, the seat of Christendom. Even when he went on to become a chemical technician and literature teacher, these were not direct paths to the priestly frock and the flock.

Except for the few luckiest of the luckiest in this world – as, say, members of the British royal family – it is hard for any of us to predict from the cradle our future station in life. Of course they say if you work hard in life, you'll make it. In general terms that's true, but in some situations that would not apply. There are what they call circumstances beyond our control. These circumstances have the capacity to change the courses of our histories. And none of us has any hand in it – can't have a hand in it, even if we try. It is destiny. Our destination charted by supernatural forces. Our fate. Providence. The hand of God.

Bergoglio's path to his providential station all started from his 'confession' experience at age 16 when he believed he had the call to become a priest. CNN Religion Editor Daniel Burke, in an article titled 'The Pope's Dark Night Of The Soul', would narrate the incidence thus: "Bergoglio's call to priesthood was mysterious but strong, interrupting an otherwise ordinary adolescence. It was a spring day in Buenos Aires when he passed a church and was lured like a fish to a line. The 16-year-old entered a dark booth where a priest was hearing the sacrament of penance. 'Something strange happened to me in that Confession,' he later said. 'I don't know what it was, but it changed my life.' It was Bergoglio's first shock from the 'God of surprises,' a deity who lies in wait and springs upon souls unawares."

Austen Ivereigh, in his biography of the Pope titled 'Francis The Great Reformer', quoted the pontiff's description of that day: "I looked, it was dark, it was a morning in September, perhaps 9 o'clock, and I saw a priest walking, I didn't know him, he was not part of the priests of the parish. And he sat down in one of the Confessionals, the last one on the left when one looks at the altar. I don't know at all what happened next. I had the impression that someone pushed me to enter the Confessional. Of course I told him certain things, I went to Confession — but I don't know what happened… I knew there that I would become a priest. I was sure and certain of it. Instead of going out with the others, I returned to the house because I was submerged. Afterwards, I pursued my studies and all the rest, but I now knew where I was going."

Yet, even when he had been 'called' out of the world to become a priest, it was obvious Jorge Bergoglio did not go into priesthood with an ambition to become a Pope – the Pope. It could have been remotely entertained – since it was a possibility for any priest – but it was far removed from any certainty, looking at his background. Popes did not come from his ilk within Catholic circles. He was a member of the once very controversial 'Society of Jesus' (Jesuits) within the Catholic Church – a group that was proscribed by Pope Clement for its radicalism and had since not been favoured by the Church authorities. Ivereigh is worth quoting again to underline the fact that Bergoglio did not set his eyes on the bishopric of Rome: "He confided to Oscar Crespo, of the chemistry laboratory where he worked: 'I'm going to finish the Technical College with you, the lads. However, I won't be a chemist. I'll be a priest, but not a priest *in a Basilica*. I will be a Jesuit because I want to go out to the districts, to the *villas*, to be with the people."

No Jesuit had ever been accorded a chance to become a Pope. Until now – until Bergoglio came around through a miracle! A most unexpected miracle.

After all, Bergoglio had already lost out. His chances of ever becoming a Pope were sealed and thrown into the trash bin when he lost to Pope Benedict in the 2005 conclave election on who should succeed the deceased Pope John Paul II. As the papacy was structured to be headed by a Pope until his death, Bergoglio's defeat at the age of 75 was a sure way of saying goodbye to any dream of heading the Catholic Church. But then we all believe – or should now believe – in miracles; when what seems impossible is made possible.

The impossible happened. Jorge Bergoglio became a Pope – at last! Out of the blue, with even the most sanguine Catholics not predicting it, Pope Benedict woke up one morning to announce his resignation barely eight years in office. This was an event that had not happened in centuries. The last time a Pope resigned was over 500 years ago in 1415 when Pope Gregory XII was forced out to end the 'western schism' of rival papacy. That was foreseen or schemed out. In this case, no one saw it coming; because Pope Benedict did it on his own volition (suffice it to say the rival Pope that caused Gregory's resignation was his namesake called Benedict XIII).

Therefore, the world was stunned by the news of Pope Benedict XVI's resignation on 28 February 2013 (first announced on 11 February). The universal Catholic Church was bemused – except apparently the Makeni Diocese whose laity was exhilarated for the news because they were contesting Pope Benedict's choice of a bishop for their diocese. And when Bergoglio decided to take the papal title of 'Francis', the recalcitrant Makeni laity interpreted it positively – that it was probably in recognition of their diocese, which had both primary and secondary schools bearing the name 'Saint Francis'.

That's how far men can go to turn or interpret events in their favour! They did not even know – or rather they were not bothered to know; they didn't want to know – that the Makeni St. Francis schools were not named after Francis of Assisi (the patron saint whom Pope Francis was emulating and had adopted); but after Francis Xavier! That would not matter to Makeni Catholics, would it? A Francis is a Francis. A saint is a saint! St Francis is St Francis. Assisi or Xavier didn't matter. After all, in fact, Pope Francis was, as mentioned earlier, a member of the 'Society of Jesus' (also known as the Jesuits), of which Francis Xavier was one of its founders! So it was Francis's palm-oil that was spilt in Francis's rice – the Makeni Franciscans would eat in relish. And when Pope Francis would later succumb to the demands of the Makeni laity to replace the rejected Bishop Aruna as one of his first major decisions, the conspiracy theorists had a field day!

It could not have actually been any succumbing. It was, perhaps, just the nature of the new Pope – a Pope that loved the poor, just like Francis of Assisi. Pope Francis has lived up to the expectations of the poor; he is living up to their expectations. The world has generally hailed his every move since his inauguration and has not faced any fierce criticisms like his immediate predecessor. Pope Francis has not only proclaimed himself as a friend of the poor, he has actually acted it out. A Pope that would kiss the feet of Muslim refugees from war-torn Syria and adopt some and actually bring them to stay in the Vatican must be an extraordinarily loved figure. A Pope who had no qualms about entering into mosques or reaching out to the breakaway Orthodox Church must be an endearing and much-loved figure. He would enter prisons to pray with prisoners – even washing their feet! One of the twelve prisoners whose feet the pontiff washed at Rome's Regina Coeli Prison was a Sierra Leonean! And those prisoners were not all Catholic: two were Muslim, one Orthodox, and one was a Buddhist.

Being the first Jesuit Pope, the first from the Americas, the first from the southern hemisphere and the first non-European Pope since the Syrian Gregory III (731-741), Pope Francis's ascension to the papacy was certainly a turning point in Christian, nay Catholic, history. The poor man's pastor had emerged, urging the Church to be more open and welcoming to the downtrodden. His sense of humility was displayed when, just after his election, he refused to follow the tradition of sitting down to greet the cardinals but stood up in respect of them; then he chose to reside in the moderate Domus Sanctae Marthae guesthouse in the Vatican instead of at the papal apartments of the Apostolic palace as was done by his predecessors. He also opted for simple vestments with no ornamentation, particularly refusing to wear the papal mozetta cape after his election, choosing silver instead of gold for his piscatory ring, and continuing to use the same pectoral cross he used as a cardinal. He also retained his Episcopal motto 'Eligendo atque miserando,' loosely translated as 'by mercifully choosing,' patterned after Christ's mercy and choice of Matthew the tax collector as His disciple.

Making his first pronouncement as Pope from the balcony of the Central Loggia of the Hall of Benedictions to the waiting crowd of tens of thousands in St. Peter's Square, Pope Francis stated, "As you know, the duty of the conclave was to appoint a bishop of Rome. It seems to me that my brother cardinals have gone almost to the ends of the earth to find him. . . . Here I am. I would like to thank you for your embrace." And the people embraced him in their hearts!

Time Magazine named him Person of the Year 2013 because, among other things, he had the "ability to alter the minds of so many people who had given up on the Catholic Church in such a short period of time." The magazine's Howard Chua-Eoan and Elizabeth Dias titled their biographical article on him on 11 December 2013 as 'Pope Francis: The People's Pope.'

The BBC's Carolyn Wyatt called him 'Pope of the poor' when reporting his 2015 visit to Africa.

In his first book published as Pope, 'The Name Of God Is Mercy' (2016), Pope Francis revealed the poor-man's-friend character in him, alluding that he might have ended up a prisoner and not Pope had it not been for God's mercy. "The Church does not exist to condemn people but to bring about an encounter with the visceral love of God's mercy," he wrote. He also stated that "Every time I go through the gates into a prison to celebrate Mass or for a visit, I always think: Why them and not me? I should be here. I deserve to be here. Their fall could have been mine."

In essence, in many senses, Pope Francis has tried to portray himself more as a pastor than a conventional Pope. And many Catholics are delighted in calling him pastor. The pope is in actual fact a pastor. According to Catholic Canon Law, the Pope is 'the pastor of the universal Church on earth'. But that title became drowned over the centuries in the pontifical paraphernalia displaying royalty and the accorded reverence that followed the holder of the office wherever he went. In reality, or in accordance with the original 'great commission' and in view of the fact that he is holding the position of a disciple of Christ, a pastor is who a Pope really is, or should be. He is a preacher, an apostle of Jesus, a shepherd of the flock on behalf of Him who called him to be a pastor! Therefore, Pope Francis asked for prayers so that he would be 'a pastor according to the heart of Christ'. And when you hear his messages, you will know he is, indeed, a pastor – preaching from the heart, challenging the priests to live up to their calling. When asking for the forgiveness of the past in Church schisms, especially the backlash of the Reformation, Pope Francis said on 25 January 2016: "As the bishop of Rome and pastor of the Catholic Church, I would like to invoke mercy and forgiveness for the non-evangelical behaviour of Catholics toward Christians of other churches. At the same time, I invite all Catholic brothers and sisters to forgive if today, or in the past, they have suffered offense by other Christians."

And this pastoral duty is what is required of all heads of Church in other denominations – Anglican, Wesleyan, Lutheran, Methodist, Baptist, Presbyterian etc etc who would have started as elementary pastor/priest before assuming the highest office. The greatest distinction, though, is that, while all these other Church leaders claim sovereignty and independence and direct access to God just as the Pope, none has assumed that title. Some have gone ahead to call themselves bishops or apostles or prophets. Even the King-Henry-VIII-created 'Supreme Head of the Church of England' merely stopped at assuming the title of 'the Archbishop of Canterbury': perhaps in view of the fact that the British monarch is actually the 'Supreme Governor of the Church of England'. Therefore, while the Pope has a Church-state within a state (the Vatican in Italy), the Church is in the state in the United Kingdom under the Queen.

In these other denominations, therefore, the Church-head position is not so awe-striking and mystery-surrounded – not least because the Roman Catholic Church basks in the fame of being the 'oldest Church' or 'mother Church' and also of being the richest in terms of material and other possessions across the universe. Furthermore, in the protestant Churches, the position of 'head of Church' has term-limits (with the exception of the head of the Orthodox Church and the British Monarch as the 'defender of the Anglican faith' – both of whom also hold their positions for life). Another exception would be the one-man/one-woman-founded evangelical Churches sprouting and mushrooming everywhere today like those of tele-evangelists like Matthew Ashimolowo, Benny Hinn, Joyce Myer, T.D. Jakes, T.B. Joshua (who perhaps is as well-known in the Philippines as in his native Nigeria – and the Filipinos may well be forgiven if they see the Nigerian pastor as a living and more appealing representative of 'the black Nazarene', for whom they have held an annual event with a life-sized wooden statue of a 'black Jesus' being paraded in designated parts of Manila City since they got Pope Innocent X's authorisation in the seventeenth century) or those of local – meaning Sierra Leonean – evangelists like Mammy Dora

Dumbuya, Victor Ajisafe, Abu Koroma, Julius Lagga, or the Pastor-called-to-business Joe Abass Bangura and many others. Their leadership tenures are 'papal' in longevity, in the sense of remaining the undisputed and unchallengeable heads of their Churches 'until God knows when'.

* * *

With all the history that the Roman Catholic Church carries on its back as the 'original or first Church', accompanied by the powers, pomp, majesty and wealth at the disposal of the Bishop of Rome (the ex-officio position to which he is elected and by which he automatically becomes the Pope), the primary duty of the pontiff as pastor has had to fade over the centuries into the background to a pale shadow of its former self – thereby making the Pope look more like a political or world leader than a pastor.

Therefore, Bergoglio's choice of Francis of Assisi as his patron saint and adopting his name as title (for the first time a Pope is named Francis) expressed a clear desire to go back to basics. The Jesus way. Because, arguably, Francis of Assisi was regarded as the greatest imitator of Christ in living the life of a poor man to reach the poor (bringing to mind Jesus' classic 'foxes have holes and the birds of the air have nests, but the Son of Man has nowhere to lay His head' – the Son of God has nowhere to lay His head? What selflessness!). Francis of Assisi was the son of wealthy merchants but abandoned affluence to live the life of a poor man with the poor in order to spread the Gospel of Jesus Christ.

During his maiden papal encounter with journalists on 16 March 2013, in which he clarified that his papal name was neither after St. Francis Xavier nor St. Francis De Sales, Pope Francis said he had chosen St. Francis of Assisi as his patron saint because he was "especially concerned for the well being of the poor". "Francis is also the man of peace. That is how the name came into my heart: Francis of Assisi. For me, he is the man of poverty, the man of peace; the man who loves and protects creation...gives us this spirit of peace, the poor man who wanted a poor church. How I would love a church that is poor and for the poor," he stated. He went further to say that Francis of Assisi "brought to Christianity an idea of poverty against the luxury, pride, [and] vanity of the civil and ecclesiastical powers of the time. He changed history".

Pope Francis himself is changing history in his own way. No surprise he preached in one of his sermons against Christians who say "it's always been done that way" and are not prepared to change. Speaking at the Casa Santa Marta (or St Martha's house) at the Vatican, he reminded them of Jesus's message of putting "new wine in new wineskins, not new wine in old wineskins – for if you do, both the wine and the wineskin would be ruined as the new bursts open the old". Pope Francis said those who refused change would never arrive at the fullness of truth. That message came from the head of the once-monolithic Roman Catholic Church which abhorred and proscribed the Reformation. The Pope is now talking about accepting change. How times have changed!

Far be it from the truth that Pope Francis does not have critics. Catholic conservatives are not comfortable with him to say the least. A fierce critic is Monsignor Antonio Livi (a professor of philosophy, former dean at the Lateran University in Rome, and a presbyter of the Diocese of Rome) who accuses the Pope of 'protestantising the Church,' and disagrees with him on issues of marriage and divorce, among other things. In the secular media, *New York Times* columnist Ross Douthat has been most pronounced in his criticism of the Pope. Francis's papacy has been a continual subject of his national column.

He also released a book, *To Change the Church: Pope Francis and the Future of Catholicism* (2018), in which he criticised the pontiff for preaching 'liberal Catholicism'.

This opposition culminated into the August 2018 allegations made by Archbishop Carlo Maria Viganò, the former Vatican Ambassador to the United States, just in time to coincide with the Pope's visit to Ireland where he had just apologised for the 'sins' of the Church which included those of priests involved in child sex abuse. Perhaps if the allegations of a pontifical 'cover-up' had come from a source other than the Italian Archbishop, they would have carried much weight. The Pope dismissed them and told journalists on the flight from Ireland back to the Vatican: "I will not say a single word about this. I believe the statement speaks for itself. And you have the sufficient journalistic ability to make your conclusions. It's an act of trust."

The world press and the public seemed to have trusted Pope Francis on that. There had not been backing for Viganò from any major quarter. Daniel Burke, CNN Religion Editor, attributively called it 'The coup against Pope Francis' in their 28 August 2018 edition. Quoting Vatican sources, the analytical report narrated how Viganò (who was apparently pressured to resign in 2017) already had pent-up misgivings about having been marginalised. He felt Pope Francis was giving leeway to the liberal wing of the Vatican. Viganò's conservatism was clashing with the 'homosexual networks'. He appeared in an anti-gay marriage rally in the US. For this – or, on this – Viganò had many supporters, especially in the Protestant community, even if silently.

But he might have just gone overboard in stating his point. On allegations that Pope Francis covered for the named and shamed Cardinal Theodore McCarrick, former Archbishop of Washington, CNN wrote: "But the Pope didn't cover for McCarrick. Unlike his predecessors, Francis forced the former cardinal to resign in July," and further quoted John Thavis, former Rome bureau chief for Catholic News Service, to have said of Viganò: "But he also had a persecution complex. He saw conspiracy theories all around him." "The fact that most of the bishops Viganò criticizes are well-known liberals has led some church experts to suspect his motives... And Thavis said Viganò's assertions about Benedict putting restrictions on McCarrick, including not allowing him to participate in church events or celebrate Mass in public, are patently false," the CNN report stated.

And then it summarised everything in the words of Massimo Faggioli, a professor of Catholic history and theology at Villanova University in Pennsylvania: "This is a coup operation against Pope Francis. It is a stunning convergence between the personal agenda of Viganò and the theological agenda of those who do not like Pope Francis."

Yet, the question that remains is, why or how has such a mass network of sex abuse in a most depraved manner occurred in the Catholic Church, of all Churches? It has become a hindrance to many to receiving the Gospel: a practical example being the low turn-out (130,000 at Phoenix Park, Dublin – partially blaming torrents of rain and poor weather) during the August 2018 visit of Pope Francis to Ireland. Pope John Paul II's famed 1979 visit there (the first by a Pope) attracted 2.5 million at the same spot, and the "American spiritual hymn 'He's Got the Whole World in His Hands' became the background music and anthem of his visit", according to the *Irish Examiner* of August 23 2018, doing a 'special retrospective supplement on the Papal Visit in 1979' just as Pope Francis was visiting.

The sex-abuse priests have become a stumbling block! Pharisees!

Wouldn't it be better to marry then? Or, rather, should the debate on Church-sanctioned celibacy not be rekindled, at least to a certain level? Apostle Paul himself wrote in 1 Corinthians 7:9: "But if they cannot control themselves, they should marry, for it is better to marry than to burn with passion." Those who can, can be celibate; but those who can't, please leave the kids alone – joining Pope Francis in the call. That it has happened on such a large scale and at such a long time (spanning decades) in different countries is a cause for grave concern. It's more than a scandal. It reveals the sinful nature of man and, as Pope Francis put it in Ireland, "remains a source of pain and shame for the Catholic community". The mere atmosphere that has been created of everybody else suspecting somebody else as if someone else is going to be caught at some other place the next moment is itself nauseating – whether they are only trying to undermine the Pope or not. It's a tough fight for the Pope to reverse the trend.

Martin Luther, who believed "if ever a monk got to heaven by his monkery, it was I", ended up marrying run-away nun Katharina von Bora – though he actually had the bold mind (what a man could he have been) to have written to a friend a few days after the wedding: "I feel neither passionate love nor burning for my spouse, but I will cherish her." And he did the latter. Therefore, of the marriage itself, he had written to another friend: "I have made the angels laugh and the devil weep," believing that "the best medicine against fornication *[in this case, child sex abuse]* is to get married" (italics mine) – according to Catholic journalist Peter Stanford in his book *Martin Luther Catholic Dissident* (2017, Hodder & Stoughton).

In marking the 500 years of Luther's revolution, Andrew Curry in an October 20 2017 article 'How A Runaway Nun Helped An Outlaw Monk Change The World' in the *National Geographic* online, stated that Luther would eventually describe his wife as 'the boss of Zulsdorf,' (the farm they owned), and the 'morning star' of Wittenberg "up earlier than anyone else in town to manage a staff of nearly a dozen servants, look after their six children, and manage the equivalent of a mid-sized company." The Wikipedia entry for Katharina Luther (nee von Bora – exactly sounding like my maternal grandmother's name, Tha Bora) states: "The marriage of Katharina von Bora to Martin Luther was extremely important to the development of the Protestant Church, specifically in regards to its stance on marriage and the roles each spouse should concern themselves with... She respected him as a higher vessel and called him formally 'Sir Doctor' throughout her life". He reciprocated by at times calling her 'My lord Katie' and was famously quoted to have said to her: "You convince me of whatever you please. You have complete control. I concede to you the control of the household, providing my rights are preserved. Female government has never done any good."

Andrew Curry quoted Sabine Kramer, Lutheran minister and historian who wrote her doctoral dissertation on the female Luther, in stating the point that it should never be mistaken that the success of the Reformation was a one-man project: "[Martin]Luther played his role in the Reformation, but it's important to remember that she [Katharina] played hers too. There wouldn't have been table talks if she hadn't provided the table." That's exactly what I would say of my mother's contribution to my father's pastoral work, at their own level.

Back to the Vatican story...

Pope Francis always insists that nothing that he does is for or about himself. Profoundly shifting the focus away from himself to Whom he was representing (while insisting that both Benedict's resignation and the 115 Cardinals' choice of a successor was the work of the Holy Spirit), Pope Francis told the 5,000 journalists during the March 16 2013 Vatican press conference, "Christ is the centre, not the successor of Peter. Christ is the reference point at the heart of the Church; without Him, Peter and the Church would not exist." And then he preached to the journalists as well, telling them that their profession "calls for careful preparation, sensitivity and experience, like so many other professions. But it also demands a particular concern for what is true, good and beautiful. This is something which we have in common, since the Church exists to communicate precisely this: truth, goodness and beauty. It should be apparent that all of us are called not to communicate ourselves, but this existential triad made up of truth, beauty and goodness."

During the brisk airborne press conference of 26 August 2018 from Ireland, the pontiff had stated that after the passage of time, at his own discretion, "I may speak" on Archbishop Viganò's allegations. There is no pressure on him at all.

He has gone on to take on a more lethal force: the mafia, some members of which claim to be Christians. Speaking at Sicily's Palermo's Piazza Europa on 15 September 2018, paying homage to Father Giuseppe Puglisi who was shot dead by the mafia 25 years ago for his opposition to mobsters, Pope Francis was unequivocal: "A person who is a Mafioso does not live as a Christian because with his life he blasphemes against the name of God. Change, brothers and sisters! Stop thinking about yourselves and your money… Convert yourselves to the real God."

He was maintaining his original theme on the subject-matter, because as early as March 2014, while addressing bereaved families of mafia killings, the pontiff had stated: "Blood-stained money, blood-stained power, you can't bring it with you to your next life. Repent."

Pope Francis, the people's pastor has emerged, indeed.

Chapter Sixteen

Ernest Koroma's Presidency

A 'Wesleyan Leadership' With Inter-religious And Secular Tinges; American Wesleyan Jo Anne Lyon's Instrumentality; Sam-Sumana, A Politico-Religious Scapegoat? The Hajj-gate Black Spot

Former President Ernest Bai Koroma is a most unlikely politician in an African setting: he is a man who does not talk much, likes following processes and does not want to hurt a fly. He is too much of a gentleman, his die-hard supporters say. Many have attributed this to his upbringing – his Wesleyan heritage! His parents were regarded as pioneers in the Wesleyan Church: his father was a lay preacher and teacher who rose to become the National Secretary of the Church, while his mother was a women's leader at some point and also an evangelist who actually took to the pulpit to preach on the Sunday before her demise on 6 July 2012 (at the height of her son's presidency).

Ernest Koroma was born and nurtured in the Church. In his own words, during an interview I conducted with him two years before he left office: 'I am a product of the Wesleyan Church. What I am today is due largely to how I was moulded by the Church." And he says the line runs right back to his grandparents. His maternal grandparents embraced westernisation by acquiring education: the grandfather was a colonial chiefdom clerk, while the grandmother was a midwife. They were 'missionary products'. They gave birth to his mother, Alice (christened by missionaries), who understandably became more immersed in the Church as she attended mission schools including the then-very famous Kamabai Secondary School (a boarding home for girls) in Bombali District, and she subsequently became a teacher.

The President's father had sterling credentials as an educationist, also nurtured in the Wesleyan tradition from another part of Bombali District. Pa Sylvanus' mother had the unique privilege, even from a mere human sense, of having been buried in the memorable spot where the original American Wesleyan missionaries who died of a strange disease were interred at Kunsho – underlining her attachment to the new faith. The President's father attended school up to what was then called Standard Six level – the highest point of primary education during their time. He then proceeded to the missionary Bible School at Gbendembu, and thereafter went to Fourah Bay College where he obtained a Teacher's Certificate. On graduation, he lectured at the Magburaka Teachers College (about 16 miles from Makeni). He would later relocate to Makeni to become Head Teacher of the Anglican Sierra Leone Church (SLC) Primary School – the same school where his wife taught. The former President still remembers how his paternal grandmother (for whom he was a favourite grandchild) used to take him along on visitation to the surrounding villages on foot to trade and preach.

President Koroma relishes talking about how the relationship between his father and mother was actually arranged by the American missionaries who guided young Christians through youth camps and seminars, identifying and pairing them. "The missionaries saw this beautiful intelligent girl and also found this bright and handsome young man, and paired them. The result today is this President sitting here," he told me during the interview at State House. And this story is well known in Wesleyan circles at home and abroad.

Little wonder then that when he became President in 2007, the USA-based Wesleyan global leadership was quick to recognise that one of its own had risen to the highest position possible in Sierra Leone. An invitation was immediately extended to him to attend and address the General World Conference (the highest gathering in the Church) in Orlando, Florida. Apart from that, delegations of Wesleyans from USA and their complimentary organisations like the humanitarian-focused World Hope International had unfettered access to State House – especially with me as Press Secretary to the President – to thank God for a Wesleyan presidency in Sierra Leone and pray with him. The first major delegation in early 2008 was from Houghton College, whose graduates were among the first Wesleyan missionaries sent to – and died in – Sierra Leone in 1889. Led by their president, Shirley Mullen, I facilitated their meeting with President Koroma. They, of course, visited the missionary gravesite at Kunsho. They also visited Mabanta!

Love for the Koroma regime was not by coincidence though. And it was not a sudden acknowledgement. There was a catalyst in addition to the 'natural' Wesleyan background. During his campaign for the presidency in 2007, the future

President made it a point of duty to visit the local Wesleyan Church in Washington any time he was in America. At that time – as God would have it – Jo Anne Lyon, an American Wesleyan leader who had worked in Sierra Leone and knew the President's family well, was co-pastoring the Washington church with her husband Wayne Lyon. It is worth recalling that, after the civil war, Jo Anne Lyon's World Hope International had played a prominent part in practically healing wounds by providing prosthetic limbs for amputees. Perhaps that's a reason why the Unity Wesleyan Church in Washington (actually in Alexandria, Virginia) had a sizeable and influential Sierra Leonean congregation. The future President would be given the podium to speak to his people – at one time bursting into worship with his familiar favourite song, 'Have faith in God… Wonderful things will happen to you if you have faith in God."

Therefore, when President Koroma eventually won the 2007 elections, Jo Anne Lyon wasted no time in connecting with his development agenda: she would be very instrumental in attracting investors to Sierra Leone, including the opening of a fruit juice factory at Newton in the outskirts of Freetown. Coincidentally, in less than a year into President Koroma's tenure, Jo Anne Lyon was elected as General Superintendent of the Wesleyan Church Globally at the Orlando conference where both the newly elected President and I were invited. Though the President could not attend, he sent a video-recorded message with me to represent him. The prayers offered for him and the nation of Sierra Leone at that conference by representatives of the Wesleyan Church from around the world in June 2008 still metaphorically reverberate in my ears as I write! Jo Anne Lyon retired in 2016, but her World Hope International continues to do marvellous work in Sierra Leone by providing medical support, educational assistance, micro finance, and drilled water-wells to poor communities across the country.

If the Wesleyan leadership at the international arena was elated for Ernest Koroma's presidency, the local leaders and members were certainly also very pleased. A denomination which was hitherto less known or lowly in Freetown (albeit Rev. Y. M. Kroma first gave it national visibility) suddenly took extraordinary national significance for having produced a President – not least because he identified himself with the Church from the beginning. Arguably, no other Sierra Leonean leader has ever been claimed as being owned by a Church in such a manner – with local preachers making him a theme in their sermons as either a David, or a Moses, or a Joshua, or a Joseph, as the case may be. And the claim became more authentic in seeing him bringing a good number of Wesleyan sons and daughters into government – myself (son of a Wesleyan pastor), Richard Konteh (son of a Wesleyan teacher), Frank Kargbo (son of a Wesleyan lay leader), Lovell Thomas (son from the Wesleyan Bible School town of Gbendembu), Martina Kroma (daughter of a former Wesleyan National Superintendent), Joseph Fitzgerald Kamara (born and bred in the same Rogbaneh Church as the President), among many others in different fields. Even Alimamy Petito Koroma's appointment had Wesleyan roots, as his father-in-law, Rev. J. S. Mans, who subsequently helped found and led the Sierra Leone chapter of the Baptist Mission, was originally a well-known Wesleyan pastor who worked with the President's father and – as I mentioned earlier – mentored my father.

Apparently, the missionary 'seed' of the American Wesleyan Mission (AWM) which later became the Sierra Leone Wesleyan Church (SLWC) and later still changed to the Wesleyan Church of Sierra Leone (WCSL), has grown to heights and has become a shrub that attracts all types of birds to build nests. Evangelism has come full circle! In recognition of this, the Kissy Dockyard Wesleyan Church organised what they referred to as a 'Wesleyan Hero' service in honour of the new President and those other Wesleyans he had appointed in government on Sunday 12 October 2008. Four years later, the Wesleyan Church of Panlap (where the paramount chief of our chiefdom resided) organised a special service "in honour of four years of dedicated service" on Sunday 2 October 2011 (which was coincidentally the President's birthday). The Wesleyan national leadership made it a point of duty to introduce formally any new National Superintendent to the President – the last being Rev. John A. Baminhoma on 1 June 2017. And they would invite him as a special guest of honour at their annual gatherings.

Reciprocating the goodwill gestures, President Koroma would support the Wesleyan Church in several ways: he made huge financial contributions for the modernisation of the Kissy Dockyard Church (where he was registered and had always been a member), he made donations to different auxiliaries including the purchase of a modern musical band-set for the national youth group. If he was away in other parts of the country, like Port Loko or Kabala, he made it a point of duty to attend the local Wesleyan churches there.

* * *

It has to be said though that despite all his 'Wesleyanism', President Koroma's presidency ran the affairs of state with a full realisation of the 'Christian state, Muslim country' notion – or, to put it more appropriately, as a secular state. A democracy. His government was not essentially Wesleyan or Christian tilted. He had more Muslims in Cabinet, apparently as per population ratio.

Consequently, he became the President that promoted the Islamic pilgrimage to Mecca to its highest and largest ever proportions with chartered flights and scholarships (meaning free sponsorship) to hundreds of 'hajas' and 'alhajis'. At the early stages of his presidency, Muslims were allowed to pray at State House on almost every Friday; and the President joined them once on a while. He would send gifts to mosques and to Muslims in general, particularly during the month of Ramadan. In some of his speeches, he would make special appeals to Christians and Muslims, and at least on one occasion he used the word 'Allah' to emphasise 'brotherhood' with Islam (but one thing I never saw him do was to call Muslim clerics to pray for him as he would do with Christian leaders of different denominations). He definitely had no compunctions entering mosques especially for funerals or weddings. He also developed the practice of joining Muslims in grand public settings like the Siaka Stevens Stadium particularly during 'pray day' at the end of fasting. (But this went on to a point that it angered some Wesleyans, and even caused some serious rumblings within high-level Wesleyan circles! The discontinuation of the Muslim Friday prayers at State House could not have been unconnected.) The President introduced the position of and appointed a Special Assistant on Social Affairs who was by and large at State House mainly for Muslim affairs and was the secretary of the hajj committee.

President Koroma was happy to talk about the cordial relationship he had with the Muslim 'clergy', with a particular reference to the Gaddafi mosque in eastern Freetown where perhaps he attended 'prayer' the most, and was always welcomed with enthusiastic ecstasy by mosque leaders and attendees. And Muslim clerics themselves, when interviewed, had immense respect and love for the President – one called him 'a believer and a child of the Way'. They adored him more than his predecessor President Ahmed Tejan Kabbah who was a Muslim. Moreover, President Kabbah was a very frugal man as opposed to his generous successor – and the Muslim clerics overwhelmingly noticed the huge difference in largesse and donations.

At the international scene, President Koroma accepted the nominal label of Sierra Leone as a Muslim country by cooperating and participating in Islamic activities, particularly with the membership of the Organisation of Islamic Conference (when I was his Press Secretary, I attended a couple of such meetings with him abroad).

But what I would surmise as my assessment of the President's overt attachment to the Muslims would stem from events that only unfolded later in his presidency. They had to do with his then-Vice President Samuel Sam Sumana. The revelations came later to the public, but I would think the President had an inkling of, or rather suspected, some deception about his Vice President's claims of being a Muslim just for political reasons. It was customary in Sierra Leone for the President and the Vice President not to belong in the same religion as a way of balancing power in the sphere of faith. Therefore, President Koroma, I suspected, wanted to mitigate the consequences of any revelations about the Vice President's religious orientation. If President Koroma had not done what he did by closely associating with Muslims, then when it later came out that Sumana was 'not a real or original Muslim' (as claimed by some members from his hometown, but that he was a Christian), the fallout for the government would have been disastrous. Because we are talking here about 75% of the population; and if they had not had that solace in the President identifying with them before the revelations of Sumana's questionable religious leanings, the Muslims would have felt thoroughly conned.

A school of thought, however, believed that Sumana's troubles had nothing to do with religion: that they were generated by a bitter power-struggle between political clans in his Kono hometown. Indeed, most of those who testified against Sumana in an inquiry set up on a charge of 'anti-party activities' went ahead to allege that he was desperate to take over power and wished his boss dead. Sumana's denials and protestations fell on deaf ears. And the controversy only became more topical when, in fact, he was replaced with a Christian, Victor Bockarie Foh (who humorously described himself as a 'Chris-Mus' in an effort to assuage the suspicions of Muslims).

However, all the efforts President Koroma poured in endearing his administration to Sierra Leonean Muslims flew out of the window when the flagship hajj scholarship programme became enmeshed in alleged massive corruption. Millions of dollars were alleged to be involved, as people were obviously conned and left out from attending the pilgrimage. The first to have raised the alarm a year before was the then-Minister of Social Welfare, Sylvia Blyden, who used surreptitious methods to record a telephone conversation of some unauthorised withdrawals of money from the hajj account at the government-owned Sierra Leone Commercial Bank. No known action was taken, as the methods she used were deemed unconventional and unofficial – particularly by making the recording public before consulting with the bosses. She was deemed bitter for not being given a free hand to run the show as the minister in charge of religious affairs.

And then the big one came: would-be pilgrims, who had already said goodbye to their relatives, were left stranded either in Freetown or at the Lungi airport.

There was bitterness and wailing in the Muslim community. Happening just months before the 2018 elections, the President's party was apparently punished for this when it lost to the opposition. Victor Bockarie Foh, the man with whom he controversially replaced Sam Sumana as Vice President, being the supervisor of the hajj committee, was eventually arrested and charged by the new government. Also charged for the same alleged crime was the Deputy Leader of the party, Minkhailu Mansaray, who was the chairman of the committee. It came closer to the presidency when a man who had been working at State House all these years was also named and eventually charged – Alhaji Sheka Kamara, Special Assistant to the President on Social Affairs, who in actual fact coordinated Muslim affairs and was the secretary of the hajj committee.

There was this confusion of my name being associated with the hajj-gate owing to the latter's name – mainly because he had also adopted the 'Shekito' nickname that I had been using in my journalistic writings. When some newspapers screamed with headlines like 'Shekito In Hajj-gate Scandal', 'Shekito Ordered To Return From Mecca', it only caused more confusion. Thankfully, I was in England at the time the scandal broke out, while the alleged culprit (we were close when I was Press Secretary to the President and we used to argue over the nom de guerre) was in Mecca.

But perhaps my being out of the country at the same time added to the controversy as well. A former university classmate staying in London, Saidu Kaye Sesay, had to take to social media to diffuse the confusion, publishing a photograph of him and me on Facebook. He simply confirmed that I had been in England days before the hajj, and above all I was a Christian who would not have anything to do with the pilgrimage's arrangements! But it was a huge embarrassment for the government.

All the work of the previous years went under the bridge, overshadowed by the scandal.

* * *

I have already noted that President Koroma's Christian roots were well grounded, and that he had received a Christian upbringing. This was further illuminated by his attendance of the Magburaka Boys Secondary School at a time when the charismatic Christian preacher, Rev. Canon Modupeh Taylor-Pearce, was Principal. The future President, who became head boy of the school, was so attached to his Principal (with a tinge of physical resemblance) that he was actually nicknamed 'Taylor Pearce' by his school peers (they also gave him a more Christ-like nickname 'Ka lomeh ka Kuru', a Temne phrase meaning 'lamb of God' in apparent recognition of his meek character). I have in an earlier chapter mentioned the traditional rivalry that existed between the Wesleyan Church and the Catholic Church in Makeni. Wesleyan Ernest Koroma developed a very healthy working relationship with Catholics – calming nerves, foiling fears.

The clergy and laity of the Catholic Church in Makeni could not have asked for a better President. No wonder most described the rapport between their denomination and the Wesleyan President as excellent. And it was visible. He had a personal affinity with the then Diocesan Bishop George Biguzzi who had unencumbered access to him. And when the idea of establishing a Catholic-owned University of Makeni was born, the President fast-tracked its implementation by not only offering hundreds of acres of land at his paternal home village of Yoni (a couple of kilometres from Makeni) but he actually poured in huge financial resources, including personally funding the construction of the residence of the Chancellor of the University.

In a further extension of his Christian-oriented tentacles, President Koroma was the main benefactor for the construction of modern blocks for the Anglican-owned Sierra Leone Church Primary School where his father was head teacher, where his mother was a teacher and the President himself did his primary schooling (interestingly, my mother was his classmate at this school). He succeeded in giving it also a junior secondary school. Filial gratitude, one would say!

Yet still, President Koroma's Christian affection spread even further to the evangelical and charismatic spectrum. He had a sentimental liking for the evangelical activities of the non-conformist Sister Wisdom Veronica Conteh, a young female 'apostle' who was fired up for evangelisation with no recourse to a higher earthly authority – a scenario no Catholic Pope accepts! The President financially supported her evangelising programmes, as I can testify to having been the courier on some occasions! It was such unalloyed fervour and passion for unrestricted evangelisation that caused the President to honour invitations to formally open two of the most famous charismatic churches in Sierra Leone: Victor Ajisafe's Sanctuary Praise Church (also known as the Solution Cathedral, but more famously known as 'Let my gate be opened!) and Bishop Abu Koroma's Flaming Evangelical Ministries mega church. Each of these men of God saw himself as a pope in his own right! Furthermore, President Koroma had tremendous respect for 'the Body of Christ', a conglomerate of various churches, whose leadership intervened during the virtual stalemate of the 2012 elections outcome to bring the then-defeated candidate Julius Maada Bio (who would win the subsequent 2018 election) and the President together at State House for general national acceptability of the results. It worked.

* * *

Even with all this mainstream religious manifestation of his open-mindedness as a leader who embraced all religions, the fact of the existence of 'African traditional religion' was not lost on President Koroma. He fully recognised the activities of the traditional and pseudo-cultural activities of the male poro society and the female bondo society. Other cultural groupings like orjeh and hunting societies all had their place and attention in the President's agenda. One would be privileged and exhilarated to be present when the President, as a member, would discuss issues of the poro society with other members in informal settings – the debate over personal supremacy or knowledge of the details or the quasi magical stunts. Yet, all was done more from a social perspective than in any belief in the superstitious. Sierra Leoneans generally saw secret societies as social or cultural phenomena much in the same way as people in the western world would regard Halloween or sorority/ fraternity clubs – with certain 'secrets' reserved for members. Many Christians also complained about the President being too closely associated with these 'worldly' groups.

* * *

Assessing President Koroma's presidential stewardship, National Superintendent Emeritus of the Wesleyan Church, Rev. J. Y. Konteh (or Pa JY, as he was fondly called), told me he remained very proud, calling the former President "an ambassador of Christ". He mentioned sterling humane characteristics, apart from the general socio-economic transformation of the country like the road infrastructure and electricity provision especially to Freetown which was once described as 'the darkest city in the world.' Pa JY believed the most glaring show of President Koroma's Christian orientation was in the area of human rights: he set the record of not holding any political prisoners and no executions of opponents for the first time in post-independent Sierra Leone. Pa JY also had admiration for the President's calm fortitude in marshalling the nation for prayer and collaboration during the fight against the virulent Ebola disease.

The clergyman also commended the former President's ability to easily forgive his opponents and detractors even when they had clearly crossed certain barriers. It was admirable how he maintained his university friendship with key opposition party leaders like John Benjamin of the SLPP. He was also admired for turning around once-acidic critics like medical-graduate-turned-newspaper-publisher/editor Dr. Sylvia Blyden (she was a personal friend of mine before my appointment and we have tried to remain so to this day…).

Sylvia had used her newspaper, *Awareness Times*, from an opposition standpoint not only to deride the government but to personally attack the President with a caricature of devilish horns on his head. Her paper continually harped that the elections were rigged by Chief Electoral Commissioner Christiana Thorpe in collusion with foreign collaborators in favour of President Koroma (the same argument she would put against her former allies ten years later on the same 'regime change' concept). It was part of my job, as Press Secretary to the President, to try to contain or correct any apparently sentimental journalism and unsubstantiated reportage on the presidency. She would not prove that she received emails from Zimbabwe describing President Koroma as being a worse dictator than Robert Mugabe when I took her to the Independent Media Commission to do just that. She faked it, the Commission concluded after engaging the services of IT experts who established that the supposed varied sources quoted by the newspaper could all be traced to the IP address of one computer in Sierra Leone, not in Zimbabwe. We had a few more spats, one of which led her to take me to court for 'defamation' over an online banter – the case was dismissed on a *nolle prosequi*. She realised the futility of continuing the fight. Her love affair with the opposition apparently ended when her preferred candidate for the SLPP presidential ticket for the 2012 elections did not win. She switched sides!

President Koroma would later appoint Dr Blyden as his Special Executive Assistant, from which position she resigned after controversies with other State House officials; and later still appointed as a Cabinet Minister, from which she was sacked following a radio spat with her Deputy. To her credit, she became one of President Koroma's most ardent defenders particularly after he left office. She anchored her new zealousness on ancestral political spirits – drawing inspiration from the role her forbears played in party affairs. Indeed, she has a fine political genealogy in the APC.

The general view around the country was that President Koroma did not want to hurt a fly, could not hurt anyone, and would always want to turn the other cheek when slapped! And this could be his undoing, believed a certain school of thought, when some of those around him used a pretext of primitive loyalty to deceive him. It culminated to the 'hajjgate' scandal.

* * *

From a personal perception of President Koroma's religious orientation, he once told me that the first thing he would do whenever he entered his office at State House was to pray, on his knees. There was no reason to doubt that.

Even if I had doubted that, I wouldn't have doubted it was divine direction that took him to Israel on a state visit in January 2017, making him the first-ever Sierra Leonean

President to visit the 'holy land'. In the typical global village that the world had become, the activities of the President were relayed virtually live on phones, computers, laptops and other news-savvy devices through email, WhatsApp, Facebook, Twitter – the social media frenzy. And then the mainstream media also was awash with reports of the visit.

It was a political visit certainly. But the President used it to send a religious message. The Jewish religion (Judaism) is intertwined with the Christian faith! The picture that went more viral and obviously captivated hearts and minds was the one which showed him praying at the 'wailing wall' with a Jewish skull-cap on his head – an open Bible in one hand, the other hand raised to touch the wall, reading Scripture.

"I prayed for the country, I prayed for peace, I prayed for peaceful elections, I prayed for my party. I prayed that the hardship should pass and for future prosperity," he would later tell me. He was fascinated by the fact that he was accorded the opportunity at a special ceremony to plant a tree in Jerusalem, with its plaque bearing his name. Doing this in his ninth year in office was like an icing on the cake of his presidency.

I was forthright in wanting to know what he was reading at the 'wailing wall'. He told me it was selected verses from Isaiah, Psalms, and Nehemiah. But he was much more delighted about having been taken to Christian-related sites on a conducted tour. And one of the places was the empty tomb of Jesus Christ. "O how amazing! I felt fulfilled," the President said.

And by way of sealing his presidency before leaving office, President Koroma himself made sure he visited Pope Francis – on the background knowledge that I had impressed on him how spiritually fulfilling an experience it was after my own visit.

We were sitting at the high table during the formal laying of the foundation stone (where I was Acting Minister of

Internal Affairs in the absence of the substantive Minister) for the construction of a police academy in Makeni just a few days after my 'Vatican pilgrimage'. Though I had already spoken to him on the phone about it, I decided to repeat the message that it was a trip worth making – that meeting the Pope was an opportunity he could use since he already had it within grasp.

"Is it?" he asked rhetorically, as he looked me straight in the eye. I straightaway knew he would do it. But it would take two years for him to do it in somewhat controversial circumstances. He led a delegation that comprised his choice as successor and the losers within his party. For the purposes of this book, I would stick to just saying that the former President also met with the Pope!

It was so exhilarating when on return he told me in the presence of the welcoming party at the State Lodge (the official residence of the President) that Pope Francis asked about me!

The last word: a few days to the end of his presidency, Koroma attended a Christian evangelisation crusade at the national stadium in Freetown (fuelling the complaints in Wesleyan circles that he had lately abandoned the leadership of his original church for the charismatic). Dressed in immaculate white on this midnight occasion, the President publicly knelt down in prayer with the pastor, Francis Mambu of the Faith Healing Bible Church. The President didn't come along with the man he had chosen to succeed him. His party didn't win eventually.

All smiles: a day never to forget

The bridal high table: (L-R) Rose, myself, bestman David Oglaza and his ex-partner

Marching on to solemnise it: bride and groom with the vicar, the Rev. Andrew Dawson

In front of the most famous house on earth: the White House

At the White House lawns with World Hope International's Ann Karl

Hobnobbing with royalty: the day I received an award from Princess Ann

As Deputy Minister of Internal Affairs, shaking hands with current UN Secretary General Antonio Guterres when he was UN High Commissioner for Refugees

When I was Deputy Minister of Information, I met with current President Julius Maada Bio in London after he had lost the 2012 elections to President Koroma

Sitting right behind the President at the UN General Assembly in New York

Happy days: shaking hands and chatting with the President at a public ceremony in Freetown

Side by side with the President: during the laying of the foundation stone for a police academy in Makeni

The chosen few: we can be seen far right, the barricades behind us, as the Pope comes near as per protocol

A large family: with Love Bridges at the centre of St. Peter's Square

With my parents: sandwiched with love

When mother was crowned 'Wesleyan Woman of the Year 2013'

Marie with her grandparents at Mabanta

Rose and Marie in London

A proud dad: with Marie and John Sheka at Mabanta

Out and about with Marie in London

Rose (sitting in the middle) with her theological class colleagues on an evangelising mission at Mabanta

A visitor from Manchester: David Oglaza visits Mabanta and poses with my parents, sister Esther, niece Becky, Rose and me

A visit to the farm: a snapshot with some members of the Mabanta Farmers' Development Association

In one of my public speaking events in Manchester

Exiled journalists from different countries: during our course at Lincoln University

At a seminar at Bristol University

Reconnecting with Manchester folks while in government: sitting with the priest who married us, his wife and other friends

Here with my former boss at the CAB, Clare Taylor, and colleague journalist Mansoor Hassan weeks before I was called to return home and work for the government

Mansoor Hassan, my colleague journalist from Pakistan: here with Rose while visiting Manchester during my days in government

With the President at State House together with company CEO Martina Gjergja, Alie D (ist right) and engineers

All work and no play: watching Croatia play at Euro 2016 in Freetown with company President Vedran Taslidzic and engineer Sasa

In a visit to Croatia, I couldn't help but take a picture with a work of art of a huge crucifix (all made with nails and barbed wire) in the city of Dubrovnik

Visiting Rose's mother in Gitwe, Rwanda

Rose graduates from the theological college in Freetown

A table for three: with Rose and Marie at a London restaurant

Representing Sierra Leone: here giving a speech at a UNHCR conference in Geneva

As minister in charge of immigration, handing over a Sierra Leone passport to former British High Commissiner Peter Penfold

Senior Kroma brother Martin and wife Hawa

All Kromas: me, Elleen, Matilda (M.A.), Admire, Benji

Girls of a kind: Martina, Elleen, M.A., Admire

Benji and Martina

Me and Martina

From the Kroma clan: Austin, Chrystabelle, Vanessa

A dynasty: Elleen, Admire, Warren, Lacee, Benji, Sylvanus (Koroma)

Heart to heart: Vanessa and Ann Marie (Kromas)

Girls of the same feather: Becky, Ann Marie (Mayo) and Marie

Tarawalie dynasty: Mother, Alice, Marie, Esther, Danny, John Sheka

Mother, Sembu, Marie

All Tarawalies: Rebecca, Alice, Marie, Esther

Home visit by legendary Sierra Leonean clergyman, the Rev. Canon Modupeh Taylor- Pearce (center), and our Bloomer family friends together with officials of the traffic lights project

Pastor Rose preaching at the Mabanta Wesleyan Church with the aid of an interpreter

Close friends of Manchester: visiting the Whethams – Baby Keziah, Mei, Rose, Me, Daniel

Tarawalie next generation: Hudson Sheka, Becky and John Sheka (Johnny)

Kroma next generation: Vanessa and the twin sisters

Rose and I on a boat ride on the River Thames in London after I completed the first draft of this book

The Lord is my Shepherd

Chapter Seventeen

Appointment As Press Secretary To The President

Setting The Stage For Highest Christian Encounters; In-depth Background On How And Why I Left Concord Times; *The AFRC Military Interregnum Explained*

It is gratifying for any member of a group to be recognised by that group's leadership. It is every believer's pleasure if he or she has an opportunity of meeting the top-most leadership of their religious order on earth.

I have no iota of doubt that if it were not for President Ernest Koroma being the Head of State and appointing me into his government, I would not have been included in an invitation for the President to attend the Wesleyan World Conference, the highest body in the Wesleyan Church's leadership pinnacle – at least not at the time I did.

I have no doubt that it's because of the same reason and

circumstance that I was able to meet Pope Francis – at least it wouldn't have been at the time I did; and in the foreseeable future. Just the thought of ever touching the Pope's hand, let alone arrange a meeting with him, would never have crossed my mind if not for my appointment into government.

Moreover, if President Koroma had not remembered me and called me from the UK (where I was seeking asylum) to return home to serve as his Press Secretary, even continuing to call myself a Wesleyan Christian would have stopped or remained in name only. For there was no known Wesleyan Church in Manchester and I had already joined a different denomination – this time of a charismatic character – and had got married in the Church of England.

So, what came to mind was the biblical saying that, all things work together for good to those who love God, who have been called according to His purpose. The President called me to return home and be his Press Secretary. I was humbled. My prayer was for God to prove Himself in me, even with all my human deficiencies!

The President appointing me as his Press Secretary immediately after his inauguration came as a surprise to some people – but not to the leadership and membership of the Wesleyan Church of Sierra Leone. To those who were surprised, it was apparently owing to the fact that I was out of the country at the time and did not participate – in person. But, of course, I had been writing articles that were published online and reproduced by pro-APC local newspapers in the campaign that saw President Koroma elected from the opposition to take over governance.

* * *

I had left Sierra Leone after a tumultuous journalistic career and I was now settling in the UK as a political asylum-seeker following my strange-bedfellow relationship with the then-ruling SLPP government of President Ahmad Tejan Kabbah – as I was thrown into prison once, thrown into 'a fugitive life' once, and then thrown into the Diaspora.

Things were already changing for the better for me in Manchester – making a name in many circles, getting married there, appearing on television, in newspapers, on radio, doing post-graduate courses at UK universities through my membership in the National Union of Journalists and the Exiled Journalists Network, and receiving an award for excellent work at the Citizens Advice Bureau (where I was a trained and certified Adviser) from no less a person than Princess Anne, Queen Elizabeth's daughter. I was, therefore, unwittingly becoming a local celebrity, and I was naturally entertaining and virtually concretising the idea that it was in Manchester where I was destined to settle and live, at least in the short and medium terms.

And then the President called! For me to come and be where he was. To be his Press Secretary. To be the bridge between him and the press. I would later like the way the Secretary to the President put it in my appointment letter: "I write to inform you that it has pleased His Excellency the President to appoint you to the position of Press Secretary… to keep the President informed about daily national and international developments, including providing analyses of their wider implications… to serve as liaison between the presidency and the press, both national and international… to attend to certain specific matters relating to the press, that require the personal attention of the President…"

The onlookers were questioning why a man living in England would be the one to have such enormous and enviable responsibilities at State House just after the elections. One Wesleyan pastor would later jokingly say my appointment was "ordained – the Wesleyan way".

I have already mentioned how the former President was the son of Wesleyan parents while they were serving as 'missionaries'. Likewise I had been born while my parents were being trained as Wesleyan 'missionaries'. It's even more striking to note that the President's father was one of the tutors of my dad at the Gbendembu Bible School. That relationship lasted, and it simmered down to us (their descendants). Ernest Koroma, the generous insurance boss who would later turn President became a role-model to many of us aspiring boys and girls from his home-district (mainly as a group of students from the Bombali District Students Association soliciting his support for our various activities, including transportation to the district to offer free tuition to various secondary schools during holidays). On graduation, he was a leading figure in financially contributing to the setting up of the newspaper I founded, *The Torchlight*. I remember very well the words of encouragement he gave me after my prison experience following my first spat with the then-Kabbah-led SLPP government – he admired my response to the experience with my first after-prison article titled 'Good Morning, MPs', and he called me to his Siaka Stevens Street office to encourage me to continue. We were a family – of sorts!

From that perspective, it would appear my appointment was more or less based on family or personal connections. Ok, it looked like that.

But it was not.

For the President to have made such a crucial decision of choosing anyone to be his liaison with a new nomenclature of

'Press Secretary' (being the first time an official at State House was being called such, away from the tradition of getting someone from the Government information bureaucracy serving as 'Press Officer') must have been informed by more than merely personal considerations. He was doing it for his own good and for the good of the country – as much as it was for my own good. He needed a journalist tried and tested, who would be able to steady the stormy media landscape that had not foreseen his victory, to put it mildly. His new regime was up against a hostile press. The appointment of a Press Secretary must, therefore, be based on merit! Someone with a patriotic commitment and loyalty.

The background story is long; but we would have to narrate it in summary.

* * *

My marriage to Rose Tarawalie (née Kabeera), a beautiful Rwandan lady, had just happened in spectacular fairy-tale fashion at St. Thomas' Anglican Church in Oldham, Greater Manchester; and we were still steeped in post-honeymoon bliss, having spent the weekend in London and were returning to Manchester that memorable November Sunday afternoon when my phone rang. A personal direct call from the newly-inaugurated President in the company of his younger brother Thomas and one of his closest long-standing allies Siray Timbo (who later passed away while serving as Ambassador), and I had to speak with all three of them in informing me that I was his choice for the position of Press Secretary. It was so unbelievable, so surreal, so out-of-this-world, so cool of the President. I asked Rose (who was driving) to pull over to the hard shoulder. She parked and the conversation continued, as she unavoidably listened.

And then you would just have expected me to have said "Yes sir, your Excellency, thank you sir for such magnanimous consideration, I'm hopping on the next flight to Freetown." But no, I didn't say that; that wouldn't have been me. My typical me. Inquisitive me. Not that I turned down the offer. I couldn't have. It's virtually impossible to turn down an offer from the President. But I wanted to water it down. It was too much of a surprise. And I had not enough time to think about this unexpected appointment. I wanted to temper it down. I wanted another job; not that one. A lower-level job, for my convenience really. So I told the President that I had just married a foreign lady and I was now in the process of settling proper. So I asked for the appointment to be changed to 'Information Attaché' at our High Commission in the UK, since I was already living there anyway.

Unwittingly, by that 'argument' on its own, I was not being grateful or courteous to the Head of State (both Thomas and Siray were telling me); and the President interjected on similar lines: "I've asked you to come; and I want you to be here with me. I believe the lady would also love to come," and then he was gone (or rather he did not say a word again), as Siray and Thomas continued scolding me for having the temerity to put up an argument. I climbed down and accepted the offer unconditionally.

Rose was listening to – or rather following – the conversation throughout. I had quickly whispered to her that it was the new president calling, and he was together with our friend Siray (whom I had always been in touch with and was already known to her by phone and photos). Her eyes of approval during the 'argument' gave me the impetus to agree. She would afterwards say she didn't see the need for me to have argued, because this was a call from the President. "If it's the President, why argue?" she asked rhetorically.

Can you imagine! I thought I was trying to please her by giving our new marriage as an excuse to ask for a London-based job. She was pleased with me standing up for her – but not to the point of arguing with the President over a job offer. We laughed about it anyway, filled with joy. "I knew you were a star when I agreed to marry you," she couldn't help but say, hugging and kissing me – just the two of us on the hard shoulder between Manchester and Birmingham. We saw the world around us changing. We felt as if we owned the world – well, we owned it: our own world. She increased the volume of the gospel music in the car stereo (we always play gospel music); and now she drove faster; with me entering Manchester no longer as the just-married asylum-seeker whose final fate or immigration status was still technically undecided, but as a sojourner who had completed his mission in the UK (even if temporarily) and was now only back to pack his bags and return home to Sierra Leone as a hero. So, so unimaginable. It was like a scene in a drama movie. I just continued beaming!

From the conversation with the President, he didn't say he had offered me the job because of any family connections. Rather, choosing me for the position of Press Secretary was based on my journalistic pedigree. I could hear the president saying he believed I was the best person for the position. He was always a man who did not mince his words. He did not say he was appointing me for family reasons or because we belonged in the same church. He said he had come to the conclusion that I was the most appropriate person for the position of Press Secretary to the President. And that he wanted me to be where he was. So it was more about my credentials and competence, although obviously informed by not merely family considerations but personal trust. And that's so essential in such appointments anywhere in the world.

Invariably, at the national level, it was the credentials that mattered. If the President had chosen a Press Secretary who did not have the requisite pedigree, the new administration could have been slain by a then-hugely anti-APC media. But I was no newcomer in Sierra Leone's politico-journalistic landscape. In fact, except for the mercies of God in whose hands our lives belong, I could have been a martyr of journalism. I would have been burnt alive like Alhaji Musa Kabia, or I could have faced a firing squad with Col. A.K. Sesay or I could have died in prison like Conrad Roy or at least I could have been on death row like Hilton Fyle.

And I would give the background.

* * *

I became a journalist by calling – by divine calling, I can boldly say. As God said about Jeremiah, He had known me before He formed me in my mother's womb – just as He knows each and every one of us. He had predetermined my profession, I believe and I know. He planted it in my DNA. Or let's say He had made me a writer ever since it started with writing Church letters for my dad. Though the President – or circumstances – would take me from journalism, but they would not take me from the pen and paper or could not take the pen and paper from me. I would always say, "I'm a journalist on loan to politics" to many of my colleagues! And I kept telling my people at Mabanta, "I'm not a politician!" Most would not understand initially; unfolding events would convince many.

* * *

Since primary school days, it was clear my academic path was charted towards the Arts as opposed to the Sciences. Not that

I was not doing well in the latter, but my instinctive favourite subjects had all revolved around reading and writing, later climaxing into an Honours degree in English Language and Literature. I was too fast in learning the Queen's language, my teachers used to say – thanks to my 'missionary' background and interaction.

At secondary school, when the time came to make the choice (interestingly, I had passed all my subjects and was qualified for any of the three streams: Arts, Science, and Commercial), you already know which I chose. Many speculated that I would be a lawyer (country people love lawyers!). In both Birch Memorial and St. Francis, I wrote articles and poems for student consumption as an extra-curricular activity. At Pa Kroma's house, I opened a home newspaper for fun; and the family generally liked it. When I entered the university, there was no longer any room for doubt left as to who I was – a student journalist. I became something like a celebrity on campus, with my articles becoming the centre of arguments almost on a daily basis within the student body. It was the last days of the APC one-party rule, and student politics was very potent, very powerful – it was like the only opposition remaining, a kind of last-man standing. You must certainly also be courageous and determined to be a student journalist, because your language was always under the strictest scrutiny.

My writings launched me into the national spotlight just after the overthrow of the APC government of JS Momoh by the NPRC military junta: the nation was in a state of euphoria, swallowing the 'revolution' hook, line and sinker; and then I came up with the article 'Captain Strasser Is Not Our Redeemer' (as narrated in chapter 12).

And even with my continuing crusading journalism (having been formally recruited as part of the 'Nigerian-boys-founded' *Concord Times* newspaper's ground-breaking 'new journalism' while I was still a student), I would eventually graduate from the university with one of the best degrees of that generation after seven of us were selected from a group of over a hundred to the Honours class for English Language & Literature. At that time, there was no Department of Mass Communication; Journalism was only incorporated as a module within the English programme.

***

And here's how FBC and *Concord Times* were connected: I had a brush with one of the Editors of that newspaper when he wrote an article about a candidate at my university's Students Union elections having lost due to 'bad English'. I wrote to the newspaper pointing out the 'bad English' in the article as well. But instead of a counter-article, what I received was a gracious invitation from the founding Managing Editor, Kingsley Lington, asking me to join his team as proofreader. Pleasant surprise; and we clicked the moment we met. I jumped in.

On graduation, I formally joined *Concord Times* as Features Editor (which included being the proofreader of the whole paper), where I introduced the later-famous 'From the Black Tank' column. At the same time, I was an English and Literature teacher at Lebanese International School for students taking the London 'O and 'A levels.

I would leave *Concord Times* to set up my own newspaper, *The Torchlight*, for editorial policy reasons – having had to come to terms with the Nigerian background of the owners when they had a dispute with their High Commission in Freetown because of me. I had written an article condemning the despotic regime of General Sanni Abacha after he carried out the execution of well-known writer and activist Ken Saro-Wiwa in November

1995 in an article titled 'What Is Wrong With The Black Man?' describing the Nigerian dictator in devilish terms.

Kingsley and Tony (young Nigerian refugee journalists from Liberia) – it must be said – brought modernity and innovations (like widening the range of issues covered other than merely politics and being the first to publish daily, except on Sunday) into the then-traditionally fretting media landscape in Sierra Leone. Perhaps, just perhaps, I might not have gone on straight to journalism from the university if they had not fished me at that early stage and got me immersed into the job three to four years before graduation. But now I had just landed them into trouble.

They were summoned, together with me, of course, to the Nigerian High Commission by High Commissioner Alhaji Mohamed Abubakarr who threatened them with deportation if such writings should ever come from *Concord Times* again. It was not a mere threat. The Abacha government had actually sent a *note verbale* to Sierra Leone's Ministry of Foreign Affairs requesting the deportation of Kingsley and Tony. The High Commissioner had a copy; hence the meeting. The deportation was only stayed when it was ascertained that they were not the authors of the article. The High Commissioner was so very visibly angry, as he remonstrated to me as well with several questions "Shekito, did Abacha kill your mother? Did he kill your father? Did you know who Saro-Wiwa was?" I did not say a single word, as my bosses kept apologising profusely. There and then I made up my mind – it was time to move on. I would prefer not to put my friends in danger, but I would not leave the vision and fervour of my journalism. "We were not jellyfish, but we were on a cliff's edge," Kingsley, now working with the United Nations in New York, would later recall for the purposes of this book.

I did not leave *Concord Times* alone. At least four other senior members followed me when they knew I was going to start my own newspaper: Tatafway Tumoe, Pasco Temple, Sorie Sudan Sesay and Ornette Turay. I snatched Sullay Adekulay and Mohamed Sankoh from an unattractive teaching field and 'play-cook' journalism respectively – plus an array of zealous reporters. And before long, as you would expect, *The Torchlight* was in trouble with the authorities.

Well, really in trouble on the first day of publication! It was a big shock to the SLPP government when *The Torchlight* hit the newsstands on 6th September 1996: a press release was immediately issued by the Ministry of Information banning the newspaper, saying it was not registered (but actually because its critical contents were talk-of-the-town: we had published a story – with a picture – about a secret meeting between President Kabbah and General Sanni Abacha in Aso Rock, Nigeria, wherein the former handed over a package to the latter, and that diamonds were part of the gift, according to our source! The story itself was never refuted!).

The then-Minister of Information, lawyer George Banda-Thomas, sincerely thought we were not registered because in actual fact his ministry was in charge of registration. Banda-Thomas (who actually had some personal liking for me and used to invite me to his office for political chit-chat) was an avid reader of newspapers and knew I had just left *Concord Times* about two weeks earlier and should not have gone through the registration process (which used to take months) within such a short duration. What he did not know was that we had done our registration with the directorate of information months before. Thankfully, the Director of Information (a trained international journalist himself and a fan of my 'Black Tank' column) did not inform the Minister, who would apparently not have approved if he were informed.

We made a loud noise about the government being arbitrary, calling on journalists – local and international – to have a look at our documentation. The government had to back down: another press release was issued on the same day lifting the ban, saying we were actually properly registered. 'Banned And Unbanned' was our next-day front-page screamer. We would never have asked for better publicity – though the government was poised to silence us through a proposed legislation crafted for the purpose.

This was how the Committee to Protect Journalists (CPJ) reported the issue on its website:

> *"September 6 – Torchlight, CENSORED*
>
> *Minister of Information George Banda Thomas banned Torchlight, a new independent newspaper that was to come out twice a week, on the same day the first issue was published. The newspaper, sponsored by the opposition United National People's Party (UNPP), was banned on the grounds that its first issue contained uncomplimentary articles about President Ahmed Tejan Kabbah. Thomas retracted the ban the same day and gave Torchlight permission to publish until after an upcoming government review of proposed changes to the press law." (https://cpj.org/attacks96/countries/africa/sierraleonelinks.html)*

But the Director of Information, Rod Mac Johnson, lost his job (I would later in life reward him by recommending him for the position of Chairman of the Independent Media Commission when I became Deputy Minister of Information and Communications). Thomas himself would be reshuffled and replaced by Abdul Thorlu Bangura. *Aluta continua!*

Our writings continued to be so revolutionary that one Cabinet Minister once confessed to me that we were preventing President Kabbah from sleeping. The President was very thin-skinned! A front-page story, a month later, that revealed how he had apparently tempered the then-vociferous stance of MPs (who had been giving him a tough time in approving his nominees) with a 'loan' which the newspaper described as a bribe, was the last straw that opened the prison doors for my entry there. An invitation to justify my story to the House of Representatives ended up being a charge of 'contempt of Parliament', with the Speaker eventually reading an already-prepared type-written verdict, sending me to jail for one month.

The game had only started. I came out of prison more revolutionary, more crusading. The 'Black Tank' had become a little more than famous – it was a household column in literate circles and beyond, pouring out weekly incisive articles to a nation in need of light. The only action that the government would now take to silence me was to introduce draconian press requirements, obviously tailored purposely to rule me out as editor through a clause increasing the number of years of experience needed in journalism to be qualified. An editor was now required to have graduated from the university and practised for at least five years. I only graduated the year before, though I had been practising for five years. I was not qualified. None of my colleagues was qualified. The government knew what it was doing. Abdul Thorlu Bangura was going to take the statutory instrument to an eagerly-awaiting parliament for a foregone-concluded approval. *The Torchlight's* time was up. A short-lived newspaper!

But then this would not materialise. The article I wrote in response to the new law, 'Goodbye SLPP', in anticipation of parting with my much-loved profession, turned out to be a valediction for the government itself. It was sent packing by a group of military officers in yet another coup. To us as a newspaper, this was not totally unexpected, as we had been highlighting the dangerously supercilious role given to a local militia (kamajors) over and above the national army (on suspicion of, and allegations that, the latter were colluding with the rebels in prosecuting the war, thereby coining the term 'sobel' – 'soldier by day, rebel by night'). The civil militia men had the effrontery to not only arrest soldiers, but actually had the audacity to attack military installations and brigades, publicly humiliating and killing soldiers at will – all with the blessings of their presumptuous traditional leader, Chief Hinga Norman, who was the Deputy Minister of Defence.

President Ahmad Tejan Kabbah himself, being the Minister of Defence, would later not mince his words in describing 'the disloyalty' of the national army when recollecting the scenario in his book *Coming Back from the Brink in Sierra Leone: A Memoir* (2010 –Excellent Publishing and Printing, Ghana). The President wrote: "Many civilians in the war-affected areas soon realised to their chagrin that elements of their own national army were turning against them. Some were colluding with the rebels. Those disloyal soldiers who collaborated with the rebels were nicknamed 'SOBELS', that is, 'soldier-cum-rebel'." He would go on to state that: "In these circumstances, some communities decided to organise their own defence mechanism by forming civil militia units... In time, the *Kamajor* militia emerged as the most formidable group. Its overall head was Chief Sam Hinga Norman, an ex-officer of the Sierra Leone Army."

There was therefore no better way to have easily courted controversy or inevitable trouble with the military by making a dismissed military-officer-turned-*Kamajor*-chieftain the Minister in charge of the Army. And this is more resonant in President Kabbah's own narration: "Relations between the Army and the civil militia units rapidly deteriorated due, in part, to the unpatriotic behaviour of the 'sobels'. By the time I became President, relations between the civil militia, particularly the *Kamajor* group, and the Army had reached an all-time low." But he never revealed 'the other part' responsible for the 'deteriorated' relations.

The former President was apparently still very angry with the Army when he wrote the book in 2010 – even though he had already executed by a firing squad 24 senior officers including a female officer in defiance of international appeals in October 1998. And even though his former Deputy Defence Minister Sam Hinga Norman had already died in 2007 at the hands of the Special Court (the hybrid United Nations/Sierra Leone Government war-crimes Court), which had arrested and charged him for war crimes and crimes against humanity. Kabbah himself would later appear in the Court as a defence witness for rebel leader Issa Sesay (who succeeded prison-deceased original leader Foday Sankoh) but could not do the same for "my close friend" Norman!

For this, he would fall out not only with a majority of his party members but with another 'close friend', Peter Penfold, the democracy-loving anti-military junta former British High Commissioner to Sierra Leone. Penfold, after he failed to convince the soldiers to reverse the coup, pitched tent with Kabbah in Guinea during the military interregnum. He went all out – perhaps went out of his way, as he lost his job over the 'Sandline' arms affair – to get Kabbah restored back to power. Penfold, crowned honorary paramount chief for his efforts, would testify at the Court on the side of Norman. (When I became Deputy Minister of Internal Affairs, I would recognise Penfold's continued attachment to Sierra Leone by facilitating his naturalisation and I officially handed over a Sierra Leone passport to him at a well-publicised ceremony).

Now, it was apparent, as in all theatres of war throughout the ages, that some soldiers might have committed atrocities (there was an attack on the residence of then-Chief Electoral

Commissioner James Jonah by soldiers, and there were shootings by NPRC boys during elections day in 1996; during the AFRC, there would be the infamous civilian massacre at the quay-side Mabela slums allegedly by soldiers). But there should be a better way of handling the matter – military tribunals would do. There were obviously those soldiers also who would be nostalgic of the junta days – but you would not play into their hands. The overwhelming and seemingly unlimited authority garnered by the Kamajors under the new Kabbah regime obviously pushed the Army as an institution into a difficult situation – backs to the wall.

Some people believed the Army was just power-thirsty, having relinquished government just over a year earlier. Such people immediately openly condemned the military take-over. President Kabbah himself had always insisted that the NPRC military junta 'grudgingly' handed over power to him due to persistent pressure from the civilian population and the international community; and that the AFRC coup was wholly and solely a military escapade to perpetuate in power. The President was not complimentary of the Police either: "I also had great difficulty relying on the Police because most of them lacked the requisite discipline and wherewithal to do a good job. They too were plagued with the same problems that confronted the Army, namely excessive politicisation and corruption." Trust was lacking would be an understatement – though a tangible peace process, rickety as it was, was handed to the government by the out-gone junta.

However, to put things in perspective, those who organised the coup were a totally different crop of soldiers from the NPRC leaders who had been given enticements and passageways 'to go study abroad'. An Inter Press Service (IPS) report of 28 April 1997 could not be more succinct or grimmer in describing the unfolding state of affairs: "In the past few months, relations between the Kamajors and the government army have plummeted. Since the signing of the Peace Accord last November between the RUF and the government to end the six-year-old conflict, the Kamajors and government troops have clashed in Moyamba, Bo and Tonkolili districts in the North. There have been casualties on both sides. The most recent incident occurred last month in the settlement of Magburaka, 20 kilometres from the northern regional capital of Makeni. Eyewitnesses said that 12 soldiers were shot dead by the Kamajors."

Half-hearted attempts at pacification did not bear fruit as long as the kamajors continued to have leverage under Norman's tutelage. This had been a poorly-equipped Army, ill-prepared for war, mainly accustomed to ceremonial duties (unless the few who had gone into peace-keeping in Liberia). When Liberia's then-rebel leader Charles Taylor carried out his threat of ensuring Sierra Leone tasted 'the bitterness of war' because our government provided a base for the regional ECOWAS forces to intervene in the Liberian civil war, our soldiers blamed the political class for ineptitude, left the war-front on the pretext of complaining for better conditions of service, overthrew the APC government of Joseph Momoh and formed the NPRC. To have fought a guerrilla warfare in which the enemy would also wear military camouflage fatigues at whim – confusing the civilian populace in the process – depicted the callousness or heartlessness of war. In some places, even the kamajors were accused of being rebels when the enemy adopted and deployed similar tactics in their mode of dressing. It was hard to tell who was who. Things had fallen apart. The centre could not hold.

In fact, the new military leader, Major Johnny Paul Koroma (a Britain/Sandhurst-trained officer who did not hold any political position in the previous military junta), was sprung from jail – having been incarcerated for several months following a fierce and bloody challenge his military unit had put up against the civil militia in the south-east in which 'over 100 kamajors' were killed.

The kamajors, either through the exasperation of war-weariness or foolhardy indoctrination, had claimed invincibility and invisibility in battle through magical powers – that bullets couldn't pierce through their charmed bodies. How on earth well-educated men could believe such a charade still beats my imagination. Why then were the South African mercenaries, Executive Outcomes, being paid millions of dollars as an auxiliary force in prosecuting the war? And why should anyone be arrested when the charms didn't work? In any case, Major Johnny Paul was charged with treason following an investigation by Nigerian soldiers brought in for the purpose – with reports of torture and at least one Sierra Leone soldier dying in the process. He was brought in while I was there; but we never managed to meet in prison. I left him there. He was awaiting trial when members of his unit struck on May 25 1997 and formed the AFRC.

And a digressing, if related, fact of this intriguing tale is that current President Julius Maada Bio of the SLPP did not support the idea of reinstating the Kabbah government through a military intervention at all. In fact, former Ambassador to the USA, John Leigh, accused Bio of working against the SLPP's efforts in favour of an international recognition for the AFRC junta. Writing in *Cocorioko* online on August 4 2018, Leigh asserted that: "Bio studied in Washington DC when I was Ambassador there. Bio supported Dr. Abass Bundu [current Speaker of Parliament] when Bundu was the Ambassador of the AFRC-RUF junta that overthrew the elected SLPP government of Tejan Kabbah." This further fueled the 'sobel' conspiracy theory! But then – adding further to the twists and turns of

Sierra Leonean politics – the same Bio would return after Kabbah's reinstatement to contest for the leadership of the SLPP. Today, he is President of an SLPP-led government…

The international community was virtually united in denouncing the AFRC coup, refusing to recognise the new regime. Their resolve was hardened by – and this I saw as the junta's own self-undoing – the virtual automatic incorporation of the rebel outfit into the new administration. Rebel leader Foday Sankoh, then in prison in Nigeria, was announced as the Deputy Chairman of the AFRC. His imprisonment was seen by the rebels as 'a coup' against the peace process, since he had been invited for peace talks in Nigeria only to be arrested for 'carrying a gun' (which they denied). The situation was not helped by the support given to the action by representatives of the RUF who had been sent from 'the bush' to Freetown in the Commission for the Consolidation of Peace. A delegation sent by the Kabbah government to talk to the rebels on why Sankoh was arrested was itself arrested by the rebels and would not be released 'until our leader Foday Sankoh is brought back to us'. They effectively resumed hostilities, attacking villages across the country, hacking people's limbs. This was more than a stalemate.

The junta leadership, therefore, saw their invitation to the rebels after overthrowing the Kabbah regime as a practical demonstration of the end of the war. But the rest of the world interpreted it otherwise – it confirmed the 'sobel' analogy. The world saw it as chaos taking over the reins of government – not helped by the uncouth behaviour of most of the rebels who had turned up in large numbers in towns and cities across the country. Their 'jungle justice' methods (like arbitrary seizure of property, public flogging, frog-marching, shooting) towards civilians on the flimsiest of accusations only generated more abhorrence from the public and the international community.

Apparently, these were the same rebels that had been carrying out some of the most rapacious and bestial atrocities like hacking off people's limbs and even splitting the bellies of pregnant women on a bet to know the sex of the baby! And now, even under the host regime, they were clashing with the soldiers in trying to establish a functional chain of command.

The military was subsequently able to restore some form of order; but that was no longer enough to turn back the hand of the clock – the Conakry-based Kabbah regime was recognised as the legitimate government of Sierra Leone and it must be restored. Full stop. Even the independent report of a visiting Ghanaian diplomat Victor Gbehu sent by the sub-regional group ECOWAS was derided. Gbehu reported that, indeed, there was more order on the streets of Freetown as he drove around without any incidence for three days – "I even went to church on Sunday," he had declared. The pro-Kabbah side went to the point of saying Gbehu, who would later become a Government Minister in his home country, was either bribed or lured 'by prostitutes'.

For Nigeria's General Abacha, as represented by his Field Commander General Victor Malu, any form of return to normalcy or restraint by the AFRC was a sign that the blockading sanctions were working and must be continued to be vigorously implemented, backed by Alfa jet bombings. A ship filled with rice that tried to berth at the Queen Elizabeth II Quay was bombed and forced to return. Some in the top hierarchy of the junta would blame their prison-sprung leader for being too sympathetic to the point that he freed all the former government functionaries who had already been arrested and were slated for execution or continued incarceration. Their freedom gave them the leeway to regroup in Guinea and lobby the international community.

The Torchlight continued to call for a peaceful, and not a military, solution.

Some people thought I knew about the coup beforehand! Honestly, I did not. But then my long relationship with the army (naturally having admirers within its ranks, having acted as a media consultant for their maiden newsletter, and having several Mabanta relatives in the force) made many people to have thought I was the civilian 'John-Benjamin-NPRC' version of the AFRC military junta. But I was not. I certainly did not take up any position in the short-lived, ill-fated regime.

The Torchlight's calling for dialogue rather than any military intervention after President Kabbah had sought refuge in neighbouring Guinea would be the catalyst for my subsequent trials and woes. I would be subsequently declared 'wanted' as a 'collaborator' after General Sanni Abacha's Nigerian army succeeded in militarily dislodging the AFRC junta and re-installing the SLPP government. This was a moment of terror for many. Anybody who was branded as an 'AFRC collaborator' could easily face jungle justice: either burnt alive or publicly mutilated or sent to prison. And the numbers were in their hundreds or thousands.

In such morbid and horrific circumstances, I had to find an escape route – obviously asking God for total guidance. My soldier 'friends' had apparently forgotten about me; it was now 'every man for himself and God for us all'. I found a laborious and risky way to my Mabanta hometown (after a three-week spell at Waterloo, in the outskirts of Freetown) and stayed in hiding there for over a year until the signing of the Lomé Peace Accord on July 7 1999. Eventually, dialogue, as *The Torchlight* had always advocated, succeeded in ending the war, with the accord calling for reconciliation and the incorporation of the leadership of the renegade AFRC/RUF regime into the governance structure. The rebel leader Foday Sankoh was given a position 'equivalent to a Vice President', while the former AFRC leader, Johnny Paul

Koroma, headed the Commission for the Consolidation of Peace.

The journalist's truth would always last.

Perhaps it was an attempt to cover this truth that made President Kabbah to leave out a key dividend of the Lome arrangement in his book *Coming Back from the Brink in Sierra Leone*: namely, the role of Johnny Paul Koroma in saving the Kabbah government from falling again in May 2000. This was as serious a threat to the state as it was on May 25 1997 (when the military overthrew President Kabbah) and January 6 1999 (the infamous invasion of Freetown by combined AFRC/RUF rebels in apparent retaliation for their dislodgement by the Nigerian army a year earlier. It was that 'Epiphany' invasion that precipitated the peace talks, as US President Bill Clinton's Special Envoy, the Rev. Jesse Jackson, came to Freetown and told President Kabbah to literally abandon the hawkish approach or be abandoned, thereby taking him to Lomé – to the chagrin of most SLPP supporters at the time who were totally against any dialogue).

This time around, the chaos was happening after the signing of the Lomé Peace Accord.

On 8 May 2000, the RUF rebels had gunned down scores of demonstrators (demonstrating for the rebel outfit's refusal to abide by the peace accord and instead capturing hundreds of UN peacekeepers) at the Freetown Spur Road residence of rebel leader Foday Sankoh. There was chaos everywhere and the government had lost control again. President Kabbah was, in his own words, on the brink again. It was déjà vu all over again for the people of Sierra Leone. It took the Chairman of the Commission for the Consolidation of Peace, Johnny Paul Koroma (the former AFRC military leader), to rise to the occasion and save the day. But this did not appear at all in Kabbah's narrative – even if just to give the devil his due!

I found it unbelievable that a man of his intellect and status would write about something that everybody knew about and tried to cover it up again. The dismissive levity with which he brushed the matter under the carpet is shocking. Those who want to write history must not write it to themselves.

In Chapter 9, 'Former Rebels in Government of National Unity and the Tragedies of 2000', President Kabbah narrated how Foday Sankoh had become bloated with his position of an equivalent of a Vice President and head of a commission in charge of mineral resources, and how the RUF had angered Sierra Leoneans by abducting 500 UN peacekeepers. He narrated about the May 8 demonstration organised by civil society and parliamentarians and how it turned bloody, the rebels killing 21 demonstrators. After that, President Kabbah's narrative was purged, muddled. It did not explain what really happened just after those ugly incidences of May 8 2000 to May 17 instant – ten days of uncertainty for the people of Sierra Leone. The following was all the former President wrote in the book in that regard: "Foday Sankoh who had gone into hiding during the 8 May 2000 incident and the killing of unarmed demonstrators was apprehended ten days later. Amid conflicting reports about who had custody of him, my government issued a statement confirming that he was in our care..."

Whoever advised or edited the book for President Kabbah did not do him any good. It depicts him as a self-serving narrator. Now, narrators can be self-serving, but it should not be to the detriment of their reputation. One can't write everything in a memoir, accepted; but it is disingenuous for clearly deliberate omissions of significant events to be made.

In reality, apart from President Kabbah's own generously pronounced gratitude to Johnny Paul Koroma at the time, there were written accounts giving the latter credit for providing leadership to his own men within the military to stand up to Sankoh's boys. The Sierra Leone web (www.sierra-leone.org) – the most reliable news portal at the time, run by former American Peace Corps volunteer married to a Sierra Leonean, Peter Anderson (who would later be the Special Court's Public Outreach Officer) – had the following entry for May 8 2000: "RUF leader Foday Sankoh's Spur Road residence has been overrun and 'comprehensively looted' by Sierra Leone Army soldiers loyal to AFRC leader Johnny Paul Koroma, BBC correspondent Barnaby Philips reported late Monday."

The BBC itself in its own May 8 2000 report online titled, 'Sierra Leone protesters shot', gave the following background: "Soldiers have since Sunday arrested several RUF members – including a government minister – in connection with an alleged coup plot against President Ahmad Tejan Kabbah... The arrest was ordered by Johnny Paul Koroma – the army commander who himself staged a coup against President Kabbah in 1997, but who has now declared his loyalty to the president following the restoration of civilian rule. Mr Koroma said the arrests had been authorised by President Kabbah 'to put things on course again' – a reference to the Lomé peace agreement. On Sunday, both the president and Mr Koroma hinted that it might be necessary for Sierra Leonean loyalists to offer armed resistance against a rebel attack."

The current Secretary General of the Sierra Leone Association of Journalists (SLAJ), Ahmed S. Nasralla, in an article titled, 'Major Johnny Paul Koroma Became Head of State the Day He was to Die!', published as late as July 2017, explained the situation thus: "On 8 May, 2000, chaos ensued as angry demonstrators marched directly to the residence/office of the RUF rebel leader Foday Sankoh at Spur Road demanding the unconditional release of more than 400 UN peacekeepers earlier held hostage by his rebel outfit in the provinces. The situation was already escalating into something akin to a coup by the rebel leader when Johnny Paul Koroma intervened (once a soldier, always a soldier). He called on the public, through the radio, to shout the holy name of the Lord Jesus Christ (in the case of Muslims, Annabi Issah) up to 10 times, for deliverance from the dreaded rebel warlord. And, like a magic spell, everybody – son, daughter, mother, and father – shouted the name of Jesus above their voices."

In fact, the next day (9 May 2000), Johnny Paul's former bitterest antagonist, Chief Sam Hinga Norman, was assisting with him. This was how the Sierra Leone web put it: "Deputy Defence Minister Sam Hinga Norman said Tuesday that his Kamajor militia and former Sierra Leone Army troops loyal to AFRC leader Johnny Paul Koroma had taken over responsibility for security. 'Our security in Sierra Leone was in the hands of the United Nations but surprisingly we have come to the conclusion that the United Nations has not been able to protect us any longer,' said Norman."

Why on earth did President Kabbah not mention any of this, even if he were going to twist it to his own benefit? And then, strangely (is it?), in the same breadth he wrote that there were "conflicting reports about who had custody of him [Foday Sankoh, after he was arrested]", apparently just so that the name of Johnny Paul would not enter in his book in any positive way whatsoever. This is not even giving the dog a bad name to hang him – the dog does not deserve a name at all. But those who were recording events had a name for him. The BBC, in its 18 May 2000 online edition, reported 'The strange tale of Sankoh's capture' thus, in part: "The naked Mr. Sankoh was taken from the scene of his arrest – outside his own ransacked house – to the compound of pro-government militia leader Johnny Paul Koroma. From there he was moved to Sierra Leone Army headquarters, and flown on to a secret location by British forces." And the Sierra Leone web of 17 May put it this way: "AFRC leader Johnny Paul Koroma confirmed Wednesday morning that his men had taken Sankoh into custody. 'He was arrested somewhere behind his house, just by the hills, and he was taken to Lumley Police Station and then finally brought to me,' he told the BBC Network Africa programme. 'It was because my men made the arrest, and they took him to the police station, and they in turn sent him to me, and I handed him over to the government." The founding editor of *Concord Times* newspaper, Kingsley Lington (now working for the UN), reported in his own newspaper as published in www.allafrica.com on 17 May 2000 that Johnny Paul Koroma's men saved the day in an article titled 'Foday Sankoh Arrested, Shot in the Leg.'

Clearly, Johnny Paul or his men might have done horrible things in the past and after these May 2000 occurrences (he escaped in January 2003 and never surfaced again after an attempt to arrest him yet again for another alleged coup – pleading his innocence in hiding – when he was already a Member of Parliament, having won a seat in the 2002 elections). But I see no reason why these events and their players should not be recorded in detail and put into perspective for posterity. Sincerely, President Kabbah erred on that again. All who knew the sequence of events and read his book will agree.

The journalist's truth lasts...

And this is not to say President Kabbah himself did not eventually end up being a good leader. Despite his personal mistakes (particularly in the first term), he was able to subsequently steady the political ship and oversee a smooth transfer of power to the Opposition, as his party's candidate lost the 2007 elections. When he ultimately extricated himself from the claws of the SLPP apparatchiks, Pa Kabbah came out and ended as a fine gentleman – enjoying the retirement he had initially come to have after leaving the UN to return home but was prevailed upon to lead the SLPP and won the presidency in 1996. Three factors, among others, stood out in Pa Kabbah's favour. First, just about a year after he assumed office, his long-time colleague at the UN, fellow West African Ghanaian-born Kofi Annan, became Secretary General of the world body. Annan, perhaps also trying to compensate for the then-alleged failure to act in the Rwanda genocide when he was head of operations, would ensure his friend was not only restored to power but gave him all the paraphernalia that the UN would provide in the post-war recovery efforts. Kabbah was, therefore, through the goodwill of the international community, able to build institutions from the ashes of war. The second factor was his strange but personally healthy affinity with Nigerian dictator Sanni Abacha. Another Machiavellian classic: a junta dislocating another junta for democracy. Going back to the friendship apparently sealed with 'the gift' Abacha received from Kabbah as published in *The Torchlight's* first-ever edition, the Nigerian government sacrificed a lot (lives and money – hundreds of casualties and one million dollars per day it was reported at one time) not only to reinstate Kabbah but to keep him in power even after Abacha's sudden demise in the middle of the military adventure. Thirdly, what helped in endearing President Kabbah to the populace was his second wife, Isatu Jabbie (IJ – we were together at the university), whom he married after his first wife, Catholic-bred highly-intellectual Lady Patricia Kabbah, passed away. IJ Kabbah's youthfulness and zealousness brought some celebrity glamour to the presidency and won the hearts of the young generation. President Ahmad Tejan Kabbah of the SLPP would, therefore, wittingly or unwittingly, go down in history as the President who ended Sierra Leone's war. And he enjoyed his retirement, as he got the protection he needed from his successor, President Ernest Bai Koroma of the APC – conspiracy theories abound, especially when Kabbah's State Chief of Protocol was maintained in office by the new government. Koroma would later accord his predecessor a lavish state funeral.

***

In a nutshell, therefore, my eventual appointment as the first-ever Press Secretary to the President in Sierra Leone was a deserved one. I knew the Sierra Leonean politico-media landscape; and the President knew I knew it well. Not only him – even his newly appointed Minister of Information at the time. They both clashed in appointing me: I was arguably the only person who received two simultaneous appointments at the start of the administration. Not knowing that the President had already called me to be his Press Secretary, Information Minister I.B. Kargbo (a veteran outstanding journalist whom I had greatly admired as a role-model) nominated me as Information Attaché to China. Kotho IB, as he was fondly called, was confused when the President scratched my name off the list he had presented without explanation. I would be the one to explain to the man with whom I would later work as Deputy Minister of Information.

Consequently, and in retrospect, it was absolutely clear that my appointment as Press Secretary to the President was the one major action that set the stage for possibly the highest earthly Christian encounters anyone in my situation would desire.

Chapter Eighteen

Previous Great Encounters

The British Monarchy/Citizens Advice Bureau, Spring Harvest 'Paradise On Earth', BBC TV, Lincoln University Course, Anglican/ Evangelical Wedding (Sierra Leone-Rwanda United); Asylum Seeker

For the vast majority of British people (except for the few anti-monarchy campaigners), their great dream and desire has always been an encounter or any meeting with royalty – not to speak of receiving an award from a member of the royal family.

For a vast majority of asylum-seekers (except for the small number of economic migrants), their continuous prayers are geared towards winning sympathetic ears and having an opportunity to relay their story via the media.

For a good number of men in England, all they wish for in life would be a good wife; and if you are an asylum-seeker, getting married in the Church of England with the approval of the Home Office is a dream come true.

I did all three with ease, with virtually no conscious effort on my part. Just the will of God, I concede or rather assert. The first of these events happened in the most unlikely of circumstances, at a time when I was supposed to be a nonentity.

Being an asylum-seeker in Britain in 2004 (perhaps at any time) was like being sub-human. You were the scum of the earth. On British television and radio and in the national newspapers, immigration was a very topical issue, and asylum-seekers were the butts of political debates. "They have come to take our jobs; they should be sent back; they are taking over Britain" and so on and so forth. The fear-mongering was worsened by the rise in Islamic militarism targeting everything the West stood for – with Britain suffering several terrorist attacks including at train stations and on buses. Fear, racism and conservatism when combined would produce hatred without borders – blanket hatred, dehumanising hatred. And it became more poignant during the 2005 elections when the Conservative Party contrived the slogan, "Are you thinking what I'm thinking?" Thinking about deporting asylum-seekers! Thank God they did not win those elections. Tony Blair and his Labour Party won. There was some respite! At least the generalised deportations that Michael Howard (then Conservative Leader who himself was the son of Jewish immigrants!) wanted were not implemented – though the unfavourable conditions (like detentions and morning raids) continued for asylum-seekers. Children were being cramped with adults in detention centres in Britain. A BBC undercover documentary exposed this shameful situation (http://news.bbc.co.uk/2/hi/programmes/real_story/4310361.stm).

People who had legitimate claims for asylum were being hounded and sent back home. A man you spoke to yesterday would today not be heard from because immigration officers had seized him overnight. Another had just committed suicide in your neighbourhood. A lady you interviewed a week ago could not turn up again for an appointment: she had gone underground out of fear, all traces lost. The harrowing stories were not in short supply.

This was the time when I was an asylum-seeker in England. This was the time when I was least expected to raise my head above waters. I had just been rejected by my daughter's mother. I had just been rejected by my friends in London. I had just gone into oblivion and had been taken to an unknown 'land' by the Home Office. I was expected to be a nonentity.

But not me; I could not be tamed. My spirit could not be dispirited. That was why with all the odds stacked against me, it was in such circumstances that I was able in my work at the Citizens Advice Bureau to attract attention for an award that I received on behalf of the unit from Princess Anne (officially known as the Princess Royal), daughter of Queen Elizabeth. Royalty recognising me, an asylum-seeker. That was what it was. God took me from the miry clay and set my feet upon a rock to stand!

* * *

I had gone to the UK following a traumatic career as a journalist, with a tragic history in my country. Not that when I was making the decision to choose (or rather accept) journalism, I had a desire to make a name (famous or infamous) for myself. It was one of those honest unwitting decisions that young men and women across the globe have to make every now and again after completion of university.

I'd gone to school. I'd gone to university. What was I going to be in life? I chose journalism against the wishes and advice of many. Some told me with a second class first division (the best for that year), I could be sure of a quick rise in the civil service; or that I could apply for a scholarship for further studies abroad; that there was no known rich journalist around town; and to have considered the fact that this was the 'dark period' of journalism in Sierra Leone, wherein each and every regime had found it a game to repress journalists and muzzle the press. Why would I have to be a journalist in a country like Sierra Leone? Why would I want to be? I didn't know exactly. I just had the simple faith that this was my calling – from God. And no human would change my mind.

But if I had been forewarned as to the litany of persecutions awaiting me, without the benefits, perhaps I would have had second thoughts about becoming a journalist in Sierra Leone at that time. It was too much (to be jailed, to be declared 'wanted'). The price was high; but, in retrospect, the prize is higher (not least the writing of this book).

I settled for the profession as innocent as a dove – the one thing being on my mind was to make this little light of mine shine, with some unexplained flame burning in me, to brighten Sierra Leone. I chose it because it was chosen for me by the One who knew me even before He formed me in the womb. That was the secret. The knowledge of Scripture: that He who was in me was greater than he who was in the world; that, no matter what, 'the truth shall set you free' (John 8:32) – the biblical verse I adopted as the motto of *The Torchlight* to read, 'The Truth Shall Set Us Free'!

But you had to be suppressed before you were set free. You had to be imprisoned before you were liberated. So to prison I was sent by the Sierra Leone Parliament under the SLPP in very murky circumstances after I had written about them having literally taken a bribe from the President via a concealed unpaid loan from the government-owned commercial bank for a softening of their tough stance in vetting presidential nominees for ministerial positions. One month in jail. Freed. And then fried.

The Kabbah-led SLPP government engaged in a series of political blunders that exacerbated the war (kamajors challenging soldiers with impunity, terminating the supply of rice to soldiers, and down-sizing the military). The President was reportedly informed about a pending coup for which he would not take action until it happened. He had a different version in his book, as if he personally intercepted the coup plans, while at the same time heaping the blame on the military leadership: “In addition to my regular meetings with the top brass of the Army… I had ordered a special military network radio capable of monitoring security related information and movements. On 23 May, I heard some unusual communication. I became suspicious. I immediately summoned the Army leadership to express my concern. They assured me that all was well.” There was a big problem of trust (and therefore of what or what not to believe) between the President and the Army (not least due to the kamajor question); but I got that information of having been given a detailed report of names and locations about the planned coup but the President taking no action from the then-Chief of Defence Staff, Brig. Hassan Conteh (who was among those subsequently executed, after Kabbah’s reinstatement, for the very coup). In fact, the coup-makers targeted senior military officers (Hassan Conteh inclusive) for having informed Kabbah about their plans. Some were beaten and placed under house arrest for a while, with houses thoroughly looted.

From his perched grounds in Guinea, President Kabbah would hatch a return plan with the help of the military junta of General Sanni Abacha hiding behind equivocal UN statements (which never amounted to, or even came near, authorising a military intervention). *The Torchlight*, along with a couple of other newspapers, denounced any illegal military intervention, while at the same time calling for a peaceful resolution of the conflict.

And that was enough to be 'charged' with 'collaboration'. That was the crime of colluding with 'the enemy', as announced by a then-newly-established-for-the-purpose pirate radio station, SLBS 98.1 FM later called Radio Democracy. And when the military intervention succeeded, the spate of lawlessness and wanton killings – people burning people alive; people dying while people were laughing and enjoying it; people crying, people singing – was surreal. An odd world. A fallen world.

That was what it was. This state of madness would have consumed me had it not been for a narrow escape. I was on the list. And they came for me. Minutes after I had sensed it, I jumped the back fence very early in the morning. They had waylaid the front gate overnight. I had suspected some movement and, therefore, did not sleep in the house but in the fowl-pen, an under-cellar, with a few belongings packed in a rucksack. The pirate station had already announced that Lumley had fallen to the Nigerian soldiers. You could be sure Juba which was a couple of miles away was the next to fall. What would I be waiting for, knowing the fate awaiting me? I had already heard the harrowing automatic punishments that had been the hallmark of the intervention since it started in the east of the city, and the melee continued as they advanced. It was obvious they would reach the far west of my Juba residence by the morning. Avoid taking risks. Better to jump the back fence than use the front gate when leaving. Find your way to your hometown. It was laid in my heart by the Spirit of God. And I followed my heart. I would later be told that the way-layers entered the house in search of me less than twenty minutes after I had left! Worthy to note that this was a period when I had already inculcated the habit of not sleeping in one place; so I had left the plotters guessing!

I eventually arrived in my hometown after walking the length and breadth of the Freetown peninsular and had to first hide in Waterloo for three weeks before taking the risk of boarding a vehicle to go into oblivion for over one year in Mabanta. But then the war raged on and on until men found no more reason to continue to kill one another and a peace deal was struck – a peaceful resolution, it was eventually accepted, was the only way out!

To cut the long story short, in view of what happened to me before and even after the peace accord had been signed, I eventually sought asylum in the UK. I had always wanted to go to the UK; I needed to. I dismissed and rejected proposals for asylum in countries such as Canada and Australia while I had a brief sojourn in The Gambia. I just wanted to go to the UK. A bid to do so through Banjul did not succeed. I had to return to Freetown and find a way.

The reason it had to be UK was simple. It had happened that the continuing hostilities between the AFRC and Nigerian Forces convinced the British Government to evacuate all British nationals. My then fiancée being a British national was qualified and we had just had a six-month old daughter, Marie, who definitely needed respite from the bombardments and jet fighters and all. I had an opportunity to go with them; but since it was too automatic a decision, I asked her to go with the daughter and I would follow later for two reasons: that my contribution as a journalist was needed at that point in time in Sierra Leone, and that I would like to inform my parents about it. They went; and immediately thereafter, all flights to and from Sierra Leone were cancelled – unfortunately. I remained in touch with them until I no longer had the opportunity while in hiding. They remained in my thoughts and prayers throughout.

When, therefore, I survived the harshest of constraints (not least that Makeni was cut off from the rest of the world after the rebels overran it) and a peace deal was struck, there was no wavering as to where I wanted to go – England. I made a first try to The Gambia, convinced by my former Deputy Editor Tatafway Tumoe, whose sister was residing there. We had a stint at the *Daily Observer* before Dr. Abass Bundu found me out and got me to manage his car rental company. I would two years later resign and return to Freetown for the main reason of finding a way to go to England. I got employed as a Research Fellow at the Freetown-based Centre for Media Education & Technology (C-MET), then-run by veteran journalist David Tam-Baryoh who previously worked with *Concord Times* while I was there.

Through my new office, I secured a visa for a conference to the UK. I informed my fiancée about it and she seemed happy, only for me to appear at her door and got rebuffed – having come with nothing. She had moved on. I couldn't even be allowed to touch my daughter. She only brought her out after I had left and was already on the ground floor while they were upstairs, calling back and saying 'Sheka, look at your daughter, Marie'.

I turned and saw the little girl. My angst disappeared temporarily as my eyes and hers met. Like the world stood still for a moment. I waved and forced a smile. That was it, as they disappeared almost immediately. Would you believe it! Any attempt to have reminded the lady that she once defiantly told her mother that she would either marry me or she would be a nun would be futile and nonsensical. Things eventually smoothened up in terms of visitation (only me visiting, no return visits) after I had relocated to Manchester – she supported my asylum bid eventually. With time and change of circumstances, things got better.

Marie herself would send a point home about a decade or so later when she would decide to do her medical internship in Manchester (with me accompanying her to tell her some stories) before she proceeded to King's College. But she would actually display her Temne gene when she would, against her mother's wishes, visit me in Sierra Leone in search of Mabanta. I would ultimately come to realise that I should not blame her mother for deciding to move on in my absence. *Nar so God say*! The best wife was in store for me… And they would love each other at first sight! Marie would later tell Rose while we were having lunch at a restaurant in Kingston, London, that the best part of her trip to Sierra Leone was the Mabanta experience – of course meeting brother, grandparents, aunts, cousins, etc etc for the first time and being treated to 'royalty' at the village located between the 'male' and 'female' hills (Wusum and Mena respectively), and exploring the rest of Makeni both day and night.

After the end of the conference – and that experience – my original plan was to return to Freetown again; but then I received information that my name was included on a list of civilians allegedly connected to another so-called aborted coup (too many coups that era – factual and fictional, but lives were lost in both). And with a resolve to do all I could to reconnect with my daughter, I had to seek asylum. I was tired; I needed respite from that trap of a hostile environment I had found myself in ever since I became a journalist in Sierra Leone.

But then the asylum itself turned out to be another hostile environment. No respite. Not just yet. The British people were being taught to hate asylum-seekers. The slogan, 'Are you thinking what I am thinking?', was a most disgraceful and dehumanising mantra designed by man to describe another man. Instead of 'Are you thinking of whom I'm thinking about,' it was 'what' not 'whom'. To the anti-immigration propagandists or extremists, an asylum-seeker was just a number, another asylum-seeker, an object! This opprobrium was heightened by the murderous strategy of Islamic militants: the most notable being the video-publicised killing of a British hostage in Iraq despite international and personal appeals by his family. Many British people thought most, if not all, asylum-seekers were Muslim! People like us would later be channels of correction for that misconception.

* * *

So I was an asylum-seeker. And I was a thing. Another number. I refused to accept that. Because it was not true. Satan was a liar. Let courage rise with danger and strength to strength oppose. Therefore, even when my lawyer, Franck Kiangala, a Kenyan-British soft-spoken fellow, told me my case was virtually impossible to win because it was highly political and that the Sierra Leone government had made representation at the Home Office through the High Commission in London for me to be returned home, I told him I would not budge. I would not give in. I would never give up. In my heart, I was singing the melody "I'm holding my Saviour's hand… Nothing can stop me from holding my Saviour's hand'. The lawyer must have looked at me and said in his own heart, "He doesn't know what he is up against!"

And for sure the Home Office letter came through: I was rejected and asked to leave the country. I appealed. I was rejected again. My lawyer reminded me of his earlier words and withdrew his service. I took up the case on my own. I wrote to the Immigration Appellate Authority. They wrote back. I wrote again. A writing competition of some sorts – which I was using to buy time. I was asked to leave the accommodation provided for me. I refused. I'd rather be thrown out or get deported than leave the house to nowhere. They budged. And then they gave me another opportunity to take another lawyer, Gary McIndoe (a white British this time, and he was based in Manchester as opposed to Kiangala who was based in London), to do a judicial review of the matter.

Meanwhile, I launched a campaign through my membership of the National Union of Journalists (NUJ) and the Exiled Journalists Network (EJN). Soon I became a speaker at anti-immigration campaign events in Manchester (where I had been taken), soon the newspapers picked up my story. Soon I was on BBC television. Soon I would become the secretary of the men's auxiliary in the church I attended. Soon I would be chosen to head a new Oldham-Council-sponsored group, the Emerging Communities Forum. Soon I had become a local celebrity of sorts for obvious reasons.

All along, I had not sat down like a condemned man waiting for a final decision on his fate. I believed within me that I would succeed – that I would not be deported. Scripture took the better part of me: the Lord who had started the good work and brought me to Britain would bring it into completion! I didn't break the rule of working illegally – like some other asylum-seekers were admittedly doing, thereby somehow justifying the claims of job-stealing (although the types of menial jobs they did were actually never being done by the British themselves). But I would not be the one to justify a deportation order against me for breaking immigration rules. At least I could write articles and get a few hundred pounds (because colleagues at the Exiled Journalists Network told me this was permissible, as the fees were occasional). The Home Office was giving me vouchers as a weekly subsistence on top of accommodation anyway. I then decided to offer my services to volunteer, in consultation with the new lady-friend I had found and would later marry, Rose (who would be a great inspiration, a great source of encouragement, a ray of light, and the appropriate biblical helper at a time when the world was dark; we met at church!).

I started volunteering first at Cancer Research UK. And then I moved on to the Citizens Advice Bureau, where I received in-depth training just like regular British employees – and I was also given a weekly monetary token to cover expenses. It was the exceptional work that I, together with some later-recruited asylum-seeker volunteers, performed here that convinced the Board through the recommendation of the local Oldham branch to give us an award which I was chosen to receive. My work was wide-ranging: I advised people on a variety of issues, but particularly excelled on asylum and housing matters. I persuaded the Home Office to rescind some decisions against asylum-seekers; I got them to give back homes to some rejected asylum-seekers. I had access to a gamut of British law, rules and regulations as made available to CAB Advisers.

I used the platform to help Afghans, Iraqis, Iranians, Somalis, among many, but interestingly never came across another Sierra Leonean asylum-seeker at the bureau – they loved London. The way I wrote my daily reports impressed management a lot. I became 'volunteer of the month' several times – sometimes in a row. It culminated in me receiving the award from the Princess Royal, being the patron of the CAB at the time, on Saturday, 30 September 2006!

The special award ceremony will always be memorable. The feeling remains indescribable. In front of an audience of hundreds, including Charles Kennedy who was then leader of the Liberal Democrats, it was announced that "Sheka Tarawalie, accompanied by Terri Nicholas (a Liberian lady who had just joined the team), will receive this award for exceptional work at the CAB in Oldham", after the citation describing the tremendous achievements registered by the local branch in recent times. As I rose from my seat to the podium amidst continuous applause, I was more than humbled, tears of joy rolled down by cheeks, thinking "was this for real? Could this be a dream? No, I shouldn't be here. I should be deported; I should have been deported, but Satan was a liar!" I received the award with trance-like joy, as Princess Anne (who had already been introduced to me moments before the ceremony and we'd had a brief chat) shook my hand (hers in gloves), smiling, handing over the plaque to me, and posing for the cameras. What a life. What a mighty God we serve!

The local newspaper *Oldham Evening Chronicle* of October 5 2006 reported the event with the headline, 'Volunteers are the toast of the nation: Oldham CAB team scoops top award'. Reporter Marina Berry stated: "Oldham Citizens Advice Bureau has scooped a top national award, thanks to a team of asylum seekers and refugees. And it was a right royal occasion when the group were presented with their award by The Princess Royal in front of 900 delegates at the charity's annual conference in York... Their efforts are worth an estimated 73 million pounds to the charity each year. CAB chief executive David Harker said: 'All our volunteers are amazing individuals who give up their time to make a contribution to the local community, but those who have picked up these awards have shown an extra special commitment'."

The newspaper had been previously following and reporting my activities (thanks to my then-CAB immediate bosses, Clare Taylor and David Oglaza): when I first gave a talk at St. Thomas Church (where I would eventually get married), Carolyn Armstrong titled her report, quoting me, 'Don't give us charity, just give us a chance' with a photograph of me and the vicar Andrew Dawson in their 2 March 2005 edition; and when I settled down as an Adviser at the CAB, Dawn Eckersley did an 'Insight' with a photograph of me attending to a client in the office titled 'Welcome to your new life in Oldham' in their 11 July 2006 edition. The royal award was the icing on the cake!

From then on, it was all clear that it would be impossible to remove me from the UK. I'd got an anchor! This other 'scheme of man' against me had failed. To put more icing on the cake, there was a Sierra Leonean attendee of the conference, Veenod Fullah, a Makeni elder acquaintance whom I had not seen in ages but who was also working for the CAB in Oxford and had even married a British lady. He made sure to find me after the event, as he was so happy for me; and we took a couple of photographs. He would later attend my wedding!

* * *

Another worth-mentioning encounter while seeking asylum was my attendance of the 'Spring Harvest' international Christian festival. Another miracle. This could be one of the greatest Christian events on earth by every stretch of the imagination: thousands of Christians from all over the world, mainly from Europe and America and Australia, converging at a resort for a whole week and engaging in all types of activities in praise of Christ Jesus. If humans had ever come close to creating heaven on earth, this was it. Let me give a brief background.

As my asylum story spread from one place to another, from one person to the other, from one group to the other – including via radio, newspaper, and television – more and more opportunities opened, as I was continuously being invited to speaking events. And this was one aspect that helped me make a distinction between the British Government and the British people.

The British government had the tendency to portray itself as an anti-asylum entity, while the British people tended to present themselves as a most hospitable and humanitarian community. The vast array of charities set up to support asylum-seekers by ordinary British people and some caring organisations told the story: the Salvation Army, Oldham Unity, Manchester Asylum Support Group, the Boaz Trust etc etc.

The British were human beings like any of us, these selfless fighters manifested themselves: they thought and felt like any of us. They were even very critical of their government for being heavy-handed on asylum-seekers; they led public campaigns for the human rights of asylum-seekers. You would find a British woman like Sheila who would tell an Immigration Officer to his face: 'You'd better deport me, than take away Fred (her adopted Ugandan orphan asylum-seeker) from me,' forcing a tear or two to run down the cheek of the Home Office messenger himself! Or you would find David Oglaza who was supposed to be my immediate boss at CAB but carved a friendship with me to the extent that he was the 'best man' at my wedding – and would eventually follow me with visits to Sierra Leone when I had returned to take up government work! Or you would find the Rev. Andrew Dawson who would come and pray with me in the morning, and would take me to speak at his church and other churches in the Manchester area. He would write letters to the Member of Parliament for the area (Michael Meacher, for whom I would later write a tribute at his demise while I was already a deputy minister and it was published in the UK's *Guardian* newspaper on 1st November 2015) to take up my case with the Prime Minister (Tony Blair, with whom I – as Press Secretary to the President – would eventually work in his post-Prime Minister life through the 'Office of Tony Blair' which was supporting the government of Sierra Leone in policy and research). And then the Rev. Dawson would eventually be the vicar to preside over my wedding ceremony.

It was this type of love that caused many British people to write letters to me after I appeared with my story on prime-time television on the BBC's 'Songs of Praise' on the beauty of waiting for God. But not only letters; some actually sent money by the post (they contacted the BBC for my address). It was so gob-smacking. Not only that, some actually invited me into their homes. The Rev. Dawson virtually adopted me. Mary Embleton in Oxford made me use her home with my new bride during my honeymoon.

It was this type of love that inspired me to travel from one event to another as a public speaker. It was at one of these events at a place in Oldham called the 'Salt Cellar' that, after my speech, a lady (Sandra Cooper, whom I was meeting for the first time) approached me and said she would like me to be part of her team at 'Spring Harvest'. I couldn't really figure out what it was; because I was hearing it for the first time. But she kept saying "You'll like it". She told me there was only one space left, and she felt the Spirit telling her it was for me. Could you believe it!

Back in Sierra Leone, as a young man I used to attend Wesleyan youth camps and I had seen crusades at the national stadium (including the life-changing one by German Evangelist Reinhard Bonnke on 4 December 1991 when I personally took the decision to surrender all to Christ), but never in my life had I seen anything like Spring Harvest in terms of both numbers and the richness of events. It was a festival, a camp of Christian pilgrims virtually from all over the globe – a heaven-like convergence of evangelical Christians.

For a whole week, we were at the seaside British resort Skegness, on the Linconshire coast. And it was all about Jesus: praising, singing, preaching; and also eating, drinking, playing. And there was an aspect of the fun part that surprised me initially: some of the attendees (particularly young people) openly drinking beer and smoking – and no one berated them. It was normal, I later learnt. Jesus said "come as you are". The Grace aspect. Jesus accepted all! There was even an unmarried couple sleeping in the same room – the girl was heavily pregnant (ok, I'd been there before). All accepted! Whosoever will, may come. And I remembered the time some Jews wanted Jesus to condemn a woman caught in adultery. He would not condemn her but told her not to sin again.

* * *

In all this, it was only appropriate that I never lost touch with my first love – Journalism. I wrote articles for both the Sierra Leone press and British media outlets. The Exiled Journalists Network had a newsletter in which I contributed greatly. A memorable article I wrote in the UK was for the *Manchester Times* magazine, edited by veteran British journalist Bob Pounder (who would later become a Unitarian pastor). Titled 'Am I Not A Man And A Brother?', I re-echoed the anti-slavery slogan, relating it to the predicament of asylum-seekers. Distributed among members of the National Union of Journalists (NUJ), of which I had become a member, the article got me to be known in the British media landscape.

But what would arguably become more beneficial to me was the fact that I was able to do a journalism course, alongside other exiled journalists, at the University of Lincoln (UK). It gave me a deeper insight into the profession not only in theory but by practically sharing experiences with journalists from various countries around the world. And doing the course with regular students made it a unique academic adventure. Perhaps more significantly, that opportunity provided me with a very important contact: one of our lecturers, Prof. Richard Keeble (who had liked my output from the outset), would later be a source of great encouragement in the writing of this book, as he read it all, line by line, giving invaluable inputs, before publication. I also did courses, including International Trade Unionism, at Oxford, Thames & Chiltern (an open college network with courses conducted at hotels in different cities in the UK).

* * *

One interesting episode in my journo-Christian life was my wedding. I could write a whole book just on that. But let me summarise here: I married a beautiful Rwandan lady, Rose, in the Church of England (Anglican) in Manchester, England, on 21 July 2007. It was obviously a marriage made in heaven. A lady from Rwanda, a once war-ravaged country which overturned history through the radical President Paul Kagame (who had the audacity to lead his nation into the adventurous journey of changing its inherited French colonial language to English and finding a place in the Commonwealth of Nations for that matter) marrying a gentleman from once war-torn Sierra Leone famed for its affinity to Britain from the days of the anti-slavery campaign to colonialism to the 'Athens of West Africa' and to 'blood diamonds'. West Africa and East Africa met and fell in love in England (the seat of the Commonwealth) and threw a sumptuous 'princely' wedding against all odds.

Rose and I met in church. As simple as that. But not that simple. As you would have known thus far, dear reader, my relationship with the Church was that of body and life – a divinely ordained joint enterprise. Therefore, wherever I found myself, there were two landmarks I looked for – a library and the church.

When I was moved to Oldham, a town in Greater Manchester, after seeking asylum in London, the first thing I did on the day after my arrival was to enquire about the church and the library. I found them. And in the church, I found Rose – a very active member of the executive.

To say Rose was beautiful would be an understatement – she was stunningly beautiful (to the extent that, on our wedding day, one of our white British godfathers – John Rawlinson, a lay leader of Oldham Family Church – publicly said in the presence of his own wife, Pauline, that if he were not already married and if I had not taken Rose, he would have done all he could to marry her. So hilarious). But it was not that I fell in love with her at first sight. I was too emotionally bruised for that.

We were in Elim Foursquare Church helping out in our different ways, fellowshipping together, as both my contributions and asylum story attracted the church leaders. And the proximity of where I lived and where she lived placed us in the same cell group. We became friends. I needed someone to talk to about especially how I had been treated by the mother of my daughter, and how she was making it difficult for me to see my daughter. Rose also had a daughter, Catherine, whose dad had passed away in Uganda (where Rose grew up as a refugee) way before she came to live in the UK. A single mother in friendship with a jilted man – it was only a matter of time.

To cut a long story short (as this is not a romance book), after I tried to suppress the feeling several times, I summed up courage to express my love for her after we went to watch a movie. She responded: 'Are you serious? I didn't see it coming!' She downplayed and brushed it off. A few days later, when she realised I was really serious, she sounded scriptural, as she asked me: 'Are you he who is to come or should I wait for another?' Immediately I knew it was a done deal. "You can't look for another, my dear," was my reply, as we embraced each other. The courtship started – one year later, we were engaged;

a few months later we were married at St. Thomas' Church, Werneth.

And here you would wonder why not Elim Church where we met. Around the time of our courtship, I received a revelation that we should leave that church. We prayed over it, and Rose also felt the same. We joined the Oldham Family Church through a Sierra Leonean friend, Osman Kamara (who, together with his son Daniel, was the first African member). The former was more of an African Church, with a few whites, led by Nigerian pastor the Reverend Willie I. Achumba, while the latter was a virtual opposite led by Englishman Paul Moores. When we left Elim, the few whites followed us to Oldham Family Church – an evangelising William-Wilberforce-like Terry-Virgo-founded New Frontiers awakening church. Very soon, it became more inter-racial and was in the news.

The *Oldham Evening Chronicle* followed me here again with another 'Insight'. Titled 'Cosmopolitan church one big family' with a photograph of me giving a talk at the church (and another photograph of my soon-wife-to-be Rose with crèche leader Pauline Rawlinson and the church kids "of different nationalities"), reporter Janice Barker wrote in their March 22 2007 edition: "A new Oldham church looks like a mini-United Nations when the congregation gets together for worship on Sundays. Oldham Family Church has members from 11 different countries – some of them have fled from their homeland because of oppression, others are here on work visas to build a new life." And the caption under my photograph was: 'Mini United Nations... Sheka Tarawalie from Sierra Leone speaking to a congregation'.

The new church, charismatic and evangelical, did not, however, have a structure of its own, as we were only using the Honeywell Community Centre for our worship services, having moved from a room space at St. John's Ambulance building in the neighbourhood just after our arrival. And they had not conducted any wedding ceremony before. Also, the Church of England was one of the few Christian entities in the UK with authority to conduct weddings that were legally recognised by the Home Office. St. Thomas' Church, shepherded by one of my chief advocates, the Rev. Andrew Dawson, was an obvious wedding choice. He was more than willing and even more excited than I expected.

He sought and secured approval from the Home Office to marry – despite me still being an asylum-seeker. Banns were read for a few weeks and the fairy-tale wedding, attended by tens of white people, not to talk about Africans and Asians, took Manchester by storm. Vicar Andrew himself had been married just a few weeks before and his new wife, Biddy, led the first part of the service while he solemnised the marriage itself. The pastor of the Family Church, Englishman Paul Moores, delivered the sermon – his daughter, Amy, was one of our bridesmaids. Les and Vera Butterworth, intimate English elderly couple of the church who provided their home and more for the bridal preparations, would later say they did not know how the food and drinks could not get finished during the reception. "It's like the story of Jesus feeding five thousand with two fish and five loaves of bread," Les joked. Austin and Anne Shaw, a white couple who moved with us from Elim, have kept reminding us to this day how we impacted their lives; while Christine Geraghty, a white lady who also came from Elim to Oldham Family Church, has become Rose's prayer partner for life. Widower Karin Whetham, in whose home we had earlier done our traditional Rwandan-style pre-nuptial, became my British mother. Her son and daughter-in-law, Daniel and Mei Whetham (missionaries), did a special song for us at the church ceremony. Another music-loving British couple, Ike and Karen

Allen, staged a wonderful performance. Zambian couple, Charles and Edna Kwalomboto, played the role of the African in-laws exquisitely. Iranian Christian convert Hassem Razael and English buddy Fran Hanley were the background friends helping to make things happen. Filipino nurse Maria Theresa Gomez was a human machine partnering with Nigerian teenager Bola Olamrewaju in house-keeping.

There could hardly be a more talked-about wedding in the community – a wedding that brought together members of the evangelical Oldham Family Church, the conservative St Thomas' Church and the African-dominated Elim Foursquare Church – as it's worth mentioning that many friends from my former church (including lay-leader Kunle Obadeyi and wife Amaka, and Men's auxiliary president George Duru and wife Chichi – all Nigerians) graced the occasion. Also present were my three Uganda buddies since Elim days: Isaac Moshen, Fred Lumu and Robert Otim.

Rose had many friends and relatives from the East African community, which included people from Rwanda, Burundi, and Uganda. Her elder brother Eliya, elder sister Sophie and cousins Jacob and Jenny were very supportive; while her niece, Mariam, and nephew, Victor, were part of the bridal party. Her friend from Uganda, Sophie Gakwaya, was a bridal adviser who provided her daughter, Allet, as a flower girl.

We had a mixture of Christian and non-Christian friends and guests.

And there were Rose's co-workers (white and Asian) from Oldham Family Crisis Group. On my side, Sierra Leonean friends and relatives like Sullay Adekulay (a school mate and former employee of my newspaper in whose London home I proposed to Rose after attending a Sierra Leone outing), Messeh Kamara (a senior school mate), Patrick Kanu (of blessed memory, another school mate), and Tedson Sesay (who by and large represented my parents as he was from Mabanta and could have been 'the Mabanta boy' for being the first to go to the university had he been brought up or had gone to school in the village) came from London, Alie Soyei (my university mate) came from Newcastle and Veenod Fullah (the elder relative who witnessed the CAB/Princess Anne award ceremony) from Oxford. That was more than enough, as they joined Osman Kamara (Osboy), another schoolmate, who was instrumental in luring me to Oldham Family Church and whose son Daniel was our page-boy. The Manchester branch of the National Union of Journalists (NUJ), of which I had become an active member, was fully represented by white, black, and Asian colleagues. I would have to make special mention of senior Pakistani journalist, Mansoor Hassan, a strong Muslim, who became a friend that guided and introduced me to many journalistic opportunities. He did not only participate in the planning of the ceremony, but his whole family attended the wedding. Of course, the Citizens Advice Bureau was very active, with my immediate boss David being the 'best man', and our overall manager Clare Taylor (a member of the Oldham Family Church) participating fully throughout. Many other friends I had made in Manchester, including asylum-seekers, were also in attendance. We catered for a hundred people; someone told me the total attendees could have doubled that number! I can't name everybody, I'm sorry – all were important at the wedding.

It, therefore, became a potpourri of an international, inter-racial, inter-denominational wedding – with Rwandese cultural performances dominating the wedding reception! Immediately after the reception, we went for our honeymoon (with the bride driving) to the seaside resort of West Kirby and to Hilbre Island – as recommended and arranged by a couple at Oldham Family Church, Ian and Helen Collinge – before being welcomed on our final leg by a compassionate lady in Oxford,

Mary Embleton, who first knew me through the BBC 'Songs of Praise' television programme and had actually sent cash for me during my trying times. We were meeting her for the first time.

We returned to Oldham to a new home we had purchased via a mortgage to sleep there for the first time as husband and wife.

And we lived happily ever after (with usual fights over 'shoes and socks', or when these APC party ladies would just appear in your compound on a Saturday morning supposedly to help in cleaning and they would start being 'too familiar' in front of your wife). It's not a bed of roses – it's a bed for Rose.

My wife would not only eventually come to live with me in Sierra Leone, but she enrolled at Freetown's The Evangelical College of Theology (TECT) for a three-year course where she trained as a pastor – with my unflinching support throughout! I would sometimes be invited as a guest of honour at some of the college's ceremonies, at times being asked to give a speech. Nothing made me feel more fulfilled in our marriage than when she first took the pulpit at the Mabanta Wesleyan Church – in the presence of its founding pastors, her parents-in-law, Reverend and Mrs John Sheka Tarawalie! The women's wing and the children fell in love with her. Rose and I printed and donated hymn books with both Temne and English songs to the Mabanta Wesleyan Church. We made huge contributions in modernising the church: changing the wooden benches to plastic chairs, getting electricity supply through the national grid, paying the monthly salary of the Assistant Pastor, and making other donations here and there to members. I would always be called upon to give a talk! I would tell Rose how it was at this very spot that I started my schooling – when it was both a church and a school in corrugated iron-sheets.

Ultimately, to me – seeing it as an act of God in terms of the providential timing of this book, which I could have written earlier – ours was a marriage with a microscopic foreshadow (at a very remote level I would insist) of the globally-acclaimed fantastical wedding of British Prince Harry (Duke of Sussex) and American actress Meghan Markle (Duchess of Sussex) which captivated the whole world eleven years later in 2018. Christian, Church of England, across-borders, multi-racial attendance (with African-American Episcopal/Anglican Presiding Bishop Michael Curry – apparently a descendant of former slaves, like the bride – preaching at the royal ceremony about the power of love in the presence of the British Monarch, the famous Queen Elizabeth, 'the head of the Church of England'). Ours at the lowest level, theirs at the highest level – but, from my perspective, both obviously pointed to Christ!

I like how the Archbishop of Canterbury (the 'pope of the Anglican Church') Justin Welby summed it up when relating the feelings of the royal family to London's *Evening Standard* newspaper of 22 May 2018 on the sermon delivered by his American Bishop: "What we saw in that is that preaching is not a past art. The use of language to communicate the good news of Jesus Christ just blew the place open. It was fantastic."

Even celebrities – who don't normally 'do' church – couldn't be left behind in the flurry of commendations for Pastor Curry. Jamaican-British star Naomi Campbell – whose modeling stardom was linked with Sierra Leone when she had to testify before a Hague tribunal on the war-time 'blood diamonds' – tweeted, 'Bishop Michael Curry giving me life.'

Peoples of all nations converging at the seat of the former British Empire – with cellist Sierra Leonean-British boy Sheku Kanneh-Mason enthralling the Windsor Castle wedding guests with his dexterity – depicting one human family, touched the hearts of many. And Sierra Leonean-fathered/Ghanaian-mothered rising Hollywood actor, Idris Elba (Beasts of No Nation star), was in church among the celebrity guests at the royal wedding.

Our world – together with the Church – has come a long way!

Chapter Nineteen

Post-Appointment Great Encounters

Wesleyan General Conference (USA), The White House, UN General Assembly, CNN Interview, Future UN Secretary General, Yamoussoukro Basilica

A Sierra Leonean friend of mine in the UK was very sceptical about me accepting my appointment as Press Secretary to the President. Not that he was not happy for me – as far as I could read him. He was concerned that the appointment was only made by telephone conversation; and that I should also consider how my 'star' was shining in the UK at that moment. He advised that I should at least ask for a written appointment letter with all the terms and conditions of service (especially the emoluments) before I would disengage and return to Sierra Leone.

He found out it was too late. I had made up my mind; and that would not change. The prospect of returning home without facing any harassment on its own was an emotional springboard that pushed me further. That I would return with no fear of being sent to jail on trumped-up accusations or the fear of any persecution was too refreshing. That I would return as a sort of vindicated hero could not be swept under the carpet of my mind. That there's no place like home could never be contested by any reasonable person. That I had an opportunity to serve my country in a new capacity and try and influence a positive change to its development brought great joy.

After consulting my immediate boss at the CAB, my good friend and wedding best man David Oglaza, I went to inform our overall boss Clare Taylor (a warmly Christian lady who was also a member of the church we went to, Oldham Family Church, and was very supportive of and participated fully at our wedding). She was happy for me.

I contacted the Home Office through my new lawyer Gary McCindoe (a very successful fellow at his trade who had helped many failed asylum-seekers secure a stay, including Fred, the Ugandan orphan who became a close friend of mine as we attended the same Elim Church). He told them I was stopping my asylum claims and voluntarily returning to Sierra Leone due to 'change of circumstances' – political circumstances back home. Friends in Manchester organised a well-attended send-off dinner for me; just as Sierra Leonean friends in London later did.

And back to Sierra Leone I went, in very high spirits, and reported for duty at State House.

Press Secretary to the President. The title on its own was nerve-wracking. That such a title had never existed in Sierra Leone before was in itself special. Before then, State House only had an Information or Press Officer (who was, by and large, a reporter) on secondment from the Ministry of Information. I was going to do a special job with virtually unfettered access to the President, having an opportunity to discuss issues of national importance with him every working day in our one-on-one 'press briefing'.

It was that position that got me to the US-based Global Wesleyan Conference, the highest hierarchical body of the leadership of the Church. And it was that position that got me to the White House, the world's most famous and most powerful presidential home – through Jo Anne Lyon, CEO of World Hope International, who demonstrated so much love for Sierra Leone through providing prosthetic limbs for war victims and thereafter embarking on various poverty-alleviating projects like micro-financing and water-wells. It was that position that took me to the UN General Assembly and to many other places that I hitherto would only dream of.

* * *

The election of President Koroma to lead Sierra Leone was definitely welcomed and perceived as a 'Wesleyan reign' by both the international and national structures of the Wesleyan Church. The son of Pa Sylvanus, a well-known lay leader who was a Wesleyan Bible School tutor and rose to become National Church Secretary, had become President. It's a Wesleyan presidency! And they would become more excited and perhaps more convinced when he appointed me as his Press Secretary, the son of a Wesleyan-converted Christian turned Wesleyan-trained pastor. The 'good guys' had finally taken over the reins of government in Sierra Leone, they believed. This was fertile ground for more missionary activity. The sacrifices made by the original American missionaries had not gone in vain; the seed they planted had borne good fruit – as the Wesleyan leadership was ready to seize and make use of the moment.

The messages of congratulations kept pouring in, and the number of Wesleyan missionaries visiting from the US suddenly increased – delegations for mainstream Wesleyan mission work as well as delegations from Wesleyan-affiliated universities and colleges. They would almost always pass through me; and the President himself, acknowledging that his was a Wesleyan presidency, would always acquiesce.

The culmination of the appreciation came about when Jo Anne Lyon (well known in Sierra Leone for her humanitarian/church work especially through her charity World Hope International) extended an invitation to President Koroma to attend the Global Wesleyan Conference in Florida (USA) scheduled for 8 to 10 June 2008. The gathering would attract representatives from all Wesleyan churches around the world. An invitation was also extended to me – with a special bonus message that arrangements had been made for me, as State House Press Secretary, to visit and tour the White House with particular reference to the work and functions of the White House Press Secretary. I couldn't believe it. Anybody in my circumstances wouldn't. I, who had never been to America before, would go to the very top! And when President Koroma would not attend and thereby gave me his blessings to represent him at the same time, there could hardly be a better way of being in the spotlight on a first visit to America.

I travelled with the then-head of the Wesleyan Church of Sierra Leone, the Rev. J. Y. Konteh (who was very integral in the whole arrangements back and forth to State House), plus his wife Ya Adama, and his would-be successor, the Rev. Usman Jesse Fornah.

President Koroma sent me with a video-recorded message which was played to the delegates at the conference. The President did not mince his words as to how he saw himself as the embodiment of Wesleyan values: born Wesleyan, brought up a Wesleyan and now a Wesleyan President. That should have been enough. But then I was called upon to again make a speech in person. I had to rise to the occasion. I had to do it. And I did it: relating the history of the Wesleyan Church of Sierra Leone and tying it to the presidency of Ernest Bai Koroma. I thanked the work of the missionaries, some of whom paid the ultimate price for the Word of God and education to be planted in northern Sierra Leone, which was at that time substantially ignored by the British. I ended my felicitations by singing the Temne version of the missionary-taught 'Take the Name of Jesus with you' telling them it was in gratitude for what they did for my father. I received a standing ovation from all! At that moment, I fought back tears as the thought that overwhelmed me was a justification of the historic decision that my grandfather (my namesake, Pa Sheka Tarawalie) made by dumping his forefathers' traditional religion for Christianity – because when my name was being called, it was like calling him; and I thought for a brief moment 'he would be smiling in heaven'.

From the conference in Florida, I was flown to Washington for the White House encounter, accommodated in Jo Anne Lyon's home in Washington. She briefed me that my meeting had been organised by a former Deputy Press Secretary, Josh Deckard, acquainted to her through her regular prayer meetings with President Bush at the White House. Deckard himself was a great Christian with whom I would later pray together and discuss Christian values. But he would not go with us to the White House as he had just resigned to take up a private consultancy: I was going to be accompanied by a Washington-based World Hope International personnel, Ann Karl (a highly intelligent young lady new to the organisation), and we would be guided by a senior White House official. We were expected at the White House: all was set for me. The day was 11 June 2008.

Visiting the White House under any circumstances for many people was a once-in-a-life-time opportunity. And I cherished the moment. It was really a conducted tour of the west wing of the White House, the working wing (not the east wing, residential part) of the presidency. The original plan was for me to have met with the then-White House Press Secretary Dana Perino; but President George Bush had a European tour to which he was accompanied by the former.

This turned out to be a great blessing in retrospect. Their absence gave me greater and easier access to all the major offices: from the Office of the Press Secretary, to the press briefing room (where the Press Secretary usually met with reporters for regular updates), to that of the Chief of Staff (Joshua Bolten, whom I met and he welcomed me to the White House), to the Vice President's Office, to the Cabinet Room, to the Situation Room, and to the great one, the Oval Office (the President's office). Ann Karl – the World Hope staff member – continuously whispered words of gratitude to me for being the reason she was entering the White House for the first time. At one point I retorted, "We thank God. We thank Jo Anne." Step by Step, the tour conductor took us to all these magnificent offices, each with its own story and functions.

But the highlight of the visit (that still sticks in my brain to this day) was when we entered the Oval Office. After showing us the small wooden presidential table (which our guide said was made out of wood from a ship captured by the Americans from the British during the War of Independence), we were taken through a door connecting with the main office to a small room full of books. And the guide said, "This is the famous library where President Clinton touched Monica Lewinsky." We all burst out laughing! This was much more than I would ever have expected to come out with from the White House. I was impressed by his frankness. But I could see politics playing out in this – if President Clinton were a Republican like President Bush, this White House official would most certainly not have shown us that library or told the story as he boldly did. Politics was politics – whether it's in Sierra Leone or Zimbabwe or South Africa or Burma or the great USA – some dirty tricks were allowed!!

But what was more important to me was that I had entered the big house, and I had got a cinematic appraisal of how to run my own Office of the Press Secretary. I would try my best to put it into action. I would later reminisce on how it would have looked like if I had another opportunity to visit the White House under President Obama (the Democrat African-American who succeeded President Bush). But then I would not visit the White House under President Obama – by the time President Koroma would make his first visit to the White House, which happened under Obama, I was no longer Press Secretary – or there was no longer a Press Secretary! It had pleased the President to abolish the position after I had served for three years and he appointed me as Deputy Minister of Information!

Meanwhile, I came from the White House tour with memorabilia – the blue blanket that journalists normally used when flying with the President on Air Force One with the White House seal emblazoned on it. I also received a pair of round silver cufflinks with the inscription 'Office of The Press Secretary - The White House' in blue encircling the seal. Furthermore, I was given a 70mm first-term bronze medallion coin whose obverse had the image of the President with his name boldly written 'GEORGE W. BUSH', and the reverse having 'the great seal of the United States of America' encircled by the words 'FORTY-THIRD PRESIDENT OF THE UNITED STATES OF AMERICA – INAUGURATED JANUARY 20 2001' – although I was visiting in 2008 and there had been another bronze medal for President Bush's second term in 2005. The certificate of authenticity for the 2001 medal, with the title 'THE OFFICIAL 2001 PRESIDENTIAL

INAUGURAL MEDAL', stated thus: "This is to certify that the Official 2001 Presidential Inaugural Medal originally accompanied by this certificate was minted in solid bronze with an antique finish by Medalcraft Mint and issued under the authority of the 2001 Inaugural Committee to commemorate the inauguration of George W. Bush as the 43th [sic] President of the United States of America… January 5 2001 CERTIFIED… Bill & Kathy DeWitt (Co-Chairs, Inaugural Committee)… Mercer & Gabrielle Reynolds (Co-Chairs, Inaugural Committee)." Above all, perhaps, I came away with literature on how to run the office of the State House Press Secretary or how the White House Press Secretary's office was run – and this on the back of me being the first-ever holder of the office in Sierra Leone. I couldn't have asked for more! I had got the foundation blocks by which I would create an enviable State House public relations outfit never before heard of in Sierra Leone.

My White House visit had a tinge of controversy afterwards when a local media furore arose as to whether I met with White House Press Secretary Dana Perino. What happened was a case of mistaken reportage. I had sent out photographs of me at the White House (and in some of those photos posing with Ann Karl, the World Hope personnel accompanying me). All I wanted to show was that I had been at the White House. That was reported; but then with the addition that the person in the pictures with me was Dana Perino. Some others argued that it was not Dana. I had to come out with a clarification; and with the original reporting media stating that I did not in the first place tell them it was Dana. They had initially contacted me to send them the photos immediately after my visit so that they would be the first to 'exclusively' publish (in the manner of the journalistic 'breaking news' scoops).

Yet the controversy in the end gave me some considerable publicity, so that many who would otherwise not have heard of my visit to the White House would get to know about it. The tens of Sierra Leoneans in the USA who thronged to hear me speak when – through online media veteran Kabs Kanu, I was implored to pass a night and address Sierra Leoneans at the Washington (actually New Jersey) suburban home of APC party stalwart Foday Mansaray – were a testimony to the celebrity status that had suddenly come upon me.

On my return home, the story 'sweetened', as personal compliments poured in. It's a never-to-be-forgotten experience that I'm sure my great-great-grand-children will be happy about.

Grateful to Jo Anne Lyon. My relationship with her became so close that I attended her son John Lyon's wedding to Katy in Terre Haute, Indiana (the city where the Wesleyan headquarters were based), in March 2011 when I would have become Deputy Minister of Information & Communications. A few days to the wedding, John and I would attend the screening in Washington DC of *War Don Don* (War is over), a movie/documentary in which RUF-rebel leader Issa Sesay somehow came out as a tragic hero in prosecuting and ending the Sierra Leone civil war. It was produced and directed by American filmmaker, Rebecca Richman Cohen, who was a Harvard law student and legal intern for the defense team during the Freetown proceedings of the Special Court ("the world's first international war crimes 'hybrid tribunal' created jointly by the United Nations and the government of Sierra Leone"). I was given an opportunity to say something after the show (wherein I thanked all those – local and international – who contributed to finding lasting peace for Sierra Leone). I afterwards had some pep talk and took some photos with Rebecca (also known for her earlier participation in the production of American film mogul Michael Moore's hugely successful 2004 documentary *Fahrenheit 9/11* which controversially detailed the war on terror under President Bush).

* * *

Since then, there would be no turning back in my pursuit of diligence in my duties. And that would eventually turn me into one of the most-travelled officials in the administration of President Ernest Bai Koroma. I became a globe-trotter: not for self, but for others; not for my glory, but for Sierra Leone's progress. As Press Secretary, I travelled with the President most times; but the high point of those travels, for me, was attending the United Nations General Assembly in New York (which I did for three consecutive times – 2008, 2009, 2010 – until I was moved to the Ministry of Information) and the privilege of sitting right behind the President in some of those sessions! Meeting, rather seeing, Heads of Government from all over the world under one roof was a spectacle too surreal to behold!

When I was appointed Deputy Minister (first Information & Communications, and then Internal Affairs), I continued the globe-trotting – for good purposes, for the benefit of the state. Meetings to get the fibre optic cable landed, to improve on ICTs, to address refugee problems worldwide, to represent Sierra Leone generally in international fora. It was in such meetings that I met and hobnobbed with António Guterres (current UN Secretary General), while he was the UN High Commissioner for Refugees. We met a couple of times at Geneva and also in Ivory Coast, where I signed on behalf of Sierra Leone the agreement on state protection for stateless persons. During one of our informal discussions, Mr. Gutterres told me he liked my 'usual succinct speeches'. He was a very humorous and down-to-earth man!

It was in one such meeting in Ivory Coast that I visited the basilica built by late Ivorien President Houghouet Boigney in Yamoussoukro, his home village turned city. Officially called the Basilica of Our Lady of Peace, it's one of the largest Catholic basilicas (none beats St. Peter's at the Vatican), and its magnificence was simply fantastic with its apostolic paintings and marble artistry. We held ministerial meetings at Yamoussoukro three times, and each time I made sure I went to the basilica. Senior tour guide, Aime Coulibaly, noticed my frequent visits and we became friends – we communicate to this day. On one occasion, the security detail attached to me were so over-excited after our basilica visit that they became indulgent and actually took me on a conducted tour of the former presidential palace, where I was able to see the grave-site of the late President (clustered with his dead family members under the same roof). I was also taken to his former bedroom (a small cubicle with the photograph of a half-naked woman pasted on the wall opposite the bed); and in his bathroom were still the toothbrush and paste he last used! I was told – and confirmed from what I saw – that he was a man who lived a simple life. On our way out, we stopped at the bridge connecting the presidential home and the village – to have a look at the crocodiles once deployed as part of the security in the lake enclosing the premises. They had become lean and hungry since the President's death, I learnt.

One more highlight I would give was the interview I did with CNN, for which I had to be flown to the Washington World Hope offices to talk about the benefits of the establishment of a fruit juice factory. It's worth mentioning not merely for the worldwide audience it attracted, but for the fact that the factory's construction was an idea that I pursued from inception to completion. When it was first floated by Jo Anne Lyon, President Koroma immediately chose me as Presidential Liaison to ensure it became a reality. I had at times to fight with government bureaucracy to get things moving faster. And so after the creation of First Step Fruit Juice Factory, the investors thought, with me as Deputy Minister of Information at the time (though we started the project while I was Press Secretary to the President), I was the best person to speak about it. It was an unforgettable experience, as the CNN technological gadgetry was moved into the World Hope office to create a temporary studio for the purpose! The interview was done by Jill Reilly and was broadcast on the CNN programme 'Marketplace Africa'. When an article on the interview was posted on the CNN website, it was credited to both Reilly and Sierra Leonean-born former CNN anchor Isha Sesay, whom I did not meet. Titled 'Juice factory could bear fruit for Sierra Leone,' (http://edition.cnn.com/2011/BUSINESS/06/29/sierra.leone.fruit.juice/index.html), Sesay's inclusion gave the article a general cross-party local appeal, since her mother (Dr. Kadie Sesay, who was my lecturer at the university) was a strong opposition figure. This was in June 2011, a year to the re-election of President Koroma (in those elections, Dr Kadie Sesay was the running-mate to now-President Maada Bio). It was so accomplishing to have worked for First Step as Country Director on a one-year contract after I was out of government in 2016.

There were numerous other interesting episodes in my representations around the world: like my frequent visits to the post-war ever-progressing Rwanda (the home country of my wife – I deliberately chose Rwanda as a model for the ICT infrastructural development), or to the beautiful 'paradise on earth' island of Mauritius, or the ancient city of Chonqing in China where I probably ate a snake or a dog, or the captivating landscape of Rio de Janeiro in Brazil, or meeting with late Col. Muammar Gaddaffi in the desert in Tripoli in the middle of the night to eat camel while discussing bilateral co-operation, or reliving one of my schooldays-favourite Shakespearean book 'Merchant of Venice' in that ancient Italian city, and many more – which were all as a result of my having been appointed into government.

Chapter Twenty

Would-be 'Co-Pilgrim' Alie Wasco (A Muslim)

A Rickety Bridge Of Friendship; Ebola Crisis Mentioned; Tribute To Muslim 'Good Samaritan' Late Ambassador Siray Timbo

Alie Wasco would not be the friend you were looking for. But once you bumped into him, you wouldn't want to look for another (or wouldn't you?) – even when you discovered that this would be a very bumpy and rough road of a relationship.

Ten chances to one, if President Koroma were not Head of State I wouldn't have known Alie Wasco. His official name was Alie Doyle Kamara (usually shortened to Alie D.), while still having yet another alias of 'Alie Gbainkfay'. But Alie Wasco, the name he said he was given during a school football match when he and President Koroma were in the same class, had stuck through the years and was the most frequently used within his immediate circle of peers. And he was close to Koroma through school into business and in politics –

until the moment of revelation came in the end for them to part ways (but that's another story). In early adulthood, they both formed a tobacco-planting company called Rokel Leaf, with the former President as the major shareholder and Alie Wasco as Managing Director. The war drove Wasco away to the US (where he eventually naturalised as a citizen) and only returned when his friend became President and appointed him as Resident Minister North, which he wittily described as 'the president of the north'.

It was obvious and inevitable that Alie and I would know each other ultimately, even if only by virtue of us being in the same government, especially with him being the minister in charge of the region I hailed from (where we all, including the President, hailed from). But it was amazing how the two of us (with a huge age disparity between us) became very close and intimate. From my perspective at the time, the obvious reason was that we both held similar views in terms of loyalty and allegiance to the President (albeit Alie would sometimes noticeably exhibit some sibling-rivalry attitude: it could have been, or should have been, him as President; after all, they sat in the same class).

It was Alie who found me – or was asked to find me. A few months after I took up office at State House as Press Secretary to the President, Alie came knocking on my office door with a message from a school-days friend of mine who had been living in the USA with him. This mutual friend, Hassan J. Koroma, was one of my closest and competitive classmates in school and would later in the university be my 'gorilla master' (a student hosting another student in the hostel until accommodation issues were sorted) for a year. When Hassan heard of my relocation from the UK to State House and saw Alie coming to take up his new post, he sent a brotherly message to me through him. And it was not so much about the message – but the humour and embellishments spiced in by the messenger made us click immediately.

The fact that President Koroma liked his hometown and would make frequent visits there, and I (also hailing from there) was obliged as one of his official aides to accompany him, and where Alie was always the host as Resident Minister, brought us closer together. At times it would only be him and I and the President in one room, discussing issues, cracking jokes, recollecting history.

Alie was not a particularly intellectual man (he didn't go to university) – though doubting his intelligence would be misplaced. He would almost always make people laugh when he made off-the-cuff statements at public gatherings. He never wasted time with the niceties of trying to find the correct pronunciation of certain words – but his general message would always be cogent and impactful. He knew his target – primarily to please the President in public. Alie's persona reminds me of Nigerian novelist Chinua Achebe's populist politician in *A Man Of The People*.

Alie Wasco Kamara adored President Koroma (though not to the end). He remained Resident Minister North (with Makeni as headquarters) until the end of the regime. They attended the same secondary school and were at one time sleeping on the same bed – as Wasco was adopted by the President's mother. Alie remained a nominal Muslim, but his admiration for President Koroma's 'Wesleyan' character was always a sing-song for him. Wasco would also once in a while say he saw the Wesleyan in me as he saw in President Koroma during their early days together. This comparison would also make me recall that the President and I belonged to the same Kissy Dockyard Wesleyan Church by virtue of me having been adopted during my university days by the then-National Superintendent of the Church, the late Rev. Y. M. Kroma, who had helped found the local branch.

* * *

Three or four or five more factors endeared me to Alie – some very personal, some very sentimental. The loyalty to our boss aside, we got on together on our own for a range of issues that acted as the ladder by which we gradually climbed – at times tripping – and clawed our way to the Vatican to see the Pope together. Through God's grace!

A big factor that made us more attached to each other was the relationship that our wives developed between themselves. My wife, Rose, being of foreign origin – Rwandan-British to be specific – needed a close friend. She found one in Alie's wife, Jemimah (also partially foreign with Nigerian lineage), with whom she could chat for long hours to the extent, at times, of virtually forgetting about our presence. And the fact that the Kamaras lived in our hometown where we regularly visited made the affinity a necessity.

Another impetus for my relationship with Alie D. was the fact that my parents lived in Makeni, his administrative jurisdiction, and he would turn out to be more than handy to them in my absence. If I needed quick material or financial or any doable support for my parents, I would just ask Alie or his wife to give them or take them to the hospital and I would settle the bill later.

Two crucial unforgettable interventions Alie did would come during the infamous Ebola outbreak and during an attempt to dethrone my father unceremoniously as acting Section Chief of Mabanta in our chiefdom. On both instances, Alie's support to my parents raised their dignity and esteem in the community. During the notorious Ebola imbroglio, I had refused to take my parents away from the community to Freetown, as a way of giving the other people reassurance to stay put (just as we did as a family during the war, while I was in hiding there).

It was a moment of confusion, and the people needed direction and hope. Alie would visit them regularly and give them whatever they needed for me to pay later. Their stay in Makeni was a magnet for me to make frequent visits during the crisis. The community people would say, 'As long as John Pastor and Marie Pastor are around, we are fine' – and there was no case of Ebola infection in the village throughout the crisis, which ravaged Sierra Leone from May 2014 to 7 November 2015 when it was officially declared over, leaving nearly 4,000 people dead (including doctors). During that same period, a conspiracy was contrived by 'Sanbalat and Tobiah' to include my dad's name (acting as Section Chief because the substantive was incapacitated by illness and he was the natural head of the Mabanta ruling house) on the list of chiefs to be dethroned for violating Ebola rules. As stated, Ebola in fact never reached at Mabanta. So I alerted Alie, and he as 'the president of the north' reversed the decision of the Panlap-based chiefdom authorities – who even took the action without the consent of the paramount chief who was already very ill at the time, and later passed away.

Another factor that bonded Alie and me was his informal function as an adviser to me when I was Press Secretary. One occasion worth mentioning was when the President had privately informed me he would move me from being his Press Secretary to become Deputy Minister of Information and Communications, but he went ahead to appoint a replacement publicly before officially announcing my new position. The new appointee (though his title was whittled down to Communications Director instead of Press Secretary to the President; meaning his authority was diminished because he was not to have direct briefings with the President but through the newly-created position of Chief of Staff) was eager to take over the office I was occupying immediately. I was under pressure from other officials, including the then-Chief of Staff to give up my position, office, and keys. Intrigues, subterfuge, shenanigans – office politics they called it. But Alie strongly advised against relinquishing anything until my new position was announced – saying one should hold on to what one had until one had something new to hold on to. He said I should be obstinate until the President clarified the matter. And I didn't budge until my new position was announced – perhaps earlier than the President had wanted. He had previously called me in to his office to ask why I had refused to move out when the matter was reported to him by his Personal Assistant. I explained. A couple of days later, the announcement came through. Alie's advice worked. Though at the time I had no reason to doubt that the President was going to keep his word, yet I could have been without an office for a whole month!

One thing you would never take from Alie Wasco was his love for and continued use of his native Temne language. He would speak it at the slightest opportunity anywhere, anytime – official or unofficial – in Sierra Leone or in the UK. It was probably this linguistic notoriety that caused the late Resident Minister East, William Juana Smith, to start calling him 'Temne Mabanta' (many Sierra Leonean non-Temnes would always want to refer to all Temnes that way – not really knowing the difference between the various dialects). Alie put up with this epithet until it reached a boiling point on a trip he and his colleague Resident Minister made to China. Both of them would later narrate the incident to me when Alie would vehemently disown the description and told Smith that 'the only Temne Mabanta in government is Sheka Tarawalie'. Thereafter, instead of the joke dying down, the three of us would just start calling each other 'Temne Mabanta' wherever and whenever we met. Sad that Smith passed away while in office, but that was another factor that spiced my relationship with Alie.

Another key ingredient that also cemented our relationship was the common fondness the President's mother had for both Alie and I. She regarded him as her son, and she took me as a kind of grandson – virtually literally. For Alie, via adoption; for me, through the love she had for my parents when my father was pastor at her Rogbaneh Wesleyan Church. So when her son, the President, appointed me as Press Secretary (I'm not sure whether she played any role in that), she became very happy with the news. I would make sure I visited her most times I was in Makeni. She would give me advice – at one time suggesting that my wife should stay with her for three months to learn more of Temne culture and language. She also liked my dad's Sunday morning radio messages (which have continued to this day), and she would express that at every given opportunity. Therefore, Alie and I became more attached when we visited her together to eat some delicious traditional food she would prepare for us.

* * *

But it would be dishonest to say my relationship with Alie was a bed of roses (in fact, it broke down before I could complete writing this book; and his relationship with the former President crashed after the 2018 elections!).

Alie was a very mercurial fellow, very temperamental and unpredictable at times, a man who liked to be praised or appreciated all the time; and if you forgot to do that, it angered him!

Alie would always like to be seen and recognised as the man 'closest' or 'most loyal' to or 'most liked' by the President, and would want to make a public show of it. If he saw that someone wanted to take that position – whoever it was – he would feel apprehensive and would devise ways of discrediting that person ('I will download him [or her] to the pa' he would say). And beyond that, he had his moments of jealousy even for the President.

One example was during the 2012 elections for the second term of the President. Alie could not sleep day and night working hard to ensure his 'brother' was re-elected. He would use all types of tactics to achieve his goals; canvassing, convincing, and even coercing. He and I travelled from one polling station to the other galvanising support and lifting morale. At the end of it all, we converged at his Makeni house (together with his biological elder brother from the village) when the results were announced declaring President Koroma as the winner. But while we were celebrating, dancing, and shouting, Alie was sitting down quietly and emotionally unmoved. I was surprised. When I ventured to ask him about his lukewarm mood, he retorted: "It's Ernest again. It's not me. It's always Ernest who shines. From school days, to business, to politics. Am I not also a human being?" That was a very telling moment to both myself and his brother (who passed away just after the 2018 elections). Human nature – the weak side – at times takes the better of us even at our best!

Alie would not leave me out for scathing criticism. And he found a classic in my attitude to Islam, particularly for having never been in a mosque. Alie said this was a big difference between me and President Koroma – and that even Pope Francis had been entering mosques. He scolded me for wanting to be 'more Catholic than the Pope!' I would remind him I was not a Catholic! He would only be more furious. My excuse that I would develop back pains if I sat on the floor for long was hogwash to him.

But I would remind him that I made no discrimination between Christian, Muslim, or poro or bondo members as far as normal human interaction was concerned. I know I am not of the world, but I'm in the world! I still continued to have long-time friends who were Muslims. One such friend was Siray Timbo (the late ambassador to the UAE, a product of Saint Francis Secondary School and would later in life become president of the Old Makeni Franciscans Association) whom I had found to be totally trustworthy: he was a social mentor who admired my writings since my university days and would not only be there for me during sunshine, but when it rained as well. Siray was more humane to me than many religious leaders, and had been a source of succour in times of great trial (including during my infamous incarceration in Pademba Road prisons by the Tejan-Kabbah SLPP government for my journalistic writings). He came through to me as the 'Good Samaritan' who in Christ's parable was more acceptable in the sight of God than the superciliously pious priests! The closeness of my relationship with him transcended religion and broke family barriers. Alie Wasco himself was able to acknowledge this! Even a university classmate – in fact a roommate –was a strong Muslim. Momodu Turay now lectures at the same university and is a 'Sheik'. That relationship has not died.

Furthermore, I would explain to Alie, whenever I did my annual donations of cows and rice to my village and at times to the neighbouring villages as well, I always gave to the leadership of the communities (with no reference to religion) and for all inhabitants. I did meet and donate to the leadership of the village mosque – coincidentally, the imam was my maternal uncle who grew up in the same hamlet with my mother! My material support to bereaved families in my village crossed religious boundaries. In his heart of hearts, therefore, I would urge, Alie Wasco should not see me as a Christian fanatic or extremist in the negative sense. I always tried to emphasise to him that, all my life, I had been brought up in a predominantly Christian environment, and that my entry into governance was not as a politician, but as a 'picked-out exiled guy' brought all the way from the UK by President Koroma. I never for once tried to pretend to be a traditional politician – as I never even organised a political rally in my village. I told Alie a day might come when I would enter a mosque like President Koroma and Pope Francis.

Despite all those character flaws, Alie was still a lovable fellow, full of humour. He loved the exuberance of life and would not allow anything to derail him from enjoying it. "I am the brother of the President. I must live that life. If I don't do it now, when?" he would rhetorically ask.

It was as if we were stuck together for the time being and were just paddling on together. Our friendship continued and deepened, and we were frequently seen together in public places. We were bound to share secrets – or rather discussions that were just between the two of us. At one time an audio of our discussions about the President's political plans was leaked on social media via my phone; and there would later be strong suspicions that Alie could have pressed the record-button while we were speaking, to water down my sterling standing in the eyes of the President – then seeing me *also* as a rival in presidential affection! But it only remained a suspicion that would never be proven.

Invariably, we assisted each other in various ways (for instance, I would help him improve his public-speaking skills and would write a speech or two for him). We introduced each other to our acquaintances, formal or informal. When I honed the concept of re-introducing traffic lights to Sierra Leone and had gained the approval of the President, Alie was the next person I discussed the plans with and gained his support to make it become a reality.

It was through such reciprocity that – by humorous irony – he introduced me to Father Ignazio, the local representative of the poor-communities-alleviating 'Love Bridges', a semi-Catholic charitable organisation that would eventually be the link to our meeting with Pope Francis.

Chapter Twenty-One

'Love Bridges' Charity

A Bridge Of Love To The Poor, To The Pope

It started in a most ineffectual way and merely as a joke. The country representative of the poverty-alleviating 'Love Bridges' charity, Father Don Ignazio Poddighe, found a strong ally in Alie Wasco apparently because the latter's position as Resident Minister helped in protecting the organisation's interests. Working in rural communities could be cumbersome; having a political cover would be helpful. And Alie himself, seeing the impact of the organisation's humanitarian support for the Lungi community (building hospitals and schools, constructing water wells, establishing feeding centres and giving scholarships to poor children), embraced them. And he was boisterous about it – he even brought the First Lady (wife of President Koroma, Sia Nyama Koroma) to do the official opening of the main hospital at the chiefdom headquarter town of Lokomasama.

The camaraderie between Minister and charity could best be found in the words of an Italian volunteer, Silvia Floris, in an article written on 30 January 2016 and published on the organisation's website. Written in Italian and titled 'Sierra Leone o la filosofia del no problem' ('Sierra Leone and the philosophy of no problem'), the lady from Cagliari had this to say:

"An old friend of the association comes to visit us, Sir Alie D. Kamara, Resident Minister of the Northern Province, with him his wife Mamie, in a sporty suit, long honeyed hair and jeans, practically a young girl.

We are all standing but the Minister is a really easy guy, he greets us and announces that a few days later we will have a meeting with the President of the Republic. Yes, you understood correctly! What are you doing, go to Sierra Leone and do not meet the President of the Republic?..."

'Love Bridges' (founded in 2008 after Don Ignazio had made a preliminary visit and saw the poverty in war-torn Sierra Leone) wants to present itself as a secular organisation. In its mission statement, it clearly states that it is "secular and independent". I would agree in so far as the discharge of its services to various communities without any religious prejudice is concerned. The two chiefdoms where they are operating – Lokomasama and Kaffu Bullom, with about 500 villages – are, in fact, predominantly Muslim. But the people themselves see the organisation more like a 'Catholic' one, with a 'Catholic father' being its head. And perhaps more telling is the name of their flagship project, the Pope John Paul II Medical Center in Lokomasama. The 50-bed facility is more advanced than most hospitals in Sierra Leone – with a first-aid room, an adjoining first-visit room, ambulances, a pharmacy, a blood-testing laboratory, medicine storage area, and an office for staff, among others. Or what about the daily feeding centre named after famed Catholic nun Mother Teresa of Calcutta?

Notwithstanding, to their all-embracing credit and living up to their secular mantra, 'Love Bridges' volunteers are not restricted to being Catholic as long as they abide by the organisation's mission of service to the communities. And local workers or volunteers are not recruited on the basis of their beliefs. It's a charity for humanity! Priding itself on the saying: "You cannot say that you really lived if you've never done something for someone who can never repay you."

Therefore, Minister Alie had become very enmeshed in their activities. He was accruing some benefits as a result – he was taken to Italy to meet with international donors on several occasions; and he received some free medical services there as well: 'One good turn deserves another' he would repeatedly quote as justification. I was brought into the picture not by human design but by accidental necessity! By the Hand of God!

It happened that, one of the varied types of support given to the communities by 'Love Bridges' was taking some of the sponsored pupils to Italy for holidays. They had been doing it for several years, but this time there was a problem. They had submitted applications for passports to be issued to some newly sponsored children at the immigration department for eventual travel to Italy. However, there was a serious shortage of passports in the country and time was running out. The pressure was mounting on Alie Wasco to use his political influence. That was when he contacted me.

I was then the Deputy Minister of Internal Affairs, the ministry directly supervising immigration and housed in the same building with that department. Alie phoned me and explained the situation, and I asked him to come to the office. He came with Father Ignazio, whom I was meeting for the first time.

I was inevitably more than willing to help. I became acquainted with Father Ignazio immediately: as he was of an outgoing, outspoken and lovable character, we jelled the moment we met. We started cracking jokes instantly, one of which was the famous saying 'When in Rome, you do as the Romans do' and I started quoting some of my Shakespearean favourites from *Julius Caesar*. We expanded it by saying that if you met the Romans dancing on one foot, you also would have to do the same. We didn't only say it, Ignazio and I started hopping each on one foot right in my office, chanting 'When in Rome do as the Romans do,' with Alie laughing uncontrollably.

I immediately called the Chief Immigration Officer and explained the issue to him. And he said: 'Consider it done sir', adding that the passports should be collected in two days! That was it. The deed was done. The relationship was sealed.

By the time we parted company, I would innocently – and just by way of peppering our conversation – tell Ignazio that it would be great not only to go to Rome (where I had never been) but also to meet the Pope. We all burst out laughing. He responded that going to Rome would not be a problem; but as for meeting the Pope, fingers crossed. And it emerged that Alie had previously but unsuccessfully tried to meet the Pope, starting from the days of Pope Benedict.

Yet, when the time came, it came. No one could stop destiny!

And which organisation would so apparently easily facilitate a meeting with the Pope if it's not Catholic?

Chapter Twenty-Two

The Prospect Of Meeting The Pope

From Fantasy To Reality; Croatia, Traffic Lights Project In The Mix Of Things

"Minister, the Pope has ticked your names. You are going to meet the Pope."

"Father, what are you talking about?"

"I said the Pope has agreed to meet you and Alie Wasco."

Could this be a cruel joke or a fantastic dream? I looked at the phone for a second time, read the exchanged messages again on the screen, and sent another WhatsApp text: 'Father, I don't understand."

"Tell Alie Wasco that you are going to meet with the Pope on November 18."

To say I saw myself over the moon would perhaps be an understatement. I saw myself as the sun eclipsing the moon!! Or like Joseph the dreamer who dreamt the sun, moon and twelve stars bowing to him! But in humility! In graciousness! In wonder! In knowing that this would only be the Lord's doing! I pinched myself several times to ascertain that I was not in a dream! I would be meeting the Pope! The sound of it made a difference; the reality of it made an ocean of a difference! Just the feeling was good enough, the fame of it – not about whether it was true about the myth that this was a man with powers to 'wipe out sins and pour earthly blessings'! I had never thought about him in those terms.

And when I informed Alie Wasco, he switched to another planet. Being a man with a mercurial personality, or a temperamental aptitude, he had the ability or propensity to switch from one extreme mood to another extreme disposition in a split second. He would have the lowly character of planet earth in one moment, and in another he would be in planet mercury's swift eccentricity.

So, earlier that morning, he was not in a good mood – I should say we were not in good moods. We'd had some petty quarrels the previous night – we always had something to quarrel about, and we were sort of used to it. So I decided to break the news to him piecemeal.

It all happened at the official residence of Edward M. Turay (commonly called Eddie Turay), Sierra Leone's High Commissioner to the United Kingdom, where we almost always put up when in London. And during this visit we were with our wives, each couple in their own room, adjacent. I knocked on his door.

"Nar who dat?"

"Nar me o koth Alie," I responded.

"Who dat?" he asked again, apparently still reeling from last night's argument; though, of course, he would have known it was me knocking, not to mention recognising the voice. But I still felt obliged to answer.

"Nar you small brother, Sheka sir."

I could sense the sluggishness of him getting out of bed to open the door. And he opened with a crumpled, sleepy face.

"Nar waetin?" he enquired, perhaps still ready for a fight.

"Father Ignazio has just sent me a message."

"Why should father send you a message and not tell me directly?" He'd obviously forgotten that when we coincidentally met in Casablanca in transit, he was the one who told Father Ignazio that he should contact us through my phone because it was on roaming. I had to remind him about that.

"E say the Pope don gree for meet with we!" I broke the news suddenly.

"What are you talking about?" he retorted; and I could now see his demeanour being transported from one extreme to the other, as he rephrased the question, "What do you mean?" "Waetin you mean by father say we dae go meet di Pope?" And he was now saying it much louder – loud enough for his wife who was still in bed to hear. Alie's demeanor had a sudden transformation from unbelief to disbelief to belief, as I showed him the exchanged WhatsApp messages between Ignazio and me (Oh how I wish that phone was not stolen! *Freetong nar city*).

Alie immediately went into a lecture of how his 'star' and my 'star' were destined to shine together, how he and I had similar characteristics of not being covetous or over-ambitious, and how my simple faith in God was as admirable as my respect for elders. He had suddenly forgotten that I was arguing with him just the previous night. His excitement had overwhelmed him, and it eclipsed my own excitement.

"You don tell Rose?" he asked, making reference to my wife; and I said no he was the first to tell.

'Jemimah, Jemimah, grap, grap; we get good news," though obviously his wife had overheard the latter part of our conversation and the story didn't need recounting to her.

'Call Rose,' he was urging me; and I did, while breaking the news to her. All four of us were there celebrating the news at the second floor of the High Commissioner's residence with nobody else present, as our host and his children were all out to work or at school. We were shouting and jumping and embracing each other: he and I embracing, my wife and I embracing, I embracing his wife, he embracing my wife, the two wives embracing. Embracing, thumbs up, palms together, knuckles together. And Alie was talking on top of his voice: "Since Sheka and I became friends, only good things have been happening to us. I like this young man so much!" And when he was able to calm himself down to quasi-normal composure, he came with his usual elderly advice – that we should not tell this to anyone, not even Eddie Turay, until we were really sure and "hundred percent certain."

I agreed. And our wives obliged!!

All this was happening just at a short time after I first met Father Ignazio and off-handedly made the request to him. It was so unreal – too surreal! Like a story from a soap opera. But I could understand Alie's cautious warning – on the background that he had tried on his own for a few times before to meet Pope Benedict, and now Pope Francis; and all had ended without fruition. Though he seemed somehow more hopeful this time, he still had his reservations from experience!

* * *

At that time we were actually just transiting through London after a trip to Croatia on a presidential project exploration for the reinstallation of traffic lights in Sierra Leone. This was certainly one of the good things Alie was referring to as having been happening since we met and made an alliance. And it was while making the trip to Croatia that we coincidentally met with Father Ignazio at Casablanca Airport, himself in transit to Italy where he was taking some of the children they were educationally supporting in Sierra Leone for holidays. We had a long chat about everything we could talk about, and I remembered still putting through my 'when in Rome do as the Romans do' request of meeting the Pope. We took several photographs before parting. Any time Don Ignazio sent pictures or a message, I would show them to Alie Wasco until we left Croatia and arrived in London.

My quarrel with Alie the night before was primarily about him complaining that I had a domineering personality; to the extent of saying I had dictatorial tendencies. I did not deny that; but justified it. I made reference to how most Croatians I spoke to still believed the late Yugoslavian dictator, Josip Tito, laid the foundation for their country's development; but that, far from that, I was a 'democratic or benevolent dictator' if it came to taking decisions in our mutual interests. Alie was reeling from the fact that I had told the Croatian investors that all correspondences about the traffic lights project must be sent to me and nobody else, as directed by the President.

"Sheka, I know, as everybody knows, you are a class A student; and I know you are the initiator of the project; but you should know that you are the younger one. You have to respect that," he started.

"But I respect that, koth Alie," I responded.

"If you respected that, why would you tell the investors that they should only communicate with you?"

"Because we have to just have one line of communication for proper reporting to the President."

"I don't take that as respect!" he stated, slamming the door.

That was how we separated the night before the news of the appointment with Pope Francis!

Alie took it that I was being domineering because the President had asked me to put the traffic lights concept together, and that he was only incorporated later after I had already written it. And indeed that was my reason – because I knew that if it ever came to the crunch, the President would ask me and not him. I knew this only too well, as I had worked more officially closely with the President as his Press Secretary (as opposed to Alie whose work with him was mainly peripheral as Resident Minister North), and also on the back of my having performed a similar role – as directed by the President – at the inception of groundbreaking projects like First Step Fruit Juice Factory, Millennium Challenge Corporation, and Bumbuna Phase II Hydro-electric Project (in all of which I acted as the first person of contact between the investors and the presidency at the very early stages). So I had to become authoritative to protect the project and ensure its continuity.

But all the animosities ended when we thought of our meeting the Pope!

While on the plane back to Freetown, I gave him a type-written paper titled 'Update To His Excellency The President On Visit To Croatia For The Traffic Lights Project.' Alie burst out laughing loudly (so being heard by other passengers) when he read how I had signed off with: 'Jointly submitted by Hon. Alie D. Kamara and Hon. Sheka Tarawalie'.

Not caring about whether we were on a flight or not, or not bothered about how the other passengers felt, he said aloud, amidst more laughter, 'Oh my benevolent dictator; oh my benevolent dictator'.... While I suppressed my own laughter...

We returned to Freetown closer and more acquainted than ever before! We had a big secret between us – lurked in our hearts, only known by our wives, both of whom we left behind in London!

Chapter Twenty-Three

Saying Goodbye To Go See The Pope

The President Didn't Really Believe Us; The Passport Contract Misunderstanding On The Sidelines; Cabinet Colleagues Versus My Press-Freedom Disposition

The thought itself was exhilarating, as I moved around Freetown with a melody in my heart, keeping my secret to myself – except sharing it with Alie Wasco on the phone, face-to-face, or in my imagination. But there was one person whom it would be impossible to keep the secret from. Our boss, the President.

According to protocol, every government minister must inform the President in writing about any travel abroad (private or official), its purpose, and must secure his approval before making such a trip. By virtue of our closeness to the President, we first informed him verbally before sending in the letters later. By administrative custom, the letters would have to be written by civil servants on our behalf. That meant these civil servants would also be let into the secret. We, therefore, decided to leave the letter-writing aspect to a few days before departure. We should go in person to inform the President first.

Alie and I argued over how to put it, how to phrase it. How would the President receive the news? Would he believe us just on our word for it? We actually had received no written invitation; apart from the WhatsApp messages from Father Ignazio. I wished the President would just believe us. We met him at State Lodge (his official residence) so we would have enough time to talk and be informal. But he was not to be drawn into our excitement. Our explanation that it was Ignazio who had arranged the meeting did not seem to impress him. He knew the happy-go-lucky priest. One could see the President wanted to ask more questions; but being the reticent man he was, he kept the apparent doubts to himself.

"Well, una go try. Ar wish una well," he retorted with a wry smile, after we had informed him we would send the letters, as officialdom required, through the Secretary to the President (another official who would inevitably be led into the secret). Both Alie and I knew the President doubted our claims of an invitation to go see the Pope. Or he doubted the manner of 'special guests' that we had presented it. And honestly we were also really not too sure of how everything would pan out. We were merely hanging on the word of Ignazio; and we would not let that go.

For now, we were happy that the President had approved our trip. But the joy was short-lived as we thought of the next steps: we had not had our tickets yet (the visit was "at no cost to Government"), and we had just virtually 'emptied our pockets' in London and were waiting for the next salary.

Alie even made that known to the President. But there was no response from the latter. He was a man of moods, and one had to meet him in the right mood, Alie would later say.

But I had another thought playing on my mind. I was at the time in the middle of an official controversy. I was in sharp contrast with my immediate boss, the Minister of Internal Affairs, over a contract for the printing of passports. I had challenged the method used in awarding the contract, the ambiguity of the players involved, the implications, and particularly the high price imposed on a passport. Increasing the price from Le 100,000 to Le 500,000 was too much for hard-pressed citizens. My assertion was that the contract was not pro-people, not pro-poor. And there were other companies that could do even a better job for less – and they had participated in the tender procedures even before our arrival in the ministry. They had been given the impression that it was a fair process. Terminating it for the company that had indicated an inability to continue was not fair. There was no need for a third party (represented by a Sierra Leonean-Lebanese) in such a securitised contract. I would not support it, I'm sorry. All this I did behind closed doors.

Civil society groups only took it up when immigration public relations officials were publicising the new price. The issue gained a media flurry. The President then called me and the Minister to his office and asked the Secretary to the President to look into the matter. The Minister accused me of undermining the government; I respectfully told him I was trying to save it. The Secretary to the President, Osho Coker, was taking notes. I would never receive any feedback from him on the findings – albeit stating in a correspondence on a separate issue that he had reported his conclusions to the President. And the President also never raised the matter again. I wrote to him that I had never received a report from the

Secretary to the President, and I was re-stating my opposition to the contract 'in its present form'. He asked the Minister to table an instrument before Parliament so the issue would be debated. The MPs eventually endorsed the contract under very controversial circumstances – without a debate. I refused to attend the 'new passport' launching ceremony which was to be officially done by the President at our ministry building housing the Immigration Department. I didn't want to be associated even in the remotest of senses to this arrangement. The President asked his Vice President, Victor Foh, to deputise for him at the last minute!

Journalists would have to be summoned to the House for 'contempt' when they insinuated that parliamentarians were bribed. None infuriated the MPs more than the then-popular gossip column 'Ariogbo' in *The Blade* newspaper, whose editors Abdul Fonti Kabia and Bampia James Bundu appeared before a special committee for "a satirical article written on Parliament for the passage of the statutory instrument on the new cost to obtain a biometric Sierra Leonean passport" – according to Parliament's own 10 September 2015 press release.

The article, titled "Shameful...Rubber Stamp Parliament", had claimed the Chief Immigration Officer was seen with a huge bag in the premises of Parliament when the session on the passport issue was on. Immediately afterwards, the Acting Speaker called for a stand-down and for a members' only meeting at Committee Room No 1 – with the Minister of Internal Affairs and the Chief Immigration Officer. When they returned, with beaming smiles, the scheduled mover of the motion (an opposition MP who previously was insinuating that he would die for the people on the matter) did not raise it up again. The debate on the passport contract died before birth, no vote taken, and the contract/statutory instrument declared approved by Parliament. The Chief Immigration

Officer – according to *The Blade's* Ariogbo – left with an empty bag.

This ignited intense public debate. And Parliament could not carry its threats to punish the journalists: sensing public disenchantment, the committee sent the matter to the Independent Media Commission, where it died a natural death. The *Salone Times* newspaper's 11 September 2015 front-page lead screamed: 'Attempts To Intimidate Journalists Backfire.' My newspaper, *The Torchlight*, did not also relent in continuing to publish on its front-page air-space that passport prices in neighbouring countries were cheaper. My wife was the proprietress, and the paper had an Editor. And the impression being given by my critics was that I was the one mobilising all these other newspapers or that *The Torchlight* initiated the investigations and ignited the controversy. Totally false.

The 04 June 2015 edition of *Sierra Loaded* newspaper, with a screamer headline 'Torchlight Newspaper Investigation Creates War As APC Sharply Split Over Lebanese Passport Contract', stated that: "Another interesting aspect of the entire unfolding episode is that *The Torchlight* newspaper which first broke the news is operated by the family members of the Deputy Minister of Internal Affairs which is [the] Ministry that signed [the] allegedly dubious contract with a Lebanese man and Thomas De La Rue."

Some key men in government were naturally not happy with me. A close confidante Minister of the President was angry that my newspaper had not toed the official line. So was Vice President Victor Foh. I had a public spat with both men on the matter. They must have informed the President about it. Or those who witnessed the spats – who included personal aides to the President – must have. It was not in me to tell the President about all the spats I had with colleague public officials about this government policy or that official line.

My summary of the situation was encapsulated in the wise words of Jesus, that: "No one uses a new piece of cloth to patch old clothes. The patch would shrink and tear a bigger hole (Matthew 9:16)." The Minister was old enough to be my grandfather – and he had served in almost every civilian government since Sierra Leone's Independence (he once was Vice President of Sierra Leone under the APC, and he once also contested in the presidential race to lead the SLPP) . We could not understand each other. The hole became bigger.

My stance on press freedom never impressed (to put it mildly) many colleagues in government: that I opposed jailing journalists or closing media houses, or that I had as friends some journalists who were apparently not government-friendly, that I could allow and support the editorial independence of the newspaper I owned even in cases of alleged corruption in the government I was serving, was all unfathomable to many government colleagues. For them, the government must be defended at all times, whether right or wrong. I would rather allow the press to do its work. It was a tight rope. And we had to walk it.

That was about the time we had to ask for approval to travel to Rome. My relationship with the President was lukewarm: he was a politician; he would not like to displease the majority. Alie's involvement as a fellow-traveller could have warmed the relationship to get the President to see us in the first place. Because nothing – or no one – would stop Alie from making a trip he had been longing for all these years. And the catch was that, as Ignazio told him, he could not go alone – after I had expressed a desire to stay behind if circumstances could not permit. It had to be the two of us or none of us.

Approaching 'Love Bridges' on the ticket issue was a no-go area – as far as Alie was concerned. After a whole day of wrangling, a 'mysterious friend' of Alie's bought the tickets for us. I had never before met this friend and might never meet him – requests to meet and thank him in person did not bear fruit. But we were both excited. For Alie, Fr Ignazio had said our names were already on the Vatican list. Go we must. It was then that he revealed how frustrated he had been since having tried and failed to secure the opportunity of meeting the Pope before (though he had been a frequent visitor to Italy through 'Love Bridges').

"Now the frustration is over. Now the hour has come to go meet the Pope. To go get some blessings," Alie announced to the world.

Another mysterious friend sent me some pocket money. All good.

Chapter Twenty-Four

Last-Minute Hitch In Transit In London

No Note Verbal *From Brussels, No Seeing The Pope*

It was coming to pass. But not just as yet. We booked our tickets to Rome via London. Naturally, as our wives were there, we spent an unforgettable night in the Queen's country. Just a night.

How happy a night it was: chatting for the most part about meeting the Pope, the prospect of meeting the Pope, the anxiety and the surrealism surrounding it all. A mere joke – OK, a mere dream – was becoming a reality.

I had a very theological discussion with my wife. She had just completed her theology course at The Evangelical College of Theology (TECT) in Freetown. She was, therefore, forthright in her evangelical approach to the visit. She was happy for me, it was clear. We talked about the differences between Catholics and us Protestants – she was particularly reserved about the Catholic veneration or deification of Mary (the Mother of Jesus), a view I shared. The issue of the Anti-Christ was an allegation made against a particular Pope in history – not to be applied to all the Popes throughout history, I would explain. "Please don't bow to any image," she would admonish gently firmly – only wives would do that. And we also discussed the similarities – or the oneness in Christ. We could not be who we were without tracing it back to the Catholic Church. Rose would ask many other questions relating to the visit. Was it a worship service? Was it going to be an encounter in an office or a public ceremony? I didn't have any of those details, I would reply. All I was sure of was going to Rome to meet the Pope. Whichever way, whichever circumstances would be communicated thereafter.

There was no problem going deep into the night. Our flight to Rome would be in the afternoon the next day. But we still woke up early enough to have a sumptuous breakfast with our host, High Commissioner Eddie Turay (whom we had now informed but still looked skeptical about the veracity of our appointment). We still had time to go do some nearby shopping – we decided.

We were on our way to the shopping mall when Alie's phone rang (having now got a UK number). He told Rahman (the High Commissioner's driver who virtually always took us around) to put off the car stereo.

"Nar fada, nar fada dae call," Alie announced.

"Yes, my dear fada. Bon jornor. I'm at your service," he stated on the line forthrightly without the routine 'hello'.

"What fada! What?"

He took the phone away from his ear, put it face downwards on his leg and whispered to me, "Fada say small problem dae o!"

He quickly put the phone back to his ear, "Yes fada what problem?" There was a long silence on this side as he listened to the explanation from Fr Ignazio, only punctuated by intermittent sighs as responses.

"So fada what do you want us to do now?" was the question he posed at last.

"Explain to Sheka, explain to Sheka," he was talking and giving me the phone at the same time.

"Yes father," I muttered, not wanting to sound hysterical having heard about the 'problem' and reading Alie's body language as well.

"Minister Shekito, we get problem for solve immediately o," he said in his adapted Krio language. "You people need to get a *note verbal* as government officials," he switched to English.

"But that should not be a problem, father; we can get it from the High Commission here even now," I replied.

"No, it has to come from the embassy that covers the Vatican," he emphatically stated.

Then, of course, I suddenly fully understood there was a problem at hand. Various thoughts rushed through my mind. What if we called Brussels and the Ambassador was not available. What if the phone was not answered? What if it did not ring? Some technical issue cropping up at the crucial moment?

We had only four hours to get this resolved. Or the dream was over. Without the *note verbal*, the meeting would be cancelled. But the programme to which we were invited would still go ahead.

"Please bear with us. We'll call you back shortly. And please don't put your phone off," I tried to joke while hanging up. Rose and Jemimah were just sitting there witnessing events. For me, the most important thing to do right now was to reach the Ambassador to Belgium, Hon. Ibrahim Sorie. His phone didn't ring. I called again, the same thing. It was off. My second option, as always, was the Press Attaché, Chernor Ojuku Sesay, a colleague journalist and long-time associate. He also had an illustrious, if chequered, career in journalism – not least because he also suffered imprisonment, got brutalised by the first Vice Chairman of the NPRC military junta in the latter's office. Ojuku too had to go into hiding at the same time as me when his name was also placed on the list of 'collaborators' during the ill-fated AFRC interregnum because his newspaper, *The Pool*, took the same anti-military intervention stance like *The Torchlight*. He picked my call.

"Hey Kito," he answered in his usual self.

"Yes orman, please this is urgent. Is Ambassador Ibrahim Sorie in Brussels?"

"Yes he is," dragging his voice. "What's the problem?"

I explained.

"Orman are you sure?" he asked. I was not sure of what he was not sure of – whether my saying that we were billed to see the Pope tomorrow, or about needing the *note verbal* at so short a notice. I could hear the strain of unbelief in his voice.

"But let me give you his number." I told him I had it but it did not ring. "No, he has another number," but before he could give it out, Alie snatched the phone from me.

"Look Ojuku, this is very very urgent. Give me Ibrahim Sorie's number so I can call him right away," pronouncing the last phrase as 'ride away' (Alie always had a way of underlining his Americanism). Ojuku didn't need to ask who it was. And, indeed, Alie finally spoke to the Ambassador on the number he was given by Ojuku.

"Ibrahim bo nar me. Nar Alie Wasco," he burst into boisterous laughter to underscore the familiarity between them. He was now being drifted into laughter and Temne greetings when I motioned to him and pointed at the watch on my left wrist, whispering "Time, time, time, koth Alie, time." He continued with courtesies. "Time dae against we,"

I said to the hearing of Rose, Jemimah and Rahman. His wife quickly joined in reminding him of the time. He immediately explained. And he was then listening to the Ambassador.

"Ibrahim, you don't believe that I am going to see the Pope?" he asked, laughing the more boisterously.

He listened again. And then said, "All I want is for you to give us the *note verbal*. And I have less than two hours for this," he said rather emphatically.

"Talk to Sheka, talk to Sheka," he again passed the phone to me. I repeated the story to the Ambassador after a brief greeting.

"But I can't just give you people a *note verbal* like that. I need some documentary proof that you are going to see the Pope," he said; and I could fathom the latent doubts beneath his voice.

"OK sir, please just keep your phone line open. We'll get back to you shortly," I stated.

I knew we had the travel clearance from the President. I checked in my hand bag and found it there. I called Ambassador Sorie back to ask for his WhatsApp number. He was not using WhatsApp. The lot fell back on Ojuku. I sent it to him and followed up with a call to confirm.

Ten or so minutes later the Ambassador called, saying the document was not sufficient for the issuance of a *note verbal*. The President had merely endorsed our request for permission to go meet the Pope. This was good. But not good enough. The Ambassador wanted a document from the Vatican stating that we had been invited there.

He had a point. A valid point. We needed to call Fr Ignazio again.

"OK. I'll get something to send to you via email," were the reassuring words from the always-friendly priest. "Or you can send me the details of the person to contact in Brussels so I can send it directly, while copying you."

That was brilliant. It would only make things more authentic to our Brussels diplomats.

By now, there was really just over an hour left for us to be leaving for the airport. Father Ignazio sent the letter about thirty minutes later. Fifteen minutes after, the *note verbal* had been provided by Ambassador Sorie.

Hurray! And hurry!

When we went back to the Jewish-populated Golders Green plush residence of the Sierra Leone High Commissioner to the UK, it was all about rush-rush: we collected our already-packed baggage; couldn't eat lunch – we'll eat on the plane, I justified; kissed and hugged our wives. And off we went to Heathrow airport, bound for Rome.

The Pope was beckoning.

Chapter Twenty-Five

Eve

From London Heathrow To Rome's Leonardo da Vinci Airport; Register With Secretary Of State At The Vatican

The flight from London Heathrow to Rome's Leonardo da Vinci or Fiumicino Airport was a short one – just over two hours. Alie and I hardly spoke to each other once airborne. Everybody was deep in thought. We would exchange a few glances here and there. We spoke when the food was served – it was too small, he said; I agreed. And then a short nap followed. Next the announcement came through that we were to fasten our seat belts as we were starting our descent into Rome. I watched through the window and had a view of the sea and the scenery of Fiumicino.

Fr. Ignazio was there waiting for us. As we came through the usual immigration / customs checks, passports stamped, we found him smiling in the arrivals area and then laughing and hopping on one foot: I also hopped as we hugged – 'when in Rome you do as the Romans do.' And then a longer hug for

Alie – 'buona sera' 'buona sera' they kept saying to each other with louder laughter.

There was a thirty-minute drive from the airport to our accommodation. This gave us an opportunity to talk about the excitement and the anxiety, especially the hitch about the *note verbal*. He told us how the whole scenario was surreal to him too: the miracle of accepting our names at the first request, through the Archbishop of Sardinia (Ignazio's own hometown), and the fast pace at which everything moved to today. He informed us he had invited a support group of the organisation drawn from its bases in Italy to come and witness the ceremony, and that the Lokomasama boys on holiday in Rome had also been incorporated to present their products from Sierra Leone to the Pope. Everything sounding good. Ignazio showed us various landmarks on the way: farms, ancient buildings, war history, and papal tradition. He then informed us that we had to register formally with the Secretary of State (the political head of the Vatican who was like a Prime Minister appointed by the Pope, and officially known as the Secretary of State of His Holiness the Pope or the Cardinal Secretary of State). We had to confirm our arrival officially and secure a copy of the programme. And that should happen today – the occasion would be tomorrow, 18 November 2015. We would have to just drop our bags at our allotted accommodation, refresh for twenty minutes, and go straight to the Vatican. A pre-visit before the visit! That sounded good.

The other great news Fr Ignazio had for us was that our 'guest house' was actually within the vicinity of the Vatican. And the apartments were officially called 'Vatican Villas.' It sounded like music in my ears.

Even as the music on the car radio was still playing amid the conversation, it was easy to tell we had arrived in the vicinity of the Vatican. Before Ignazio could announce it, the great Vatican wall was spread in front of us. Amazing.

Alie would whisper to me that this was the work of African slaves. I never bothered to ask for his sources of information on the matter.

Fr. Ignazio took us to the guest house, located just across the road on the west side of the Vatican wall. Almost directly opposite the entrance to the Vatican museum was a security gate: you could only go through by entering a numeric code into a device. Ignazio already had it. 'Villa Vaticana' was boldly written at the top. Soon we were at the reception. Keys with room numbers and business cards were handed over to us. On the cards: 'Villa Vaticana, bed and breakfast, viale Vaticano, 96, 00136, Roma (Italy), Phone: + 39 0697603468, info@villavaticana.it, www.villavaticana.it.'

I clutched everything as a young Italian lady, Sylvia (many Italian ladies do like that name, I would come to conclude), took us to our respective rooms to do the courtesy introduction of each his own: how this worked, how that worked, the wifi password, the telephone code etc. Mine was Room 3. I was amused: from Villa 33 (Hill Station) in Freetown to Villa Vaticana 3. Villa, Villa, *Voila*! Ignazio introduced us to our co-guests, Stefano and his wife (hotel-owning rich members of 'Love Bridges', here for tomorrow's programme also, as part of the organisation's support group). They were in Room 4. Alie 2; Ignazio 1.

Big, spacious, decent, modern rooms – with all the facilities of a hotel. Four-star I would guess. A peep at their website would explain: "With its exceptional location, in front of the Vatican Museums, Vatican Villa offers the chance to stay on a relaxing and comfortable place, feeling the sensation of living in the heart of the Eternal City... all rooms are newly renovated and furnished in Art Nouveau... All the rooms have a private bathroom, air conditioning, free WiFi, flat screen TV, mini bar…"

Left on my own, I dropped on my knees and prayed, "Papa God you too much o." He is also a humorous God!

I quickly refreshed and changed. And soon there was Ignazio's knock on the door. We needed to leave now. It was a five-minute walk away. And we soon arrived there.

The pillars at the main gates to the Vatican were just awesome – all built in stone. "Our forefather slaves severely suffered to build these structures," Alie would whisper again. "Especially during winter," I finally responded, sending him into tantrums of laughter. "Many could have perished in the process," I stated, as if I was wholly buying Alie's African-slaves-built-Vatican story.

At that time, Ignazio was busy talking with the personnel manning the security scanning machines. There were a few other people queuing, including nuns. But Ignazio had thrown the magic wand: he called us to the front and we quickly went through the gates. We immediately found ourselves in the vastness of St. Peter's Square: the most distinguishable feature being the huge superhuman statues of Jesus Christ and His disciples placed at the top of the mammoth front building. From where we entered was a fountain with a constant flow of water in colours and contours.

From the gate to the entrance of the basilica itself – St Peter's Basilica – was a long walk. Perhaps as long as the distance to Villa Vaticana. And here, there were decks of stairs to climb. There was another security gate. It was here that we first saw the Swiss Guards: anciently dressed, in brightly embroidered and immaculate ceremonial uniforms; with thick matching boots; and metallic helmets. Standing still, as statues themselves. Even eyes not shaking? Until you looked longer and saw a wink. They were human. This time we didn't have to jump the queue. There were fewer people here: obviously tourists or pilgrims. There were a few other gates to use to enter.

Inside was serene. Certainly spiritually-inspiring: the visual can also inspire the spiritual in humans. We were in St Peter's Basilica, Ignazio would tell us, the church built on top of the grave of the Apostle Peter (the first Pope; martyred). This was the largest church in the world, which British writer James Lees-Milne described as "holding a unique position in the Christian world!" They wanted us to proceed, but I begged that they gave me a few minutes. I went and sat on one of the pews for a moment of reflection. For about three minutes I sat there, facing the candle-lit pulpit. And I bowed my head in total wonderment. I was amazed by Grace.

I came back and found Ignazio and Alie chatting. "I'm sorry," I said. Alie replied that I should not delay them again, that I should wait for the Pope's prayers. Ignazio took us to a few other churches or chapels within the Vatican. We passed through – but no 'delay' here – the Sistine Chapel, the church where Popes were crowned. Ignazio showed us impressive works of art: paintings of famous artists such as Michelangelo and Botticelli. He underlined the advantage of doing this: that this was the only opportunity we had, as far as this trip was concerned. Tomorrow's ceremony would take place at the public square; we would have no opportunity to go inside; and we would leave Rome the next day.

It was worth it.

The Cardinal Secretary of State's office was located further up, having to go through a couple more of gates only manned by Swiss Guards, without the scanning machines. Their eyes did the scanning. And that was enough.

We finally found the secretariat – almost an hour done at the Vatican. We met an administrative assistant of the Secretary of State. Confirmation was done. We were present in person. The programme was handed over to us with special badges to be worn tomorrow. Ignazio couldn't hide his excitement: "Look, your names are there," as he pointed at the bottom of the paper written in Italian for tomorrow's papal mass or 'general audience'. Our names were boldly written there: and Ignazio would further explain that it was more than a ministerial visit or even a presidential one – which normally took place behind closed doors, in officialdom. Ours would be a ceremonial public encounter that would be preceded by a general mass, and a Swiss-Guard brass band would herald our presence. The excitement reached its equilibrium. On our way out, Ignazio would tell us more about the Vatican: how hundreds of people were living there; and it even had its own railway service.

When we came out, we found a totally different public square. Preparations were well underway for tomorrow: thousands of chairs were being arranged in rows, security barriers were being erected at different locations, a raised tent-covered canopy had been set up, and all types of workmen were doing things here and there. Tomorrow would be a great day. Alie and I took photographs in front of one of the two double-decked fountains before we left.

We had dinner in one of the restaurants just outside the gates of the public square. Alie tried to familiarise with a waiter in his broken Italian. 'Buon giorno,' he had said. There was a big laughter from Ignazio. Apparently, Alie had got his Italian mixed up: 'Buon giorno' actually meant 'Good morning.' We had a very lively discussion over dinner about tomorrow.

We walked back to Villa Vaticana to prepare early. But after Ignazio had retired to his room, trust Alie, he came back to my room to do a pre-event chat. He was overwhelmed by the fact that "we are sleeping in the same place where the

Pope sleeps". I dared not say that was an exaggeration. As far as he was concerned, we had become trailblazers of the government regarding Vatican relations. This would become more poignant when two years later President Koroma would find it necessary – even at the twilight of his administration, accompanied by an array of political lieutenants – to make a state visit to the Vatican.

Alie advised we prepared our suits before we slept. Mine was ready during the twenty-minute interval before leaving the guest house for the Cardinal Secretary of State's office.

"Good night koth Alie," closing the door. I jumped into bed, with a smile, and yet another prayer.

Chapter Twenty-Six

Bad News On D-Day Morning

Islamic State Threatens To Attack The Vatican

To say I woke up very early would be an understatement. I simply didn't sleep – couldn't sleep. Too much was going through my head – all revolving around the question: 'Is this for real?'

And then I thought of my wife's reservations: "Please don't bow down to any image. Just allow the Holy Spirit to guide you," and so on and so forth in lovely and loving tones.

And then I had my own independent journalistic thoughts: look for a story wherever the opportunity availed itself (with flash recollections of the blasphemous conspiracy-theory-filled novel of Dan Brown, *The Da Vinci Code,* which I read in 2004, popping up). Plus my own individual religious inclinations: the Catholic Church could be vilified by Protestantism, but this was the root of our Christianity; it's worth exploring, it's worth connecting with.

In-between these whirlwind nocturnal thoughts, I certainly had what would only have amounted to a catnap. It could have lasted for less than thirty minutes. And I was awake again inside Villa Vaticana. I now firmly believed it was not a dream. It was for real. I looked at my nicely-ironed black striped suit, with my wedding lilac waist-coat (meaning, it was the same I wore on my wedding day) and its accompanying tie, and a blue-and-white-striped shirt. I did some polishing on the black shoes again. The socks were ready. White underwear – vest and brief. Black belt. Come take me, Ignazio, I'm ready.

Not just yet. I showered slowly and thoroughly, with a melody to match – as if I was going for newness. But that was what it was: newness. The newness of meeting the Pope for the first – and perhaps the last – time.

It was about 7:30 am. I was all dressed up. Perfumed. All set. To meet the Pope.

Not as yet. There was some bad news. From Islamic State; also known as ISIS or ISIL (former British Prime Minister David Cameron, whose tenure was plagued with a rise in terrorism, preferred calling them by their derogatory Arabic acronym, Daesh). They were planning to attack the Vatican, specifically St. Peter's Basilica, according to US intelligence agencies. The information was passed on to the Italian authorities this morning. The security threat level in Rome was raised to red alert. And our programme could be cancelled?

* * *

When US Navy SEALS on 2 May 2011, authorised by President Barack Obama, executed the dare-devil operation that killed Osama Bin Laden (the fugitive leader of the similarly daring Al Qaeda terrorist group), the world heaved a big sigh of relief. The terror group had executed the apocalyptic 11 September 2001 invasion using hijacked passenger aircrafts to inflict the worst terror attack on US soil (about 3,000 killed and 6,000 more injured – a female Sierra Leonean school-teacher turned American, Hilda Taylor, was among the dead). Pope John Paul II, shocked by the horror, had told the American Ambassador to the Holy See, James Nicholson, two days after the attack, that: "This was an attack, not just on the United States, but on all of humanity. We must stop these people who kill in the name of God." But, Bin Laden, the mastermind behind the 9/11 attack (as it came to be known) had eluded an international manhunt declared by then-sitting President George W. Bush – until the Saudi-born terrorist was located ten years later under Obama in a hideout in Abbottabad (Pakistan), killed, and buried at sea (according to the official line). And the world was at peace again.

That was what we thought!

Terrorism has a way of recreating itself ever since it was birthed. Even as it could be as old as humanity (Esau's action against Jacob was obviously terrorism), Walter Laqueur in *The Age Of Terrorism* (1987, Weidenfeld & Nicolson) stated that: "One of the earliest-known examples of a terrorist movement is the *sicarri*, a highly organized religious sect consisting of men of lower orders active in the Zealot struggle in Palestine (AD 66-73)."

This was long before Islam's Mohammed was born!

Using crude methods like mingling with crowds and unleashing violence with swords hidden under their cloths, these early Jewish terrorists also burnt public places and houses, including 'the house of Ananias, the high priest'. Laqueur went further to describe them thus: "They are also mentioned in Tacitus and in the rabbinical authorities as having burned granaries and sabotaged Jerusalem's water supplies. They were the extremist, nationalist, anti-Roman party and their victims both in Palestine and in the Egyptian diaspora were the moderates, the Jewish peace party."

And then Islam eventually came on the scene – on a string of wars between Medina and Mecca. Ever since, at one time or another, there has been a strain of violence associated with the religion – though mostly denounced by its many followers. Laqueur believed that what would eventually be labelled as 'Islamic terrorism' in contemporary times had its greatest pioneer in the late Libyan dictator: "Muamar al Qadhafi emerged in the 1970s as one of the most active, and certainly the loudest, supporter of international terrorism... His aim was the unification of the Arab world, close collaboration with all Muslim countries and eventually the revolutionary transformation of the whole world, whatever that may have meant. His political ideas which he publicized in some detail in his 'Green Book', the first part of which appeared in 1975, were based on Islam..." Eventually, Laqueur stated, "Modern technology is giving them [terrorists] powerful weapons"; and he therefore concluded that "present-day terrorist groups have quite clearly acquired the characteristics once attributed to tyranny, *atrox et notoria injuria*. The tyrant wants to impose his will on society and wants to keep it at ransom, and so do terrorists".

And so – coming back to the present story – Al Qaeda's successor terror group held the world spellbound by its share effrontery and brazenness in carrying out mayhem.

The Islamic State launched its first international attack on a Jewish museum in Belgium in May 2014. It appeared to be a one-off. But then came another assault. Yet another. In different countries: in the Middle East, Africa, Europe, Australia, and America. And then the world realised that a terrorist outfit bigger than Al Qaeda, in terms of the worldwide network of recruits and money, had emerged. They were here to proclaim a global caliphate, to rule the world via Sharia law. In fact they traced the genealogy of their leader, Iraqi-born Abu Bakr al-

Baghdadi, to the founder of Islam himself, Mohammed. They found canon-fodder territory in war-torn Iraq and eastern Syria. Their capacity and capability to brainwash, radicalise, and attract even young people in Western countries, including USA and UK, using modern technology like the internet, made world leaders take serious notice. Using gory video messages circulated worldwide within seconds, Islamic State made the world shudder: their attacks on train stations, airports and other public places using very simple but effective methods like plowing vehicles into targets, made it a very difficult terrorist group to combat.

Their ultimate aim was to annihilate Christianity and the Romans (their own description of all Europeans). And their eyes were set on destroying the seat of Christendom in Rome. It would not take long to know that both the Pope and the Vatican were top on their destructive agenda. The Iraqi Ambassador to the Holy See (the Vatican's politico-diplomatic name), Habeeb Al Sadr, was the first to blow the whistle when he stated on 16 September 2014 that according to intelligence on the ground in Iraq, the Islamic State was targeting to assassinate Pope Francis. A month later, on 13 October 2014, ISIS actually released a Photo-Shopped picture (published on the front cover of their English language propaganda magazine, *Dabiq*, with the headline 'The Failed Crusade') showing their 'black standard' flag superimposed over the obelisk at St. Peter's Square in the Vatican. In the article, their spokesman, Mohammed al-Adnani, was quoted as saying they were on their way to Rome. On 22 February 2015, ISIS released a video (alongside images of beheaded Egyptian Coptic Christians) stating that its forces were in the 'south of Rome'. In response, the Italian authorities deported about 200 suspected militants between February and August 2015.

The threats were real – though they could not disrupt or alter the Western way of life: trains would still run, planes would still fly, and public parties would still go ahead.

Just a few days before our scheduled Vatican visit, on Friday 13 November 2015 (Black Friday), ISIS carried out one of the largest internationally coordinated attacks (shootings, suicide bombings, grenade attacks, hostage taking) in different locations at almost the same time in Paris, killing over 100 and wounding more than 300. This caused the whole of Europe to be placed on high alert. Germany cancelled a football match it would have had with the Netherlands on 17 November – understandable, taking into consideration that the German football team was actually in a Paris stadium where one of the coordinated attacks took place on Black Friday. Therefore, there was heightened security in Rome when we arrived on November 17. But we did not expect it to be further heightened. We did not expect ISIS to make a direct threat to the Vatican on our day – on the very day that we were to meet the Pope.

* * *

By now, it was very clear that Fr Ignazio was much more than the laughing priest we had always known. He was a highly influential, well-connected man in the Vatican administrative tapestry. When he knocked on my Villa Vaticana door, I obviously – naturally – thought everything was normal and on course for the big ceremony. Until he said there was some bad news. His countenance was downcast. The Islamic State terrorists had put the Vatican on a list of a few places to attack in Italy. He was telling me first before telling Alie – "because you are the journalist and you would know how to handle the news". But it was still not known publicly; it remained a secret within the intelligence community, from the Americans to the Italian government and the Holy See. Then I understood, because I had listened to the BBC via my phone radio and there was nothing like that in the news.

"But will that get our programme cancelled?" I asked.

"I don't think so. We are going. Those I spoke to said the Pope will not cancel."

That was some great relief in itself. If ISIS would bomb us at the Vatican, so be it.

When we approached Alie, therefore, we gave him a watered-down version, without mentioning Islamic State (I would only imagine how he could have reacted). We just told him that we should expect more security because it would be a big occasion and the threats of terrorists generally would not be underestimated. We didn't discuss it over our light breakfast at all; but obviously our original excitement was a bit subdued.

The moment we came out of Villa Vaticana, the obvious was noticeable: there were soldiers, not police, on guard. It would later be known that between 700 and 1000 soldiers were deployed to back up the police across Rome. At the same time, there were tens of thousands (St Peter's Square has a capacity of about 300,000; but official reports stated that just over 20,000 were present that day) of people streaming to attend the Pope's general audience. We were not afraid. We were emboldened. The chain effect of seeing other humans in the same mood! Our programme was on course! Nothing would stop it. Not ISIS.

The official statement that would be released later that day by the US embassy in Rome, indeed, confirmed that the Vatican was one of ISIS's proposed targets; but it was more a precautionary message to American citizens in Italy to be wary of these places than a specific threat of an attack on that very day. Among those who would be present at St Peter's Square to witness the occasion were many Americans, some carrying their country's flag. But nothing was taken for granted, as indeed the whole Vatican security was tightened and the Pope's own bodyguard contingent reinforced.

British journalist Rosie Scammell would report the Vatican

security alert in the *Religion News Service* on 19 November with a humorous headline 'Want To See The Pope? Get In Line At The Security Checkpoint' (with an accompanying photograph of a nun being scanned by security officers at a Vatican gate). She reported: "Even nuns in habits were subjected to a security checkpoint Wednesday (Nov. 18) during Pope Francis' general audience, a weekly event that attracts thousands. Hundreds of others were also searched before being allowed into the square. The high state of alert follows a statement from the U.S. Embassy in Rome, identifying St. Peter's Basilica as a potential target for terrorists. 'The Italian authorities are aware of these threats,' said the note, published Wednesday."

We were exempted from the 'Get In Line' part of Scammell's report. The VIP badges given to us at the office of the Cardinal Secretary of State made us an exception to the rule. Not that we didn't go through the security scanners – there was no other way to go through – but we didn't get in the long line. Scammell didn't have a CCTV. The exception could not be reported.

* * *

Islamic State itself is merely a shadow of its former self as I write now. The concerted efforts of the international community, including well-known Muslim nations, have succeeded in virtually decimating an entity that just over two years before made the world to quiver. Of their leader al-Baghdadi, there are varied accounts about his whereabouts: wounded or hiding or wandering in villages or killed. But what is clear is that the roaming remnants of ISIS terrorists now only control about 2% of the territory they controlled two years ago. Their radicalised Western collaborators have either been captured or have abandoned their project and some are facing death-penalty sentences in the US.

The Vatican, or any part of Italy, has not been attacked by Islamic State!

* * *

Though Islamic State, or Islamic terrorists in general, use the Quran as their supposed source of inspiration (quoting suras here and there to suit their fundamentalism, with a promise of 'paradise'), mainstream Muslims vehemently condemn them, denouncing, decrying and dissociating themselves from the terror groups. Writing in London's *Evening Standard* of Wednesday 6 June 2018, the Secretary General of the Muslim Council of Britain, Harun Khan, asserted that 'terrorists who claim to be Muslims are twisting our religion' – in much the same ways as Sierra Leonean clerics have been stating the point. Khan was lending support to a speech by Britain's first Muslim/Pakistani-background Home Secretary, Sajid Javid, in which the latter referred to terrorists as non-Muslims. "These murderers called themselves Muslims… they were invoking the religion of my parents, and my grandparents, and countless generations of Javids before them. Of course, I know they are not true Muslims, but there's no avoiding the fact that these people self-identify as Muslims," Javid (who does not himself practise Islam) had said while unveiling his anti-terror strategy, Contest, on 4 June 2018. In his support letter, the Muslim Council's Khan stated: "As he launched the Government's latest counter-terrorism strategy, Home Secretary Sajid Javid was right to say that those who killed supposedly on behalf of Islam represent no one but themselves. … The fact that one would-be terrorist was caught with a copy of *Islam for Dummies* in his baggage tells us that these people have little or no roots in the faith they wish to kill for."

But perhaps an interesting quality, rather ironically, about the war against Islamic State was its capacity to create too many enemies; and in the process even bringing together in collaboration against them otherwise strange-bedfellow nations: America, Britain, Iran, Russia, Saudi Arabia, Turkey (under Recep Tayyip Erdoğan – I passed through Istanbul's Ataturk airport from a conference in Antalya just three days before Islamic State attacked there on 28 June 2016), Syria (under the Arab-Spring surviving Bashar al-Assad), the Philippines under the highly controversial Rodrigo Duterte, all fighting the common enemy, Daesh. Very interesting.

It is worthy to note though that a direct by-product of Islamic fundamentalism has been a rise in extremist islamophobia. There have certainly been suspicions or even somewhat hatred for Muslims in certain parts of the western world for a considerable time now for various reasons. But it was only after the al Qaeda/ISIL menaces that we started seeing the loathing against Muslims turning into violent mass 'retaliation' from 'white extremists' adopting the same or similar methods used by the 'Islamic terrorists'. One such example was the June 2017 Finsbury Park attack in London in which Welshman Darren Osborne hired a van from Cardiff and drove it all the way to the English City (a three-hour driving distance) to ram it into a group of Muslims coming from the Finsbury Park Mosque, just a couple of weeks after alleged Islamic militants rammed a van into pedestrians on London Bridge. Darren killed one and left at least nine injured – while the three ISIS-inspired London-Bridge militants (Pakistani-born British Khuram Shazad Butt and the two Morrocans Rachid Redouane and Youssef Zaghba) had succeeded in killing eight and wounding at least forty-eight when, after abandoning their vehicle, they went on a stabbing spree in and around pubs and restaurants in the nearby Borough Market area.

But back to the Vatican story...

Chapter Twenty-Seven

It Happens

Face-to-Face With Pope Francis – 'The Love Of Christ Lives In Us' Medal

It was after we had passed through the security gate that I would realise or recall that this was the first time I was seeing Fr Ignazio in his priestly dress: a black cassock with a matching white collar. I had noticed briefly when he came in the morning, but with the news he brought my initial impression immediately evaporated. And during the five-minute walk from Villa Vaticana, the focus was on the security detail of soldiers clutching Kalashnikovs with fully-equipped military vans standing by. Next attraction was the long queues we had to pass.

It was only now, in the Square, that I had a thorough look again at the man who, since I met him, had always sported jeans and a shirt or t-shirt – always casual. Today, he was a priest *par excellence* – dressed for it. We would only have to follow him. There would be no other way of meandering through the now-labyrinthine Square.

The whole place had now been compartmentalised by barricades with giant screens installed for those who were farther from the papal dais in front of the basilica. It's all changed. Yesterday we saw work being done; today the work was done. And it looked totally different, were it not for the landmark physical structures. There were people everywhere.

The four Lokomasama boys were brought by the support group; and so Ignazio led us first to where they had arranged to be picked up – by the obelisk, the indisputably tall Egyptian treasure standing in the middle of the square. And then we formed a group of seven, moving slowly: Ignazio in front, the boys in the middle, Alie and I at the back. The security personnel were noticeable, and we had to pass through another final security detail to where we had been allotted to sit. With Ignazio, there was no problem.

But what would be incredibly unbelievable to us was where we were to sit. By now, we had known we were some special guests, of course; but for our seats to be at the very top of the platform on the right side of where the Pope would sit, with no barrier between him and us, was gobsmacking. Everybody else was behind a barricade – except the cardinals who were sitting in the same position as us on the left side of the Pope, plus Vatican officials and security and selected photographers. And those behind the barricades included diplomats representing their countries at the Holy See. Ignazio introduced us to Rogelio Francisco Emilio Pfirter, the Ambassador from Argentina (the Pope's home country) who was seated right behind us, but separated by a barricade. Even most of the journalists were behind the barrier – they would only be let in to take pictures of us and the Pope when the time would come!

We were guided by security to our seats: Alie was seated first; I sat next to him, followed by Ignazio; and then the four boys. Two Swiss Guards stood right next to us. If ever it was not real, now it certainly was. This was around 9am and the programme was scheduled to start at 10am. We had one hour to absorb everything and talk to each other. Alie and I could not stop praising Ignazio for an excellent job: we admired his connections, his influence, his belonging in the 'inner circle' of the Vatican. Soon he would leave us to walk through the detailed security to meet the support group who were by now positioned somewhere at the front on the cardinals' side, with a huge space in-between and behind a barricade – displaying a large 'Love bridges' banner. Ignazio would come back with messages of joy and fun and laughter.

We were now sure we would see the Pope today. But actually we did not know how we would meet. We did not know what to do when we met. Ignazio said we should just wait and see. He was good at suspense. We didn't mind. Alie would say: 'No matter what, the witches have failed.' I didn't know who these witches were, but he was certainly not referring to Islamic State. But, with the passage of time, quintessential Alie, he soon drummed up a conspiracy theory about 'if the Pope does not come.' The pontiff could change his mind, or his security could advise him not to come. Though it was a chilly morning, Alie said he had started sweating. A very interesting fellow; he kept making me laugh. And it was my turn to tell him that nothing could turn back the clock now: our day to meet the Pope had come, 'no matter what, the witches have failed'.

But then when it reached 10am and the pontiff did not appear, I also became a bit tormented inside, my mind gnawing at Alie's conspiracy theories. Could the Pope have changed his mind? As per the Islamic State threat? It was while I was pondering on this, that three officials entered from the basilica end and were coming straight to us. Ignazio immediately alerted us that the one in the middle was the Cardinal Secretary of State. We shook hands, as Ignazio did the introduction. He was in theory our host, and had come to recognise our presence and welcome us. He left for the papal dais, but the other officials stayed. Just a few minutes into the courtesies with them, a white automobile appeared from the right corner of where we stood – and there was Pope Francis in white apparel standing in the open vehicle. Shrieks and screams from the crowds welcomed him into the square, with security detail on foot chasing the vehicle wherever it went, through the pathways divided by the barricades.

Even here and now, my heart was in my mouth. The scene was majestic and surreal. The people were ecstatic. But what if… The Islamic State threat came to mind again. May it not happen, Lord. It was here, at this same St. Peter's Square, that Pope John Paul II was shot (he survived after surgery) on 13 May 1981 while riding in his automobile in a similar ceremony. But then there were no sophisticated security weapon-detecting scanners in 1981.

Dressed in an immaculate white gown with a skull cap to match, Pope Francis alighted from the automobile (or, as they call it, popemobile) – as the Square's foreground was constructed in such a way as to prevent vehicular access to the dais area – and walked his way up. He headed straight to the Vatican officials who were still standing by us. It was not impromptu. This was the usual protocol, Ignazio would subsequently explain. They exchanged a couple of courtesies. The Pope merely waved to us, and then waved to the crowds behind us. He walked towards the dais (followed by these officials who were standing by us), turned and waved to the throngs of people in the middle of the square. Cheers were the response. He went up and took his seat, with two cardinals sitting by his left and right – only three of them under the canopy. The one on the right, on our side, was the Secretary of State, while the other was more of his personal aide, it appeared: moving the microphone, giving and taking papers, straightening the skullcap on the pontiff's head etc...

Alie thought that was it. We had seen the Pope; he waved to us; he had taken his seat. After that he would leave. That was our encounter with the Pope. We had achieved our goal. Did we? Had we? What about the goal of shaking his hand? No talk with him? Ignazio, the father of suspense, would let us grope for answers all by ourselves. If that was it, then it was still fine, I would tell Alie. "No one would say we didn't meet the Pope," he replied in a consolation tone.

And now the ceremonial service would begin: the papal general audience. As Pope Francis sat in the middle of the canopy, the aide lowered the microphone placed in front of him to suit the sitting position. The formal ceremony started solemnly with a prayer, and then a song (which was like a lullaby to me – I felt nostalgic of 'praise and worship' in the melodious Protestant way, like a Pastor-Pete-Dalton-directed performance by a boisterously rhythmic Brookfields Wesleyan choir or a pop-star-like 'Onward To The Cross' solo display by Kissy Dockyard's Daniel Solomon Bangura or a taste of the good-for-all Nigerian gospel songs like Sinach's 'I Know Who I Am' and Mercy Chinwo's 'Excess Love/Jesus You Love Me Too Much O' or Ghanaian singing pastor Sonnie Badu's 'Baba/Open The Floodgates' or world-acclaimed Australian Hillsong choir just doing 'Touching Heaven, Changing Earth' or our own Millicent Rhodes doing her gospel medley to shake the place – as we say in Sierra Leone).

After the song, in the Vatican 'order of service', followed the reading of Scripture in different languages – in virtually all the major languages in the world, including Latin, English, French and Arabic. Each read by a native-speaker Cardinal or priest.

Then it was time for the homily from the Pope. I braced myself up to hear. For me, this was the defining moment of the visit. From this message, I would assess the Catholic Church as to whether it was a Christian Church or the alleged Antichrist. Was the message going to be about rituals? Would he talk about the terrorist threat? Was it going to be about Mary? Or was it about the Gospel of Jesus Christ.

And from the moment Pope Francis opened with the Italian greeting of 'Bongiorno' with the reciprocal massive response from the crowds, I was virtually held spellbound to the end. With Ignazio being an intermittent interpreter, Alie's attempts to interject with whatever he was saying never entered my ears. I was consuming the Pope's message word by word. He did it with passion, in fashion: I could tell he was doing it from his heart, with accompanying gesticulations. He sat through it all. It took about forty minutes (and I wanted to see every second of it): the pontiff read in Latin interspersed with Italian; and the translation was subsequently done in English and the other major languages.

It was an amazing and touching message. He titled it 'The Welcoming Door'. Using the books of John and Revelation as references, he presented Jesus Christ as the Door and the Good Shepherd. Opening with a reference to the pending Jubilee (or the Holy Year of Mercy starting on 8 December 2015 by the symbolic opening of the 'Holy Door' at St. Peter's Basilica), he started with, "The Door is before us, not just the Holy Door, but another: the great Door of the Mercy of God — and that is a beautiful Door! — which embraces our penance, offering the grace of His forgiveness. The Door is generously open, it takes a little courage on our part to cross the threshold. Each of us has burdensome things within ourselves. We are all sinners! Let us take advantage of this coming moment and cross the threshold of this mercy of God who never tires of forgiving, never tires of waiting for us! He watches us, He is always beside us. Take heart! Let us enter through this Door!"

I was now gripped to hear more, pen and notebook in hand, scribbling away. He went on to plead with "our churches, our communities, our parishes, our institutions, our dioceses" similarly to open their doors to all peoples "because this is how we can all go out to bring this mercy of God". Reflecting on the book of Revelation where Jesus said "I stand at the door and knock; if any one hears my voice and opens the door, I will come in to him and eat with him, and he with me", the Pope stated: "Let us imagine the Lord knocking at the door of our heart! In the last great vision of the Book of Revelation, the City of God is prophesied like this: 'its gates shall never be shut by day', which means for ever, because 'there shall be no night there'." He then asserted: "An inhospitable Church, like a family closed off within itself, mortifies the Gospel and withers the world. No armoured doors in the Church, none! Completely open!" A one-time bouncer-doorkeeper himself, Pope Francis then paid tribute to doorkeepers (now actually Christian doorkeepers) everywhere because "tending the door requires careful discernment and, at the same time, must inspire great faith".

Then the crux of the message: "In truth, we are well aware that we too are watchmen and servants of the Door of God, and what is the name of the Door of God? Jesus! He lights up all of life's doors for us, including those of our birth and of our death. He Himself affirmed it: 'I am the Door; if any one enters by Me, he will be saved, and will go in and out and find pasture'. Jesus is the Door that lets us go in and out. Because God's sheepfold is a refuge, it isn't a prison! The house of God is a refuge, it isn't a prison, and the Door is called Jesus! If the Door is closed, we say: 'Lord, open the Door!' Jesus is the Door and lets us go in and out."

That was it. I had got what I had been waiting for. It was all about Jesus. That was no Antichrist speaking. That was not different from the Wesleyan missionary message. Only that the Pope was sitting down and delivering his message in a gentle, lowered, though impassioned, tone. If it were my father preaching, he would pace up and down in a high-toned voice and would hit the lectern for the message to sink in the congregation. That's the Wesleyan way, the Protestant way. Give the same message to American tele-evangelist T.D. Jakes; he would rain down brimstone and fire, sweating profusely. I would often think perhaps the solemnity of the Catholic Church emanated from a somewhat guilty conscience, of always having to be reminded particularly of the disgraceful killings of Apostles Peter and Paul in Rome. The ancestral guilt still haunting succeeding generations, solemnity was the only answer during Catholic mass – as opposed to the exuberant Protestant worship services celebrating the resurrected Christ. It's just my opinion.

Then followed in the Pope's homily what I would describe as a veiled description of terrorists couched in the profundity of the message: "Those who try to avoid the Door are thieves: it's curious, thieves always try to enter by another way, by the window, by the roof, but they avoid the door, because they have evil intentions, and they sneak into the sheepfold in order to deceive the sheep and take advantage of them. We must enter through the door and listen to Jesus' voice: if we hear the tone of His voice, we are certain, we are saved. We can go in without fear and go out without danger."

However, this was balanced by the fact that the Pope also had some subtle criticism for the Church which, pointing to the same Gospel of John, was the gatekeeper whose task it was to open the door for the Good Shepherd: "If the gatekeeper hears the Shepherd's voice, he opens and lets in all of the sheep that the Shepherd brings, all of them, including those lost in the wood, whom the Good Shepherd went to get back. The sheep are not chosen by the gatekeeper, they are not chosen by the parish secretary or parish administrator; the sheep are all called, they are chosen by the Good Shepherd. The gatekeeper – he too – obeys the Shepherd's voice. Thus, we can well say that we must be like that gatekeeper. The Church is the gatekeeper of the house of the Lord; she is not the proprietor of the Lord's house."

He ended the message by saying that God would not close the door on anyone who knocked "with the excuse that you are not part of the household. With this spirit let us approach the Jubilee: there will be the Holy Door, but there is the Door of the great mercy of God. May there also be the door of our heart for all to receive God's forgiveness and to give, in our turn, our forgiveness, welcoming all those who knock at our door".

Thereafter, he proceeded to convey special greetings to particular groups present. And here again Ignazio and his organisation proved how powerful and influential they were in Vatican terms. Because even though, as I would check the prepared speech later, 'Love Bridges' was not in the original script, it might have been inserted at the last moment. The pontiff actually called out 'Love Bridges' and 'Sierra Leone' among those he welcomed, together with "English-speaking pilgrims and visitors taking part in today's Audience, including those from England and the United States of America" – deflating the terrorist warning for the latter to avoid the Vatican. He also prayed for young people, the sick and newlyweds.

Love Bridges was naturally elated for this pontifical recognition during the general audience and did not mince its words in its reportage of the event on its website: "Today Love Bridges, with a large group of volunteers, took part in the General Audience of Pope Francis in St. Peter's Square. All the members of our delegation are grateful to the Holy Father for having publicly thanked us for our presence, but above all for having given us words of hope and courage to continue on the path of cooperation in Sierra Leone. At the end of the Audience, Don Ignazio Poddighe presented to the Holy Father the delegation of the two ministers of Sierra Leone, Alie Kamara (Resident Minister of the North), Sheka Tarawalie (Deputy Minister of Internal Affairs) and the four children participating in the post-Ebola welcome project (Foday, Bambay, Lamin and Israel), with a warm exchange of gifts." (Translated; as it was written in Italian on their website, www.associazionelovebridges.it).

It was through the Pope's special greetings that I knew that in actual fact this was a very special day in the Catholic calendar and, therefore, could not have been postponed for any terrorist threat: "On this day, on which we are celebrating the dedication of the Basilicas of Sts Peter and Paul, I hope for everyone that the visit to the tombs of the Apostles may strengthen the joy of the faith." We could not visit the basilica where St Paul was buried because it was not situated at the Vatican, and there was not enough time for us.

Perhaps speaking in his role as the political head of the Holy See, the Pope reminded his audience that two days ahead (20 November) would be the International Children's Rights Day and he, therefore, appealed to the International Community to "carefully watch over the living conditions of children, especially where they are exposed to recruitment by armed groups; likewise may it help families to guarantee to every boy and girl the right to school and to education".

Indeed, Pope Francis mentioned Mary, but just as a reminder that 21 November would be the anniversary of the "Presentation of the Blessed Virgin Mary in the Temple, a time to remember men and women in hermitages, monasteries, or cloisters."

And that was it. The priest on the Pope's left hand collected the speech from him and withdrew the microphone. The ceremony had finished. But not just yet. Only now, Ignazio would inform us: "Your time has come." "What do you mean?" I would immediately ask. Before Alie could join in, as his body language indicated, Ignazio explained that the moment we were waiting for was now – to actually meet with the Pope – that, we would soon be called upon to do just that. Incredible. Adding honour to beauty. The welcoming door!

Indeed, within minutes, two protocol officers approached us and asked us to follow them. Alie and I were led to the front of the canopy, standing side by side. And then the Lokomasama boys were also brought and made to stand behind us. Ignazio was now mingling with the Vatican officials. The amazement was too much for us. Alie went back to his hallucination and kept asking: "Could this be us really standing here?" And we would have to stand there for a while, because the cardinals who were sitting on the left side were scheduled to come forward and shake the Pope's hand first. They were more than twenty: and not all would be satisfied with mere hand-shaking; a few would have to say a few words, greetings or commendations – some having come from afar and were actually seeing the Pope face-to-face for the first time, as Ignazio would later explain. Alie was very impatient during this interregnum: he feared that the Pope could feel tired; therefore, when a certain cardinal would linger on with the Pope, Alie would mutter under his breath statements like "Could you please try and leave the Pope for us?" or "Can't you make an appointment to talk with the Pope later?" I had to suppress my laughter. "This cannot change again, Koth Alie," I would admonish in very low tones.

Certainly, the moment arrived. The last cardinal had made his courtesies with the pontiff. It was our turn. No, we were not meant to go meet the Pope. He would come to meet us. He walked directly to us, followed by a small retinue of officials, including Ignazio. Just as they approached us, Ignazio took the lead to do the introduction and the translation. But then two important activities could not go unnoticed: a group of journalists and photographers were let in through the barrier to come and take position almost exactly where we were sitting during the homily; and then the Corpo della Gendarmeria (Vatican police, an affiliate of the Swiss Guards) brass band trumpeted a signatory tune heralding the presence of visiting dignitaries! This was wow!

Ignazio started the introduction with Alie, who could not contain his emotions. The moment the Pope stretched out his hand and started a conversation, Alie jumped on him in a full and tight embrace, followed by his normal boisterous laughter, the photographers clicking away. As the virtual head of delegation, Alie conveyed greetings from President Koroma, thanked the Pope for the support and prayers during the Ebola crisis, while informing him that the country was now recovering and stabilising again. Alie also expressed appreciation for "the good work that Love Bridges is doing in Sierra Leone especially in the health and education sectors". The Pope then signalled to one of the officials who came with a small bag from which he removed a small box and handed it over to the Pope, who in turn gave it to Alie. It was a gift.

And then it was my turn to be introduced. Trust Ignazio, he would add something about passports facilitation. I was mesmerised while profusely shaking the Pope's hand with both hands. But the moment I opened my mouth to speak, I regained my natural boldness. I did not speak politics or about government again. I was focused on theology. I started telling the Pope how his message was very appropriate and how it touched my heart, now holding his hand with my right hand while the left was placed by the position of my heart. I told him I was not Catholic but Wesleyan; and that this encounter had only further strengthened my faith in the Lord. While I was talking, the Pope leaned on Ignazio and whispered something, pointing to me severally. The Pope then asked about my profession apart from being a government minister. I said "journalist"; and his response, according to Ignazio's interpretation, was "I knew it". I further told him I heard the information about the Islamic State threat (I would definitely not leave that out), but that "Christ has built His Church and the gates of hell shall never prevail against it." This was more than just being a journalist; and then I told him my father was a Pastor. "There you go, there you," the Pope spoke directly in English, nodding several times. He then got the same or rather similar small gift box and gave it to me with a big smile. I immediately put it in the inside pocket of my coat. The photographers could not stop the incessant flashing.

Ignazio then led him to the Lokomasama boys behind us. We all just now formed a kind of circle in the middle of St Peter's Square with everybody else watching either directly or via the giant screens or via the live Catholic TV coverage for those at home or in their offices. The pontiff gave a rosary to each of the boys and touched their heads, while they gave him a gift of soap products from the 'Love Bridges' factory in Sierra Leone. Alie would also ask the Pope to touch his head as well. The pontiff obliged. I shook my own head in laughter.

Finally, that was it. And it was more than we ever dreamt of. Together, we had about fifteen minutes with Pope Francis.

The Pope now left us and walked down the way he had come to his popemobile. But he would not just leave yet; it was a moment to go round the cheering crowds waving and passing on blessings, stopping here and there to touch a sick person or hold a child or bless a newly-wedded couple. He also stopped briefly and did the 'sign of the cross' in front of the huge banner with the inscription 'ASSOCIAZIONE LOVE BRIDGES: SIERRA LEONE.'

And then he disappeared, with the always-present jogging security round the popemobile, to the same direction from where he had initially entered the Square. And the crowd became tumultuous – everybody would now have to find their way. We had a couple of security with us and we had to join the support group. That should not be hard because they were in the front row.

But it would not be that easy. We had not fully realised what had happened and did not know how it impacted us. But as we tried to find our way down, we were reminded. As we made our way down, many people would stop us: some just wanting to shake our hands, some asking us where we were from, some requesting a photo opportunity with us, and even some newlyweds asking us to bless them. This was crazy. And we eventually managed to reach the 'Love Bridges' group. They also – well, naturally – wanted us to take pictures. And we did. And the onlookers would soon still jump in. They also wanted pictures with us. It went on and on even after the Love Bridges people and the Lokomasama boys had departed. We were exhausted as it was already lunch time; but they would not just let us go. People of all kinds of nationalities and races. Suddenly, we had become celebrities. But we were trapped with these people. Alie asked Ignazio to call on the security to help us leave. "I'm pressed. I want to use the rest room," he shouted. Only then could we be shoved away into the toilets near the gates. Alie gave a big laugh when we were in, saying: "What kind of thing is this?" Ignazio only retorted with a rhetorical question: "You don't know what has happened to you people?" Alie then asked that we lingered in the toilet for a while to allow the crowds to disperse. Alas, when we came out there were still a few who needed our attention. One woman, who looked Korean, asked that we just took a photograph with her nephew who was on a wheelchair. We couldn't say no. But after that, we were determined it was enough. We rushed out and refused any further entreaties from anyone. We were tired. We were hungry.

* * *

It was during lunch that we would open the gifts from the Pope. At the top of the white boxes was written 'MEDAGLIA PONTIFICIA – ANNO III.' Encased inside were bronze medals in coins. So lovely. Ignazio would quickly grab mine to have a thorough look. He was over-excited about it. "This is treasure," he said, noting that he wished the Pope had given him one too. He said these were medals that the Pope hardly gave out except to very important personalities and on special occasions.

And then the real thing: what was written on, and about, the medal. 'AMOREM CHRISTI IN ANIMO TENEAMVS' (translated as 'THE LOVE OF CHRIST LIVES IN US') was on one side of the coin, and the Pope's full name written on the other side with the year of his reign, 'FRANCISCVS PONT MAX ANNO III.' And then there was the accompanying explanatory brochure placed inside the box. Its front cover stated (and in English), "SECRETARIAT OF STATE – OFFICIAL ANNUAL MEDAL OF YEAR 3 OF THE PONTIFICATE OF HIS HOLINESS POPE FRANCIS – 2015 issue – Medal struck in bronze – Certificate of Authenticity – No. 0021 /4000." The inside page of the cover had what was titled 'ARTISTIC FEATURE' with the following explanation:

"*On the Front*: The Coat-of-Arms of His Holiness Pope Francis, around which is written FRANCISCUS P.M, ANNO III. Beneath is written the name of the artist... *On the Edge:* E CIVITATE VATICANA is inscribed, with the number of the medal... *On the Reverse:* The ecstasy of Saint Teresa of Avila, based on the marble statuary by Gian Lorenzo Bernini (1598-1680), located in the Church of Santa Maria della Vittoria in Rome (1647). This work evokes Saint Teresa's experience of the pure love of God. The inscription *amorem Christi in animo teneamus* is a powerful invitation to keep the love of Christ present in every circumstance of life, as 'love calls for love'. The medal was coined during the 500th anniversary of the birth of Saint Teresa of Avila, Virgin and Doctor of the Church." The next two pages read thus: "The Secretary of State Vatican City attests that this bronze medal was issued in 4,000 copies numbered from 0001 /4000 to 4000/4000" and "The Italian Polygraphic Institute and State Mint attests that the Mint has struck this medal in the declared number and with the following specifications: metal = bronze; diameter = 44 mm; weight = 40 gr." And at the back of this page was a biographical sketch of the artist, an Italian lady by the name of Alessia Di Giuseppe, born in Rome in 1990.

We were overwhelmed. I couldn't take it all in at the same time. We went back to Villa Vaticana as different people. Even multi-millionaire Stefano and his wife, with whom we had lunch together, were now more reverential to us. Our communication with them was very limited because they could hardly speak English; but they paid for the lunch. (They would on a subsequent trip invite and accommodate me at their luxurious Sardinia Island hotel). Alie was over the moon. Why not? When I sent out the information and pictures of our meeting with Pope Francis via WhatsApp and Facebook, the responses from all and sundry were just out-of-this-world. Sierra Leone, UK, America, Italy, Croatia, Australia, Thailand etc etc, even people I never knew before were sending congratulatory messages. Freetown newspapers carried these reports. No wonder the next day the then-State Chief of Protocol called me up saying we were all over the papers. She only called to ask when we would return home.

In the evening would be the time to have dinner with the support group of 'Love Bridges', meaning the whole executive was present. It was all about the great achievement registered through this historic encounter with the Pope. And each of them was thanking us: that if it were not for us, they wouldn't have received such papal recognition. But my response was to say: 'If it were not for you, we wouldn't have met the Pope.' More laughter. More drinks, more food. At some point in-between, Fr Ignazio (I was sitting next to him at table) would keep saying only to my hearing, 'Shekito, you'll go places'. Ignazio said apart from the official encounter, he thought the Pope liked what I said. How would I respond? Had I not gone places already? Was it not wonderful for the Pope to like what I said? "Nar God," I said. Ignazio also replied in Krio "Nar God o," with his infectious laugh.

We all went to bed feeling fulfilled.

* * *

It would be a year later at Banana Island in Sierra Leone (where Love Bridges has a touristic outlet) that Ignazio would tell me what Pope Francis whispered to him during our conversation. It was over a roasted crab in the quietness of the evening beach only disturbed by the waves on the shore; and Rose was meeting him for the first time.

Obviously, the meeting with the Pope had its firm roots to the presidency of Ernest Bai Koroma. We did not go to the

Vatican as real pilgrims pushed by a religious zeal. I would not have qualified, since I was not Catholic; nor would Alie Wasco, as he was a Muslim. We met the Pope as government officials with a travel clearance from the President and a *note verbale* from Sierra Leone's embassy in Brussels. The organisation that facilitated the encounter, 'Love Bridges', invited us on the basis of us having used our official positions to support their work in Sierra Leone, particularly through a relationship created with its country representative, Father Ignazio Poddighe.

Chapter Twenty-Eight

Back To Freetown, Back To Work

'Not A Saint Yet' Speech To The Sierra Leone Police As Acting Minister In Charge Of Security, In The President's Presence

The next morning we left Rome heads held high. We flew to London without incident – I slept all the way. Alie continued on to Freetown, as his wife had already gone. I would stay behind for a few days to do some official engagements and also to accompany my wife to the hospital – plus to have our now-regular get-together with daughter Marie, now a young lady studying Medicine at King's College (a leading UK and worldwide university).

On Saturday 21 November, the Permanent Secretary in the Ministry of Internal Affairs called me to enquire about when I would return (this ministry was in charge of the police, the prisons, the fire force, and immigration, among others – a counterpart of the Home Office in Britain).

"Tomorrow," I told him. "That's good sir, because we have some programmes at hand," he replied.

My wife and daughter and all our friends were very happy for me: everybody asking how I felt; or how it felt. I tried to explain; but I always said it would not be the same as when you experienced it yourself.

On Sunday, I left for Sierra Leone, my wife staying behind for a medical. But we had also been discussing my position in government. We both knew it was shaky, taking into consideration the continued strained relationship with my immediate boss, the Minister, over how to run the affairs of the ministry. It was clear that though the President had listened to my explanation, my objection, he was looking at the numbers in support of the Minister. These included leading members of the Cabinet, the leadership of the police, and the Chief Immigration Officer. Plus a powerful Lebanese man. The Lebanese, who had originally come to Sierra Leone as refugees, eventually had a stranglehold over the Sierra Leone economy – thanks to a deliberate colonial policy as punishment to the Creole merchants for their support for the 'Hut Tax War' rebellion and the post-Independence chicanery of local politicians. As Cambridge University Press-published scholar William Reno, in his book *Corruption And State Politics In Sierra Leone* (1995), in a chapter titled 'The Shadow State and international commerce,' wrote: "Lebanese businessmen increasingly acted as patrons to their politician partner-clients in this expanded Shadow-State-protected market… At the same time Lebanese businessmen extended their own economic interests which undermined the institutions and authority of state power…" My senior colleagues were in the majority in Cabinet, but as to whether their views on the passports issue resonated with the masses was a totally different question. Civil society groups advocated against the passport contract all the way to Parliament.

I told my wife I thought I might lose my job (though I didn't tell her I had written a letter of disengagement to the President). She didn't disagree – she witnessed some of the drama while in Freetown. She just prayed it would be smooth.

On the flight, quite a good number of familiar faces recognised me and were talking about the papal meeting. We reached Freetown to the same scenario of people welcoming me with gusto for having met with the Pope. At home, the boys were ecstatic: my son John Sheka (named after my father – still another of my early blessings, he is now in the same university I attended) and nephew Danny (my immediate elder sister Alice's son, also in the same university) had started WhatsApping me since I was in Rome and would not hide their admiration when I arrived. My niece Marie (whom we nicknamed Mayo, Danny's younger sister) was also on holiday. And it was all joy, joy, joy, for being in the news for the right reasons.

Monday morning I was back at work. The Permanent Secretary told me the Minister travelled out of the country and that there was a scheduled programme in Makeni to lay the foundation stone for the building of a police academy – a project we had been working on for two years. I would have to step in to give the ministerial speech, as the President would be the guest of honour.

"Great," I muttered to myself, and asked the Permanent Secretary to give me speaking notes. By the time he brought them four hours later, I had already prepared my speech – civil servants were too slow for my comfort throughout my government experience or experiment. I only added a point or two of interest from his notes. This was a decisive moment in my governance sojourn. I would say what I wanted to say and damn the expected consequences.

* * *

There was no love lost between me and the leadership of the police. This was one institution that definitely needed reform if Sierra Leone were to progress. I was very scathing about the police during my early journalistic days, especially in my 'Black Tank' column, continually holding them into account over various issues like bribery, vehicular over-speeding and over-loading, accidents, armed robbery, and treatment of suspects. And ever since I was re-assigned to the Ministry of Internal Affairs, the police bosses had found me a thorn in their sides. I would speak against corruption at meetings and urge for reforms. I would press for the enactment of the law establishing the Independent Police Complaints Board (IPCB), which most in the top leadership did not want. They thought that with the IPCB being headed by a civilian, the police force was being demeaned in the eyes of the public. I insisted it was for their good as well as for the public good. The President supported the idea, and it became a reality.

As I was chairman of the occasion to launch formally the pre-legislative nation-wide sensitisation for the setting up of the IPCB on 23 May 2013 at the British Council in Freetown, I was categorical in my speech: "The current status quo in Sierra Leone of the police investigating the police through the CDIID is certainly not enough. The public will never be satisfied if their complaints against police officers are just handled by police officers. They hardly know the difference. The problem is compounded by the fact that serving in any department in the police is rotational or moveable, meaning a police officer who is a head of Traffic today would be head of CDIID tomorrow or vice versa. The public is therefore wary of the current set up." I knew many at the top of the force were not happy with me.

They would be angrier when I stated in a well-publicised interview that police officers should not see their institution as a 'secret society'. Speaking after a nation-wide tour informing the public about the necessity of the IPCB, I told the press, published as a front-page lead ('The Police Force Is Not A Secret Society') in *The Torchlight* on 6 June 2013: "We must admit that there was or has been a great chasm, a sea of suspicion, between the people and the police. The general public is apprehensive of the police; and some police officers have not helped matters by seeing themselves as members of a secret society who should stand by their colleagues at all cost… If a policeman sees another policeman wronging civilians, let him stand up to his colleague, and not cover him up just because they are all wearing the same uniform or because they want to protect the image of the police. That is not how to protect the image of the police. You protect the image of the police by telling those who are undermining its ideals to stop or go out of the force. You don't do a cover-up and think you are protecting the image of the police. You are merely exposing your institution to public ridicule and derision."

I would also have problems with the police with regards the procurement of security scanners which turned out to be faulty. I refused to sign the PETS forms to effect payment. They had to take them to the Minister. And then when I broached the idea of bringing traffic lights to replace or reduce the traffic police officers on the streets, it was like waging a war. There was too much opposition from some sections of the police, because I wanted to 'take bread from their mouth'. The police in Sierra Leone were known for collecting bribes from drivers and had amassed ill-gotten wealth through that – a much-publicised 2016 report titled CRITICAL PERSPECTIVES OF GOVERNANCE (VOL. 6), sub-titled 'Corruption Stops With Us: Ending Bribery For Traffic Offences In Sierra Leone' by a coalition of civil society and media activists, the Citizens Agenda for Prosperity (CAP), stated, among other things: "An estimated Le81 billion was paid to traffic officials in bribes to settle traffic offences in the last twelve months. This means that government is losing Le700 billion of domestic revenue from unpaid fines as the monies do not go through official revenue channels." The traffic lights idea would, consequently, asphyxiate their daily bread (as if they were not on salary – in fact, they were even being provided with a monthly bag of rice each like the soldiers plus other amenities including new sets of uniform). It was, therefore, a herculean task to get them on board. But the President had bought the idea and gave it the go-ahead, under the supervision of first the Office of the Chief of Staff and later the Strategy & Policy Unit at State House.

While some sections of the police were never happy with me, it must be stated that the then-Inspector General of Police, Francis Munu, was very cooperative and ensured his officials participated in all the processes and meetings. By his directives, the police even provided storage for the equipment. The opponents within the force were, however, disproportionately in the majority. Some were so desperate that they even crossed administrative boundaries and took sides on the passports issue.

And now I would have to address the Sierra Leone Police (SLP) in the presence of the President for the first time. When would such an opportunity arise again? I knew only too well that it would never come that easy again – if it ever would. In actual fact, the Minister, being an old man, hardly travelled (I would remember only having to attend Cabinet twice throughout my tenure, because those were the only times he missed it). Beyond that, my future in government was clearly hanging in the balance: the forces against me were too many and too powerful – and the President had read the situation in line with the axiom of politics being a game of numbers. Our body languages were adrift of each other even in conversation – but he never told me I did, or was doing, anything wrong. That was who he was. Therefore, whatever I ever wanted to say to the police, I had to say it in this speech – knowing that the President could act on my letter at any time. It was a tough call; but it was not as tough as having had to go to jail for writing articles. Here, they would be angry; but they would not arrest me.

Speech read, re-read, ready. Makeni, here I come.

I arrived on the morning of the very Tuesday. The President had a couple of other programmes lined up for the morning; ours was in the afternoon. So I had time to go to see my parents first. They were so excited about the Rome visit, as I took time to explain the biblical connection: about the book of Romans in the Bible, about Apostles Peter and Paul having been buried there, about the Pope being like the modern-day Peter, about the grandeur of the Vatican etc etc. And my sister Rebecca's son, Sembu (staying with my parents and in senior secondary school), would ask questions whose answers had already been given in the explanation – with my younger sister, Esther (I call her 'a missionary nurse' because she treats many with illneses in the village without pay) listening attentively in the background without a question.

I spoke to the President on the phone through Alie who was with him (as always when the President was in Makeni), telling him about the papal encounter and that I would go ahead to the foundation stone ceremony instead of attending the morning programmes. He agreed.

* * *

The whole leadership of the Sierra Leone Police – east, west, north, and south – was present. Dignitaries, foreign and local, diplomats and academics, were in attendance. Ministers, Members of Parliament, all the retinue of supporters and praise-singers that followed the President everywhere were on call. I arrived early enough to have a chit-chat with the Permanent Secretary and the Inspector General of Police. They showed me the programme and told me I would have to take the ministerial salute from a dais created for the occasion during a police march-past at some point, but that I would be alerted. They showed me my seat – next to the President, on his right hand; the Inspector General would be on his left. Very soon I was called upon to mount the dais. I stood there as the police brass band and a column of the rank and file marched past, faces turning to me, right hands in salute position by the foreheads. That was done with. Back to my seat.

Before long, the President and entourage arrived. I stood up to greet him as the national anthem was played as per protocol. As we took our seats, I started a conversation about the papal visit immediately. I told him it was in itself refreshing and it was worth taking. He looked me straight in the eye and nodded. He was going to say something; but at that very moment his ADC called his attention to something else, whispering in his ear. The next moment, the occasion was called to order; the programme started. The Chairman of the occasion was the then-Minister of Information, Alpha Kanu, known for his colourful oratory. He would intersperse the programme with jokes and stories. Various speakers came before me, including the Inspector General and the Pro-Chancellor of the University of Sierra Leone. The President would speak after me.

So the moment, my moment, arrived. I opened my presentation, Roman-style, with 'Friends, Sierra Leoneans, Countrymen…' and maintained the Mark-Anthony style to the end. The speech which, indeed, received applauses from some members of the general audience, is worth producing verbatim. The police were stung; stunned, my informants within the force would later update me. I spoke with an evangelical voice – the Protestant in me; knowing that this could be my last speech to them in that position. And so it turned out…

SPEECH BY THE AG. MINISTER OF INTERNAL AFFAIRS SHEKA TARAWALIE AT THE LAYING OF THE FOUNDATION STONE FOR THE CONSTRUCTION OF THE SIERRA LEONE POLICE'S PEACEKEEPING AND LAW ENFORCEMENT ACADEMY, 24 NOVEMBER 2015

His Excellency, the President Dr. Ernest Bai Koroma,

Friends, Sierra Leoneans, Countrymen

I'm just coming from Rome, so please permit me, Mr President, to do things as the Romans do.

So Friends, Sierra Leoneans, Countrymen

Though I've just come from seeing the Pope, I cannot make any attempt to play God here. Some people have now started calling me Saint Sheka (as I also hear some are calling my co-pilgrim, the Resident Minister North Alie D. Kamara, a Catholic – though the man is Muslim). But I've told them, like St. Paul of biblical times, that I've not yet attained perfection, but just striving – like all of us do – towards the goal.

Therefore, had I got the magic wand, we wouldn't have been here, as I would just have conjured up a crime-free, corrupt-free society. But we are all still just human – still living in an imperfect world; and it is for that reason we are gathered here today to turn the sod for the construction of an edifice that would serve as a reservoir from which knowledge is gotten to protect our common humanity. With this proposed peacekeeping and law-enforcement academy, the police will have more time to do a more professional job, they are going to have more time to do a more thorough job, more time to be more citizen-friendly, and more time to be more robust and proactive on crime.

This does not mean the police have not been doing a good job. They have. That's why we call them 'A force for good'. And just last Friday the President was commending the leadership of the SLP for the visible structural and infrastructural innovations in the force during the commissioning of three other laudable projects by the police in the western area. We want to doff our hats to the leadership and general personnel of the SLP. We want to also thank them for the sterling support to the nation during the Ebola outbreak. They also generally exemplified themselves as peacekeeping officers abroad.

Friends, Sierra Leoneans, countrymen

To be 'A Force for Good' is good. But our current geo- and socio-political circumstances are yearning for 'A force for Best'. That is why, in that same speech last Friday, President Koroma noted that the general populace is concerned about the seeming growing threats of gangs and cliques and other forces of darkness. The President invariably told us that despite the peace and quiet being currently maintained, there's a latent disease that must be tackled headlong. We are all not new to heartrending stories of despicable crimes – every other month or every other season we hear these stories: if you don't hear about a gang member stabbing a rival gang member, you'll hear about a DJ being murdered at a birthday party; if you don't hear about a young girl having been murdered and dumped on the beach, you'll hear about a female police officer stabbing a male officer; if you don't hear about an OSD officer shooting to death another OSD officer, you'll hear about a police couple on international peacekeeping duties bringing the whole force into disrepute in a pornographic scandal. One fish, just one herring, spoils the lot.

And this, I know, pains His Excellency the President at heart. So even though he has just recently established a functioning

Independent Police Complaints Board, the President believes that is not enough to bring out the best from our men and women in blue. Therefore, as a President who believes in being pro-active and pro-people, he has, through 'the Agenda for Prosperity', via the Ministry of Internal Affairs, gathered us here today for the laying of the foundation stone for the construction of an academy that has the potential of continually equipping police personnel with the knowledge required to do their duties in a democratic and 21st-century fashion.

Consequently, this academy will be a testament to the government's acknowledgment of the crucial role the police have to play in a democracy and how the force is strategic to our hope for the continuity of our very existence as a people. Government knows that the knowledge to be acquired from this academy, by enhancing the capacity of those entrusted with the responsibility to protect lives and property, will benefit us all.

From this academy, police officers will learn and appreciate the nobility of their profession and will know that there's more to life than the vain search for material benefits, that a good name should be preferred over materialism. This academy, when completed, will offer frequent refresher-training courses for all cadres of personnel. The leadership of the police must be commended for having come this far without a collapse of the system. And it is more commendable that the police leadership has seen the need for a police academy and that Inspector General Francis Munu and his able Executive Management Board have been working tirelessly to ensure it is implemented.

By establishing this academy, the Sierra Leone Police is putting training and development opportunities at the doorsteps of its personnel to help them reach the ideals of their noble profession, fostering a culture where learning and intellectual development will bring benefits, including:

- Increased motivation leading to increased productivity
- A competent work-force leading to fewer mistakes
- Improved working practice leading to lower operational costs
- A happier nationalistic force leading to better inter-departmental collaboration and national serenity.

Therefore, through this academy, the presence of the police should be felt by the ordinary citizens – the presence of the police should not only be felt by taxi drivers, poda-poda drivers or truck drivers. Street-to-street policing, village-to-village policing, round-the-clock random car-stopping policing, house-searching policing, stringent border policing (on our air, land, and sea borders) – in an independent, neutral and professional manner – must be felt across the length and breadth of Sierra Leone.

Friends, Sierra Leoneans, countrymen,

Recent events in Lebanon, France and Mali must wake us up to the realities of the day. We are in a global village. We are in the age of terrorism. We cannot hide from that fact; we can't run away from it; we cannot pretend ignorance. Therefore, to make ourselves more secure, and to create a more civilised society, we need a modern, knowledgeable, high-tech police force.

Just the other day I was reading in the newspapers a serialised article by the former Mayor of Freetown Winstanley Bankole Johnson, with the theme 'eternal vigilance is the price we have to pay for our liberty'. I cannot agree more. Our liberty is at stake if we do not remain eternally vigilant. We believe in God! We all believe in God, we say! Fine, great, beautiful. It's amazing to believe in God. But God has also given us the knowledge to do our humanly best for our general safety. Where would God be worshipped more piously than in the Vatican? But the place is surrounded by arguably the thickest fence in history and continually being guarded by no-nonsense, no-smiling, Swiss Guards.

So this our excuse of 'God dae' ' leh we bear,God dae', in trying to run away from our responsibilities as a nation and as a people, must not be continued to be used to sacrifice eternal vigilance. This country needs more administrative policies that have to be implemented. All those familiar with the Exodus story know that God told Moses (whom our Muslim brothers and sisters call 'Anabi Musa') to use the rod that was in his hand to part the waters so that the Israelites would pass through the Red Sea. Therefore, it is the thinking of His Excellency the President that we have to make use of our God-given abilities to make a better and prosperous Sierra Leone. He believes that faith without works is dead. In other words, 'action pass intention'.

In this day and age of terrorism, we can't afford to be taken unawares; we can't be caught sitting on our oars. We must move with the times; we must strengthen our internal surveillance system; we must boost our external networking and intelligence systems. To achieve this, we need a modern police force, we require a knowledgeable police, a force that's willing and ready to live up to the calling and rise to the occasion. President Koroma believes this academy will open the doors for such capacity-building. In that regard, this academy may well be on the path to restoring Sierra Leone's educational sector to its former 'Athens of West Africa' status, as it is poised to attract interests from other countries in the sub region. I want to believe that experts, consultants, interns, sabbatical scholars, tutors and others will be coming here from all over the world to impart knowledge of international standards in policing.

Friends, Sierra Leoneans, countrymen,

One thing I want to remind you before I take my seat is about Sierra Leone. This country was founded on the basis of being a light to other nations. We are a chosen generation, we are a special nation, we are a selected people created to make a change for generations yet unborn and for people in far-away lands. We cannot – and we should not – allow cliques and gangs and cartels, both local and foreign, both outwardly violent and passively demagogic, to hold us hostage or to hold us to ransom or to blackmail us. We must rise to the occasion. We cannot settle for less. We should not be satisfied with mediocrity. We want more. We want more development. We want more of a better Sierra Leone. We want more time.

Now, Your Excellency, permit me to quote the American Criminal Justice Police Instructor Lt. Andrew G. Hawkes who wrote: "Without properly trained police officers, our society could not successfully function. Police officers must be trained extensively in state law, evidence handling, prisoner transport, handcuffing, defensive tactics, firearms, driving, customer service and many other areas of law enforcement."

Friends, Sierra Leoneans, countrymen,

As His Excellency the President today lays the foundation stone for the construction of the Sierra Leone Police's peacekeeping and law-enforcement academy, let us not forget that the stone that the builders may want to reject can, all of a sudden, become the head of the corner.

God bless

God bless Sierra Leone

Epilogue

Out Of Government; Back To My First Love – Journalism

Corruption And The Lebanese Stranglehold; The Tribalism Conundrum; What Life Taught President Siaka Stevens; The Church Can Do Better; Still Wesleyan...

Four months after I made that speech in Makeni, I was out of government.

The writing was clearly on the wall when the State House Communications Unit (whose foundation I had laid as the first-ever Press Secretary of Sierra Leone and the last of that administration) did not mention me nor the speech I had made at the ceremony in the official report disseminated to the public. The independent press did though – the centrist *Awoko* newspaper, reporting in its 27 November 2015 edition with the headline 'President Koroma turns sod for police academy in Bombali', quoted me extensively, appropriately referring to me as 'the acting Minister of Internal Affairs'.

In a late-night Cabinet reshuffle on Sunday 13 March 2016 (earlier that day, I had gone to the same Kissy Dockyard Wesleyan Church where the President and I used to worship together), it pleased President Koroma to let me go. The official relationship had reached its tether, as at one point before that I had, on my own volition, stopped going to work – due to the growing gloomy relationship with the Minister over how to implement policies. A close confidante of the President had asked me to tender my resignation if I felt so strongly that I could no longer work within the prevailing circumstances. I told her I would not do that, as it would put me in bad light. I would rather the President took the action, as I had indicated in my letter to him. And he did. Fine by me. Interestingly, he removed the Minister as well, alongside some others.

After the announcement that night, I sent the President a text thanking him for giving me the opportunity to serve my country, and that I did it to my utmost ability, God being my helper.

But many members of the public were apparently dismayed. When I posted on Facebook a reassuring message two days later with just the words 'I know who I am', responses of support and comfort poured in from both sides of the political divide – SLPP as well as APC. Most people had seen me as 'the political son' of the President and were, therefore, surprised that he who was once the face and voice of the presidency from being Press Secretary to the President to Deputy Minister of Information and Communications and to Deputy Minister of Internal Affairs was no longer to play a part in the government. The man who had been the unofficial link between me and the President, the late Ambassador Siray Timbo (who was there that day when the President appointed me over the phone and had subsequently codenamed it as 'the tripartite relationship'), while visiting me at home, said this could be 'the gravest mistake the President has made'. It certainly was not.

But you would be surprised to know that the President and I continued to maintain a healthy personal relationship – perhaps a better one, with frequent visits. I even interviewed him for the purpose of this book after I left office. In fact, the President assured me the action was a temporary measure, as he had something in store for me. I believed him. And what nudged me on was when he allowed me to pursue my original idea of the traffic lights project as presidential liaison. This was not a paid-for job, but since I was already on a state pension, I was comfortable as long as it was to ensure my initiative came to fruition. It entailed frequently updating him on developments and bringing together all the stakeholders under the supervision of the Strategy and Policy Unit, Office of the Chief of Staff, at State House.

The President and I were opening up to each other again. Two months after the reshuffle, he nominated me as the media person in a government delegation to Turkey, led by then-Foreign Minister, Dr Samura Kamara, whom he would a few months later announce as the presidential candidate for the then-ruling APC.

* * *

But let me take a few moments to relate the intrigues and shenanigans in Sierra Leonean politics. And it still has to do with the traffic lights project. It was my initiative, as already mentioned, and endorsed by the President. But very soon others would have to be involved because it bore the nomenclature of a presidential project. Soonest, as ingrained in the Sierra Leonean sub-culture, scheming would start on how to supplant me or scrap the project or bring in another company altogether. False allegations were directed against me as if I had done something wrong – a story was dished out that I had been paid thousands of dollars for the project. The radio station, Radio Democracy FM 98.1, which was once at the forefront of calling me a 'rebel collaborator', this time round used a phantom satirical slot called 'daddy wakabot' to demonise me continually. My denial – even after explaining in person at their studios, accompanied by the company's Croatian executives – did not stop the attacks. They claimed that the equipment and services were overpriced, taunting that 'only two traffic lights cost hundreds of thousands of dollars'. Even a failed opposition presidential candidate swallowed the hoax.

The reality was that, I did not know of – nor still do I know of – any other government project that was subjected to the most stringent of scrutiny. Every relevant department or agency was involved under the auspices of State House: Ministry of Finance, Ministry of Transport, Ministry of Internal Affairs, Ministry of Energy, Ministry of Works, Sierra Leone Roads Authority, Sierra Leone Road Safety Authority, Law Officers Department, National Public Procurement Authority, and Sierra Leone Police. I was liaising. Everything was done accordingly since inception. But Radio Democracy's 'wakabot' would have none of this.

And this is in no way an attempt to dismiss or diminish the importance or popularity of Radio Democracy. If there has ever been a successful outcome to the Machiavellian theory of 'the end justifies the means', this radio station is the clearest example. Before, during and after President Kabbah was reinstated (in the name of democracy – 'democracy by force?' as asked by current Speaker of Parliament Dr Abass Bundu in his book), atrocities were committed at the radio station's behest or collusion (they read out a list of 'collaborators' to be taught a lesson). Certainly, elements of the AFRC/RUF were committing bestialities, and it was good to report them. But some of the kamajors and ECOMOG interventionist soldiers were too. One of the Nigerian soldiers was notoriously nicknamed 'evil spirit' for his impetuosity in extra-judicial killings. But all was covered up, nothing ever reported by Radio Democracy until UK-based Sierra Leonean journalist Sorious Samura sneaked into the country and did a documentary, 'Cry Freetown', which exposed the interventionists' atrocities to the outside world.

Notwithstanding, the eventual reversal of the AFRC coup via foreign military intervention (even without a UN legal mandate and therefore 'illegal' – like then-UN Secretary General Kofi Annan would later describe the US-led intervention in Iraq in 2003) was as much a credit to Radio Democracy as it was to General Sanni Abacha's Nigerian forces. However circuitous and painful the route, when the history of the democracy that we ended up with and are enjoying today is written, they will be remembered in some section. And, to this day, the station's 'Good Morning Salone' programme remains the most listened-to by Sierra Leoneans at home and abroad. However, either by design or by coincidence, there was an apparent campaign of calumny against me – before and now – the radio station being the conduit. Interestingly, Station Manager Asmaa James is a friend (her husband a university pal), just as Julius Spencer (Station Manager during the war) was a well-liked university lecturer of mine! It made me wonder more about human nature in both instances – although the character playing the part of 'daddy wakabot' was later changed, not knowing though for what reason.

Some powerful men in government and some Lebanese businessmen were also behind this. It was in vain to have continued denying. I just kept my cool, not responding to the attacks – knowing the truth. I didn't want to put the investors on a collision course with the authorities. All I knew was that – as it was proven in two audits set up to that effect, on top of an endorsement by the procurement authority – the company presented reasonable and internationally competitive prices.

And interestingly, in the end, when the APC lost the 2018 elections, the story about 'the traffic lights scandal' had become so ingrained as truth that the new SLPP government's transition report, indeed, stated that money had been paid. Though neither my name nor the Croatian company, Elektromodul Promet, was mentioned in the report. Elektromodul had, in fact, demonstrated tremendous goodwill by honouring government's request to pre-finance the pilot phase. This was to showcase the project's necessity and advantages, and to teach the public on how to use them. Traffic lights disappeared in Sierra Leone during the war – a whole new generation of drivers or road users in general, not conversant with the rules, had emerged. In short, until the time the new government came in, not a single cent had been paid to the company. Both the Ministry of Finance and the Ministry of Transport were embarrassed by the GTT (Government Transition Team) report, as officials told the visiting Chief Executive Officer of the company, Martina Gjergja, that they were not consulted before publication.

In Sierra Leone, there is what they call the 'PHD (Pull Him Down)' syndrome. It was at play here.

Thankfully, the leadership of Elektromodul had faith in my integrity. They knew that, if anything, it had been my own money that I had been using to meet local needs, just to ensure that the project succeeded. They, therefore, rejected all suggestions to the contrary. Those who planned to abort the project failed, because the lights came on and functioned effectively ('daddy wakabot's litany of lies included a claim that the lights were installed without roads authority permission and that they were mal-functional – to its credit, the station sent a reporter when the lights were turned on). The new government was obliged to pay – having already written in the transition report that the lights had been paid for! And, graciously, they saw the need and advantages of continuing with the project and included it in the 2019 budget. You can't have a wife from Rwanda and not think progressively to catch up with your in-laws! The 'Pull Him Down' syndrome had failed here!

Though undaunted, I was a bit flabbergasted about the traffic lights affair. I wondered why such a public-friendly 'presidential' project was being subjected to rather inexplicable hurdles, even at official level. A project which was supposed to have started full-scale within months couldn't get its pilot phase paid-for two years down the line. I was flabbergasted. A powerful cabal was trying to smother a fine project.

In retrospect, however, I would fall back on my belief in God's hand in my affairs. Had the previous government actually paid and proven, it was clear that my name would have been on the list of former government officials banned from travelling. I would have also been slated for a commission of enquiry by the new administration through the self-same transition report's recommendations. In fact, my exoneration was double-edged: the report was scathing about the passport contract, which was described in terms of being against the state's interests. The Minister had passed away before the elections that brought in the Bio government, which set out to review the contract.

* * *

Notwithstanding the circumstances, I was personally in support of the APC party's choice of a presidential candidate purely as a form of political loyalty. I was, however, not at the forefront of campaigning (I was away for most of that period and only returned three days to polling day). My newspaper was unequivocal in promoting Dr Samura Kamara, who, I must reveal, was the first to tell me about his ambition to succeed President Koroma during our trip to Turkey. I had supported him on the basis of being the 'cleaner' candidate in terms of past activities in government (Bio's first stint was riddled with corruption allegations – not least to have come from the man who took over from him, President Tejan Kabbah of the very SLPP which Bio is leading today).

But I had great misgivings about Samura during the first-ever 'official' presidential debate. He made startling revelations that, when he was Financial Secretary, about 18 million dollars had been squandered by Bio as then-military Head of State. 'Why has Samura not made this revelation all these years?' was my instinctive question – and was even generally topical and debated afterwards. It gave me goose-bumps. Apart from that, I had a few reservations about our candidate: in his long career in governance, he had never portrayed himself as a politician (apart from building an APC office in his hometown) but as a technocrat. Perhaps my greatest personal unease about a potential Samura presidency was my having refused a membership offer to the Masonic lodge. He tried to convince me in Turkey, with photographs. I was certainly impressed by the immaculate dresses, but I said I could not. This was purely based on my personal religious beliefs. I had refused to join any fraternity club at the university – though approaches were made. I would not now. Not when I had read Brooke Kroeger's *Undercover Reporting – The Truth About Deception* (Northwestern University Press, 2012) which was far from complimentary about the Masonic lodges in America with regards the revelations of William Morgan and newspaper publisher David Cade Miller. Of course, in Sierra Leone membership of a Masonic lodge is more a social thing.

But the question still lurked in me: if Dr Samura Kamara became President, how would I be? I just trusted God while supporting! But I was not as enthusiastic as I had been known before. I was not included in his campaign's media team anyway.

However, Samura cannot be regarded as down and out in the politics of Sierra Leone – though having been named in the transition report. He has this amiable and meek character, soft-spoken as well, that easily endears him to the ordinary man and woman. How he emerged as candidate from nowhere and nearly won the elections was incredible. Maybe if the internal post-elections rumblings within the APC subside and he again re-emerges as candidate, it is very possible that he can do better than last time – if there is no Guy Warrington or Nfa Alie. Samura was in actual fact the more loveable candidate during the presidential debate – the honest one (when asked whom to blame for the extreme poverty in the country, he said 'governments'. Critics cutting the 's' off, it was used against him as the then-government candidate). The recent public show of his engagement in farming activities has made him even more endearing to the ordinary person.

But you cannot underestimate the will of current President Maada Bio to get a second term. A man who handed over power as a military man, promising to come back and did 22 years later, beating a ruling party candidate, will never be an easy opponent when he is already on the seat. He would now have the incumbency advantage, with state paraphernalia at his beck and call.

And if Samura, in his late 70s, should again emerge as APC candidate, that would be the last political fight of his life. Win or lose.

* * *

Immediately after the announcement of the results, seeing the violence that erupted and the mayhem caused on opposition (APC) supporters mainly in the south-east of the country (not sparing members of the security forces seen as supporters of the past administration), I ordered the suspension of my newspaper's operations. The Independent Media Commission tried to pursue the paper about articles that were critical of then-opposition candidate now President Bio. They wrote a summons. I made a written submission and left for the UK. They could not continue as they were all sacked by the new administration anyway – the 'wind of change' of sackings blowing across all sectors not leaving those who wanted to clutch on to the fringes of the new government.

On the post-elections violence, although President Bio belatedly formed an inter-party committee for investigation, nothing has actually come out of it. No one has been arrested nor prosecuted, even with overwhelming evidence of video-recordings and photographs circulated on social media. It's politics. Bio supporters claimed something like that happened after they lost in 2007. Does it always have to be like that?

In actual fact, I would have been tempted to take over the running of the newspaper – but by criticising the regime at such a time, I would be seen as a sore loser trying to undermine their efforts for political gains. This was more so when some of the officials of the new administration were actually my university mates – I sat in the same class with Vice President Juldeh Jalloh and Minister of Information Mohamed Rado Swarray (who was one of my closest pals in the university; as we used to visit his eastern city hometown of Kenema for fun – we are still buddies), while Chief Minister David Francis was also our senior just as earlier-mentioned-Ambassador-to-Geneva Lans Gberie. Deputy Minister of Transport Sadiq Sillah was my next-door flat-mate, Minister of Development Nabeela Tunis a faculty acquaintance, while Deputy Minister of Local Government Philip T. Tondoneh was at one time a block-mate.

Furthermore, I had over the years mentored journalists who, as a result, write quite like me. The one who prides himself on that the most – and justifiably so – is Mohamed Sankoh who uses the pen-name of 'One Drop' and now runs his own newspaper, *The Nationalist*. If there's any journalist I brought from the cradle, it's him. He was in the sixth form then and a great admirer of the 'Black Tank' (to this day he calls me 'the greatest of all the tanks'). He came looking for me at *Concord Times* to express that, and to say he was interested in writing. I swept him along into *The Torchlight* as a cub reporter. He had a start-up difficulty with sub editors, but he would seek solace in me. I liked editing late into the night: and Sankoh would sit through it with me, asking questions as to why I changed a particular word or phrase or sentence or paragraph. I would explain. He rose to become Managing Editor of the newspaper – but not before having had to flee like all the other workers of *The Torchlight* when the Abacha-led military intervention succeeded. When we survived and I eventually relocated to Manchester, Mohamed Sankoh came to ask more questions. At present, he is arguably the most prolific Sierra Leonean feature writer, churning out incisive articles week in week out in his 'One Drop' column. Just 'One Drop' from the 'Black Tank'. The man has been imitating me so much that he is today driving an old white car that looks almost exactly like the one we had (donated by Dr Abass Bundu) when we started *The Torchlight* and nicknamed it 'kamajor' (always expect engine problems and smoky) – and this imitation coming on the heels of Sankoh having worked at State House as a researcher for two years, just to keep with our mantra of better be content with what you have and sleep soundly than have many contents but can't sleep when you want to. And what I really have never understood is when he keeps saying that what he learnt from me, he never leant from universities – and that's after he had studied at FBC and the University of Leeds (UK) while working for *The Torchlight*.

Two or three more editors of newspapers are by and large my protégés. Sallieu Tejan Jalloh founded *The Times* directly from *The Torchlight* after serving for several years starting from reporter to Acting Editor. Dauda Musa Bangura, whom I brought from radio broadcasting to the newspaper world, went on to open *The Owl*. Sallieu Sesay, whom I took on while he was still at the university, would establish an online newspaper. There were other journalists telling truth to power. With them doing the criticising and holding the new leaders to account, it was better I concentrated on writing this book.

* * *

The country has now returned to normalcy, and the new regime is trying to have a foothold in governance. Their fight against corruption in the form of probing the activities of the former regime has been commended as much as condemned – depending on which side of the political divide one stands. President Bio (a political born-again in anti-corruption, if President Kabbah – or even his former Vice President Solomon Berewa who, when he was Attorney General, said he had the evidence of the former military leaders' corruption – were to be believed) does not seem to want to relent, in the midst of opposition cries of a witch-hunt. And the Catholic Bishops (his religious constituency) seem to firmly – though cautiously – be behind him on that. It was the only subject on which they quoted Pope Francis when they met with the President.

It would be a herculean task to eradicate corruption and bring genuine development to Sierra Leone. If you are to succeed with the politicians, you have to succeed with the Lebanese merchants and contractors. When former Vice President Victor Foh (later to be charged for corruption in the hajj-gate scandal) deputised for President Koroma in opening a consulate in Beirut in mid-2016, one of the issues potential Lebanese investors raised was that of the ambiguous and unscrupulous activities of some local Lebanese. The posting of a Lebanese Ambassador who wanted to change the status quo in Sierra Leone received a rude shock with open hostilities with local Lebanese leaders, causing the premature departure of the envoy. The same old Shadow State lives with us.

A notable microcosm of the bigger picture occurred as recently as September 2018 when a Lebanese man, Yusif Antar (of course, with a Sierra Leonean passport), was caught at Lungi airport trying to board an Air Maroc flight to Lebanon with a bag full of foreign currencies (hundreds of thousands of pounds, euros, and dollars) at a time when the local currency, the Leone, was suffering a battering in the foreign exchange market since the new government took over and the Central Bank had just auctioned some of its foreign currencies to try to salvage the falling Leone. Leonbanon – journalist Olu Gordon would say.

Though Sierra Leone hosts thousands of Lebanese, there has been little sign of integration. Most, if not all, fluently speak the Krio language (and for those in the provinces an additional local language of the area) – but that's about where the integration stops. They claim to be Sierra Leonean, but marriage with locals, especially for the females, is strictly forbidden. A big barrier to real integration. Marriage can change perceptions; and there is hardly an institution better than the family in sharing values (on very rare occasions one would hear about a lone Lebanese woman breaking taboo to marry a Sierra Leonean man – with all the risks of ostracism involved). Most, if not all, of their children attend Lebanese International School (the name by itself is racially discriminatory) from primary to secondary school. Patterned after the London GCSE, not the West African curriculum, I taught there for one year. Being one of the best-paid jobs for a graduate (I preferred it to a Teaching Assistant offer at the university), I needed some money to bail out my struggling parents. Being a very expensive private school, only the children/wards of wealthy Sierra Leoneans could afford it. They were very few. I resigned, to the dismay of the female Lebanese Principal Najat Suleiman. She offered to pay me more to stay – but I respectfully turned down the offer in order to concentrate on journalism. Teaching English and Literature, marking papers was boring for me. I wanted self-satisfaction, which I could only find in journalism, in writing.

* * *

Celebrated Sierra Leonean journalist, the late Olu Gordon, termed Sierra Leone's socio-political state of affairs as 'Leonbanon' (that Sierra Leone, a country in Africa, was virtually owned by the Lebanese). Gordon's campaign, in the Paul-Kamara-edited *For Di People* newspaper, was simple: Sierra Leone would not claim true independence without economic independence; and that the economy remaining in the hands of the Lebanese was neo-colonialism. Having transformed themselves from coral-beads street-selling refugees to the wealthiest class through a British colonial bank-loan scheme that favoured them, the Lebanese can today stand up to anybody, perhaps to any government. The cries of local domestic workers (or of those taken to Lebanon, or of Sierra Leonean girls in relationships with Lebanese men) about bullying, racism, and poor welfare have gone largely ignored by the ruling class.

University-don-turned-journalist Olu Gordon was saying that praying against this alone was not enough; some practical action would have to be taken. This reminded me poignantly of something South African liberation struggle icon Nelson Mandela wrote in his book, *Long Walk To Freedom*. Mandela was referring to an occasion when he addressed pastors in Cape Town (South Africa) in the struggle against apartheid. This was what he wrote in part six titled, 'The Black Pimpernel' (Chapter 40): "The opening prayer of one of the ministers has stayed with me over these many years and was a source of strength at a difficult time. He thanked the Lord for His bounty and goodness, for His mercy and His concern for all men. But then he took the liberty of reminding the Lord that some of His subjects were more downtrodden than others. The minister then said that if the Lord did not show a little more initiative in leading the black man to salvation, the black man would have to take matters into his own hands. Amen."

Renowned scholar William Reno's *Corruption and State Politics In Sierra Leone* was not complimentary about the status quo under first APC President Siaka Stevens (my namesake, as the policemen taking me from Parliament to prison had called him and would have felt more justified had they known that my Christian name was the alliterative 'Stephen' – which I rarely used): "Loan procurement tied the Lebanese business network and the Shadow State more closely to one another. Private dealers' management of the diamond industry, coupled with their overseas contacts, enabled them to negotiate, and in some cases provide collateral for official loans..."

Stevens himself, at the twilight of his reign, after presiding over the country's politics for about two decades, wrote a book, *What Life Has Taught Me* (1984, Kensal Press), and related a humbling experience, as he wrote: "I am convinced that God's help is freely available to all those who genuinely seek it. Rejecting it, I feel, is not a sign of strength, but one of extreme presumption bordering on reckless folly, for history is yet to identify the man or woman who never made a serious mistake and never needed moral and spiritual support from a superior force outside his or her comprehension. But life has also taught me that what most of us can expect from God is strength and guidance rather than miracles." On the plus side,

Stevens was credited to have laid the foundation for Sierra Leone's infrastructural development. A man full of common sense – one must admit (even if it was used for self-service at times) – he remains thus far the only former Sierra Leonean leader to have been Chairman of the Organisation of African Unity (OAU – later changed to African Union). The conference of Heads of State was hosted in Freetown in 1980 – the effects of which are still very much with us. The bungalows built to accommodate the visiting dignitaries are still called 'OAU villas' – now being rented out to citizens (I am a long-serving tenant, staying in the villa that was occupied by Zimbabwe's Robert Mugabe, who was the newest Head of State at the time). The area itself is still referred to as OAU Village. Furthermore, at the centre of Freetown is OAU Drive: the Vice President's Office is located there. But the Lebanese question and corruption allegations never went away, even regarding the hosting of the OAU conference itself. Stevens died a lonely man, swindled by his Lebanese friends and abandoned by his political protégés.

In a profile of Afro-Lebanese businessman Jamil Sahid Mohamed under the Stevens administration, popular local historian C. Magbaily Fyle in his book, *A Historical Dictionary of Sierra Leone*, writes that: "By the end of the 1970s, Jamil was influencing government and ministerial appointments, and he was dreaded, feared or admired, depending on the perceptions of the viewer."

Reno summarised the situation thus: "Lebanese businessmen from this financial network also organised joint ventures with foreigners to the advantage of themselves and foreign contractors. Politicians acted as partners in these deals…" Things have hardly changed since. The rumours within government circles at our time were that Lebanese contracts (or contracts where Lebanese acted as middlemen) would always be inflated five times the actual cost. No wonder they thought it would be the same for the Croatian traffic lights project!

Though late President Kabbah did not categorically name the Lebanese in his memoir, *Coming Back from the Brink in Sierra Leone,* he was apparently alluding to them when describing the state of corruption in relation to public officials: "Grand corruption is more serious because it permeates the highest levels of State and public administration, and involves high-ranking government officials, including Cabinet ministers. These people use their positions to defraud the nation of large sums of money and convert public property to their personal use. The illegal trading in diamonds and other precious minerals falls within this category. So is the practice of 'percentage' offered by unscrupulous business people..." But his actions spoke louder when he deported 22 'unscrupulous' Lebanese, stripping them of Sierra Leonean citizenship in 1998.

Kabbah's successor, President Ernest Bai Koroma, ascended to power on the twin-mantra of 'zero tolerance to corruption' and 'no sacred cow'. He started on a high by strengthening and giving autonomous powers to the Anti Corruption Commission (ACC) established by his predecessor. High-ranking government officials were charged and convicted. But the fight seemed to have lulled as time elapsed, and his success would only be determined by posterity. What was clear, though, was that the Lebanese stranglehold was still very much tight or tightened or tightening on the Sierra Leone economy at the time he left office. The Lebanese man (he doesn't like being called that – he insists he was born in Sierra Leone) who ultimately took over Jamil's Hill Station estate and turned it into a hotel, Jamal Shallop, is a 'big-time' government contractor to this day.

However, my own thinking is that the Lebanese issue would not be solved the Mandela or Olu Gordon way, as things stand now; but rather by a continuous healthy engagement with the Lebanese community itself. Minds and hearts have to be opened on both sides. There are certainly good people among the Lebanese (like the journalists-loving sports writer, Zuhair J. Kudsy who even got recognised with the national honour of the 'Order of the Rokel' by President Koroma on Independence Day 2017). A few Lebanese men have gone on to marry and maintain stable families with Sierra Leonean women – the most celebrated being the philanthropic Managing Director of Mercury betting company, Martin Michael (Barrister at law, Notary Public and Commissioner for Oaths) who has variously intervened in a most apolitical way in Sierra Leone's development especially in education, journalism and sports; and is married to outspoken fellow barrister, law lecturer and magazine producer, Basita, who is currently the president of the Sierra Leone Bar Association . A good number of them are virtual natives after generations of living in Sierra Leone. The debate has to be started – and it has to be respectful. For the good of all. For the good of Sierra Leone.

Yet, the Sierra Leone problem will never be solved if the average Serra Leonean politician continues to think North-West as against South-East, APC versus SLPP, or Temne opposed to Mende – for these are the divisions that the unscrupulous have been using to thrive upon and exploit the economy since the departure of the British colonialists.

***

The tragic seeds of this tribalism/regional menace were sown in the mysterious death of Sierra Leone's first Prime Minister, Sir Milton Margai, of the SLPP. There is yet to be a finer gentleman of a Sierra Leonean leader (the only one to have ever died in office, successful coups inclusive). He wholesomely galvanised a disparate nation and carried it upon his shoulders. With a national appeal combined with his symmetry with the British (of whom he had his wife), Margai got Sierra Leone's Independence delivered on a silver platter on 27 April 1961. But after presiding over celebrations of the country's third Independence anniversary, Margai passed away the next day on 28 April 1964. Siaka Stevens, as then-Leader of the Opposition, had this to say as a tribute to 'the father of the nation' in Parliament the following day: "Sir Milton Margai died in action. We shall not forget him and no history of Sierra Leone will be complete without a word about his continuous service. We shall miss him and we shall miss his tolerance. He has helped us and has well directed our affairs. He achieved unity among us; during a time in our history, in fact, he was the only man who could give unity to our country..."

In came his brother Albert Margai, chosen under very controversial circumstances by two Creoles (Governor-General Henry Lightfoot-Boston on the advice of Attorney General Berthan Macaulay) – a decision that was petitioned by 35 Members of Parliament, including three Ministers; but the action discontinued through 'pressure and persuasion'. The younger Margai had a little over two and half years to complete his elder brother's term and face the electorate.

Despite being a thoroughly educated man (the first Sierra Leonean lawyer from the provinces, then known as the Protectorate, and trained in London), Albert Margai only succeeded in planting bad seeds of tribal politics, and had himself to blame when his party lost the 1967 elections. Even though Governor-General Lightfoot-Boston had recognised the APC victory and thereby appointed Stevens as the new Prime Minister, Albert Margai's close friend and tribesman who was army chief, Brig. David Lansana (aided by then-Lt Hinga Norman, who would later become Deputy Defence Minister in the SLPP Government of President Tejan Kabbah some thirty years later), staged a coup to try to keep the SLPP in power. But junior officers did a counter-coup; and through yet another counter-coup Siaka Stevens was restored to power about thirteen months later after going into exile in neighbouring Guinea. That was how Sierra Leone's cycle of coups and counter-coups was put in motion. Margai's infamous introduction of the 1965 Public Order Act (which successive governments have used to clamp on the media) only made the tribalism slur uglier.

And this was how Siaka Stevens summed up, in his *What Life Has taught Me,* the leadership of a man with whom he worked very closely since their days in the SLPP to their break-away PNP (of which Margai was head) before the former founded the APC: "While stuffing his henchmen into the power-centres of politics, he was cramming every vacancy in the civil service and armed forces with fellow-tribesmen. Margai's retreat into a tribalism more divisive and a sectionalism more acute than any previously practised even by the SLPP, was the worst thing that had happened to Sierra Leone since Independence. When we needed unity most, Margai set us at each other's throats. When we most needed to set tribalism aside, Margai exploited it with frantic ruthlessness... Large numbers even of his tribesmen rejected his divisive policies and voted for us."

Stevens' views on Albert Margai's short reign were echoed by David Dalby, then of the School of Oriental and African Studies (London). Welshman Dalby, who started his long and illustrious academic career at Fourah Bay College as lecturer, wrote in the *New Society* magazine (UK) of 6 April 1967 an article titled "Sierra Leone on the brink' and stated, among other things, that: "The defeat of the ruling SLPP was not unexpected, and certainly not undeserved, and it is to the credit of the people of Sierra Leone that they should have achieved the first democratic change of government in post-colonial Africa. It is even more to their credit that they should have achieved this in the face of Margai's desperate efforts to remain in power." Albert Margai, who died of a heart attack while visiting a niece in the US, did some pretty good stuff as Minister of Finance in his elder brother's government, like establishing the central bank and changing the legal tender. But he would best be remembered for his prediction (of course in retrospect) of the war in Sierra Leone. Having seen how Siaka Stevens' APC (the Lebanese as part of the make-up) had predatorily strangled the economy, Margai, living as an exile in the UK, came to the conclusion that: "If the Stevens government does not do something to elevate the lives of the have-nots, the poor, they would one day rise to demand from the haves, the rich, their own share of the economy." It came to pass under Shaki's successor.

Tribalism was not as pronounced, even if couched, when Siaka Stevens would eventually take over – largely due to his own inter-ethnic make-up: born in the south by a northern father and southern mother, he spoke Mende fluently; and he was educated in the western area. However, there were traces of tribalism at the initial stages of APC rule (even if for the inevitability of the fact that Margai's henchmen were his tribesmen), as President Ahmad Tejan Kabbah would later recall in *Coming Back From The Brink*: "The new Prime Minister and leader of the APC Siaka Stevens seemed determined to punish any highly placed person who he believed had had some dealings with the former SLPP regime of Sir Albert Margai. I, being a strong and vocal supporter of the SLPP, happened to be one of the victims". On the backdrop of coups and counter-coups (sometimes ending fatally in executions – reintroduced for the first time since Independence), Siaka Stevens was able to hold sway over the affairs of the nation. With overwhelming support even from the South-east – it has be noted (whether out of fear or for the favours) – Shaki (as he was fondly called) ruled Sierra Leone Putin-like for nearly two decades under a One-party/APC rule until he handed over to his hand-picked successor, Joseph Saidu Momoh.

Momoh, a northerner married to a south-easterner, introduced a sort of tribalism that seemed glamorous and enticing but perhaps as dangerous as that which Margai initiated. He lent his support to his Limba tribe's association, *Ekutay* (meaning 'did you hear?' or 'have you heard?' – whatever that implied), which more or less usurped state authority and forced politicians of other tribes to either join or be left in the cold. Key state decisions were taken at meetings at Binkolo, the President's home village in the outskirts of Makeni. One politician from the east was said to have claimed ancestry from Binkolo and left some money for a certain bush to be cleared for him to build a house. When Momoh was overthrown by young military officers who formed the NPRC, the politician from the east was never again seen at Binkolo – the bush is still there. Momoh, a former Force Commander of the Sierra Leone Army, was so deep and steep in *Ekutay* stupor that he had no idea what was going on around him (I would later interview him when, having been sprung from prison as a condemned 'collaborator' under the Kabbah regime, he would be brought to my hiding place at Mabanta by the AFRC/RUF forces. He told me he had become a pastor in prison, Bible in hand. He would later die at his second wife Binta Bah's home in Guinea; pre-deceased by his first wife, Hannah).

The installation of western area-born/Krio Captain Valentine Strasser as head of the NPRC generally suppressed the South-east-versus-North political-cum-tribal rivalry. And Maada Bio's short reign after overthrowing his boss would not be gauged – except that, by his own subsequent confession, he alluded to having influenced the 1996 elections in favour of the SLPP's President Tejan Kabbah (rumours of a deal at the time later got meat when Bio would return to lead the very SLPP).

Kabbah's reign was bedeviled more with fighting the war – though his indulgence to the kamajors (the south-eastern civil defence militia) was seen as tribalism against the regular army (which was largely seen as an APC, meaning north-western, military). The saving grace was that Kabbah himself had a northern father and was born in the east to an eastern mother, and married a southerner (Patricia Kabbah nee Tucker).

His successor, President Ernest Bai Koroma, though born by northern parents (both from the same district), was not an overt tribalist: in fact, most of his tribesmen complained that he empowered more of other tribes (Mendes and Creoles in particular). However, it was a flip side for him when the *Ekutay* reared its head again in the power-play under his regime and he got associated with it. Though it was a much more watered-down version with no real authority as in the Joseph Momoh days, its re-emergence encouraged the formation of other small tribal associations like the Loko *Landorwoh* union.

One would only know how this had angered the south-easterners/Mendes when in the aftermath of the SLPP's Julius Maada Bio having been declared the successor to Koroma in early 2018, a spate of unprecedented violence and intimidation erupted in those parts of the country against northerners. I could not find another reason; since Koroma himself was not even vehemently opposed to Bio. To the contrary, Koroma even indulged Bio. But the spate of fast-tracked sackings of Koroma's appointees and being replaced by south-easterners turned the former President's seeming conciliatory attitude on its head. Bio supporters argued that all those being replaced were from the north-west. This was largely true because those from the south-east who served in Koroma's regime were either not touched at all or were promoted in the Bio administration. And perhaps what made it more pronounced was the method plus the duration: for the first time in our history, Ambassadors and High Commissioners and Attachés were sacked en masse within weeks of a change of government.

The talk of tribalism is, therefore, not dying down. And that is welcome news for those who would want to exploit politics and politicians for their selfish goals as against the nationalistic progress of the country.

The Sierra Leonean mentality has to change. We need another Sir-Milton-Margai-style of politics, drawn from the wellspring of British politics. There is, for instance, the Labour/ Conservative divide in Britain, but the British make a bridge and close ranks when it comes to national issues. The national picture should not be blurred by our natural ethnic heritage. There has to be some revolutionary nationalistic thinking. Only then will a mineral-rich geographically-beautiful Sierra Leone benefit the majority of its citizens. The 'ill-fated nation' (the title of a book – with a question mark – by Sierra Leonean university lecturer Chris Squire) has seen enough of man-made and natural disasters: military coups, a ten-year war, squander-gates, an Ebola pandemic, flooding, cholera outbreaks and mudslides that took many lives. She needs respite. She needs to progress.

* * *

I would never forget President Koroma. Serving him and giving me the opportunity to serve my country was a pleasure – the aforementioned rough edges besides. Three episodes I would particularly want to highlight for the reader.

Firstly, when I returned to Sierra Leone at his behest to be his Press Secretary, at the height of the Wesleyan Church being exuberant about his presidency, we sat side by side in the Kissy Dockyard Church during the 'Wesleyan Heroes' service. It gave me a great sense of excitement. After that, during the next-day session of my usual daily briefings with him, he told me that I should remember that the job we were doing was a 'thankless' one – that no matter what we did, we would always have critics. I noted that.

Secondly, I would always remember, very humorously, a private flight from London to Freetown when only two of us were occupying the presidential suite – his Personal Assistant and Personal Valet, being the only other passengers, sitting at the back beyond listening distance. This was mid-way in his administration. We had long discussions, stock-taking on what we had done in various areas, from government to family. It was a light-hearted conversation, as we were being served champagne by the air hostesses. Somewhere in Moroccan airspace, we had some tough turbulence troubling the small aircraft. When all subsided, the President remarked that the storm occurred because I was chatting too much with the beautiful airhostess serving us. We both burst into hilarious laughter. "I thought flirting was permitted, sir," I retorted. More laughter. More champagne.

The third highlight would be about two weeks after the 2018 elections which the APC candidate he had preferred to succeed him lost. I met the former President, together with a colleague journalist, at his Goderich residence, west of Freetown. It was a telling moment. The President admitted having made some mistakes perhaps particularly with the choice of the Chief Electoral Commissioner. Commissioner Nfa Alie Conteh was accused by many APC supporters of taking his 'independence' beyond borders and 'acted like a puppet' of the British High Commissioner. The popular notion was that High Commissioner Guy Warrington was bent on effecting 'regime change' against the will of the people (some sections of the media have gone on to label him as 'the last Colonial Governor of Sierra Leone'). This meeting with the President (or rather former President) was also light-hearted with some champagne. I had taken along the manuscript of this book for him to see how far I had gone, even as I told him I was going to London partly to concentrate on the necessary research to complete it. The President credited the decline of our official relationship to the work of 'false accusers'. He talked about those who behaved like 'Judas' and reminded us of the Greek and Roman power intrigues, and the Shakespearean tragedies in which power-hungry men were always tirelessly plotting to bring good men down... I was heartened. He gave us some money that day.

Perhaps I could add some regrets: the road to Mabanta (I've always wondered over the similarity in name with Chinua Achebe's Mbanta in *Things Fall Apart*, set in Nigeria; and the natives having similar attitudes towards the Christian Church. 'Mbanta' is actually the way the native speakers of my hometown call their enclave – *"Daykay mang wura?"* [Where are you coming from?] *"E wur Doh Mbanta."* [I'm coming from Mbanta]. Only when we went to school did we first hear it called 'Mabanta'. But if we dig further into etymology, we end up with the original pronunciation of 'Mbantha' – which loosely translated could mean 'not out of anger'. Folklore states that the founder of the village was called Pa Bantha). Ours, however, should not be confused with Mabanta in the Lower-and-Upper-Banta-Chiefdoms conundrum in Moyamba District in the South or the Yoni Mabanta of Tonkolili District in the northern fringes bordering the South – though we are certainly connected with those Mabanta Temnes at least via culture, language, and 'coincidence' of name. But the origin must have been from our Mabanta, because the territorial movement was southwards – they came from Fouta Djallon in present-day Guinea. There is a variant version of the history though! As a schoolboy, I used to go for holidays to an aunt (my father's sister, Isatu Deen – of blessed memory) who was married to a Yoni Temne at Petifu, Yonibana (Tonkolili District), bordering the Mabanta Temne of the South – there I discovered other dialects of the language. I would visit Moyamba as Deputy Minister of Internal Affairs to senstise the people on the setting up of the Independent Police Complaints Board in 2013. Upon hearing my name and background during the introduction, one of the chiefs would afterwards call me to the side to tell me, in all seriousness, how we had the same ancestors. With names of pre-historic characters to back the story up. I didn't know what to say. I accepted with a big hug, others looking obviously.

The couple-of-miles road from Makeni to Mabanta was very rough terrain; but ever since I joined the government I had been advocating for it to be modernised with asphalt. The proposal became more compelling because this road also led to the President's home village of Yoni, cutting the distance from the city by half. The idea became more attractive for the fact that a UNIMAK campus was built at Yoni, also housing the offices of the Vice Chancellor/Principal and other senior staff of the university. I pushed for the idea, and the President bought it. The contract was awarded to SALCOST and preliminary clearing was started with heavy machinery. However, work was stopped. And my reminders were no longer regarded. The road is today worse than it was before!

But the people are consoled that we tried hard and got the village (well, some parts) connected to the national grid. Makeni's famed 24-hours supply of electricity, brought by the Ernest Koroma government to a once very dark city, reaches Mabanta. It makes more practical Rev. Usman Fornah's biblical analogy (during the service to honour my mother as 'Wesleyan Woman of the Year 2013' in a well-lit Mabanta Church – now being attended by many former poro men and former 'named witches') that a people who once sat in darkness have seen a great light.

* * *

I still very much remain connected to Birch Memorial Secondary School and St Francis Secondary School. As Deputy Minister of Information & Communications, I ensured Birch was included in a selected number of schools which benefited from an ICT project that supplied computers and full internet facilities, while a similar donation of V-SAT equipment was made to the Yoni campus of UNIMAK (which by and large is an extension of St. Francis) handed over to the ever-agile former Bishop George Biguzzi.

One of my most enduring academic relationships has been with the current Principal of Birch, Shekuba R. Sesay: he taught me at primary school, taught me at secondary school, and I eventually met him at university as a student (he was adding to his array of academic credentials)!

Since the old-student network of Birch is somewhat weak, I have had to make personal donations to the school like contributing to the erection of a fence; while I was satisfied with my active membership (with financial obligations, of course) in the Old Makeni Franciscans Association (OMFA).

***

You may by now, dear reader, be wondering about what happened to, or the whereabouts of, my good friend and 'co-pilgrim' Alie Wasco. This was the man who nearly worshipped President Koroma. He always wanted to be in the President's good books and would therefore never question his actions (good or bad). He gave the impression that everything the President did was correct or was divinely ordained. I kept reminding him of some of the blunders of the administration to tell his boss, but he thought I was speaking from a 'frustrated' perspective – having been out of government (he was one of only two people I showed the letter of disengagement I wrote to the President; the other being the late Ambassador Siray Timbo. Alie said as long as I was out, I should stay out!).

Sincerely, I was wary about how President Koroma was handling the political processes in the APC in the run up to the 2018 general elections. My newspaper was particularly vociferous about the apparently irregular activities of the National Electoral Commission headed by Nfa Alie Conteh, especially as there were clear manipulations of the voter register, not least because it was not displayed for verification as by law established. But President Koroma and Alie Wasco would not listen to the newspaper of a dissident. I was also seriously concerned about the choice of Samura Kamara, knowing his non-political background (when President Koroma announced his name in the jam-packed Makeni hall, everybody was asking 'you sabi am?' [Do you know him?]).

In fact it was Alie who confirmed to me, the night before the APC 'selection' convention, that Samura Kamara would be the handpicked candidate, though twenty-odd others had been lured to believe they could be chosen through a series of well-publicised dinners and meetings held for the purpose. I had known Samura Kamara would be the one ever since he told me in Turkey – and seeing how much power he had exerted around the President privately and as Foreign Minister. I reliably learnt Samura Kamara personally dissuaded the President from any extension of his term, when party lackeys were demanding for 'more time'. I told Alie the President's choice was wrong! But I was just 'the dissident'!

I invariably had been lukewarm throughout the campaigns and did not participate in any outdoor event (well, even in no indoor one). I was in Makeni during the Convention, but I did not go to the hall at all – I stayed at home, sipping some wine intermittently, knowing the outcome already.

For Alie, everything President Koroma did was correct, even in the choice of Samura Kamara – although he was not his preferred candidate. Koth Alie was a strong supporter of Vice President Victor Foh as the natural successor. He had even started calling him 'His Excellency' and Foh would reside at Alie's residence whenever he visited Makeni. Alie would even introduce him as 'the next President'. After knowing President Koroma's decision that night, Alie switched his loyalties immediately. He started following Samura Kamara virtually everywhere.

When the results of the run-off elections were read and Julius Maada Bio of the SLPP was declared as winner, Alie was shocked beyond belief. He feared the worst and escaped to neighbouring Guinea using bush paths at night, eventually finding his way to his 'second home', the United States of America. But not before calling President Koroma to tell him how he had sold out, how he had betrayed the party. Alie said he had asked the electoral commissioner Nfa Alie Conteh, with whom he was very close, how he came to deliver the presidency to the SLPP on a silver platter while the APC had swept the majority of seats in Parliament in a country where people never divided the two at the polls. Alie said his namesake told him to ask his 'brother Ernest Koroma'. Alie said when he confronted President Koroma, the latter retorted 'what's wrong with that?' And then he asked him if he was comfortable with a Bio presidency, and the President said 'why not?'

Alie would subsequently call me to say my assessment of the President's handling of the political processes was correct all along. He was late. Too late.

Alie may not return to Sierra Leone throughout the Bio presidency; and he is not on speaking terms with his 'brother' President Ernest Bai Koroma. Father Ignazio and 'Love Bridges' would never get a better political ally. And I miss him too… But, at least, he has the Pope's 'blessings'….

* * *

Despite a somehow healthy ecumenical relationship with other Churches, the Catholic Church in Sierra Leone is assertively independent. Though a member of the Inter-Religious Council, which includes Protestant churches and Islam, the Catholic Church debars membership with purely intra-Christian organisations like the Council of Churches in Sierra Leone and the Evangelical Fellowship of Sierra Leone. This, perhaps, was mainly because the latter would be based purely on a theological relationship, while the former was more about addressing national issues. Notwithstanding, the local dynamics of religious tolerance have seen the blossoming of inter-personal as well as inter-Church relationships, especially during formal occasions and in family settings where members generally tended to follow varied religions without qualms.

My long-serving driver is a Muslim; and his name is Mohamed. My twin-like younger brother, Hudson, was the one driving me around since my return home. When he passed on to eternity in 2009, I had a bit of a struggle finding a replacement. Mohamed filled that void – he seems to like gospel music than I do now. When his own brother (also a Muslim) was seriously ill, Mohamed was one of those who rushed him to a church for prayers. The brother passed away, but that was a microcosm of the depth of the accommodating nature of Sierra Leone's religious tolerance.

To me, the Church (and here I mean Catholic and Protestant collectively) needs to do more in the affairs of the Sierra Leonean society. It has tried in the provision of schools and hospitals and other facilities, at times in the form of charities like 'Love Bridges' and World Hope International. But there is still a huge gap to be filled. As in the early Church, the rich church should do more for the poor church: Paul wrote to the Corinthians about helping poorer Christians: "Your abundance being a supply at this present time for their want, that their abundance also may become a supply for your want; that there may be equality." The Western

Church (whether in America, England or the Vatican), with all the resources available at its disposal, can do much more to change the lives of people in the developing world's Church. The latter need the practical miracle of the two fish and five loaves of bread feeding the five thousand! As Pope Francis has already apologised for the West's 'sins' during the slave trade, colonialism and the Rwandan genocide of 1994 – and forgiven – a little more charity would help.

I believe this world will be a better place when faith is backed by love. For when you love, there is no holding back. For God so loved the world that He gave His only begotten Son…

We are the world! By lending a helping hand to others, we are just saving our own lives!

In all this, as I re-take a foothold on the journalism hill to watch and record events, I remain a Wesleyan Christian – for reasons, dear reader, that you already know. But if I end up living in the UK again or perhaps decide to go to Rwanda with my wife, as the socio-political meteorological forecast indicates, then a church is a church. There is no Wesleyan Church in either place. In Sierra Leone, there is this well-liked equality-establishing adage that, there are many other churches besides St. George's Cathedral. Christ is for all!

And if Pope Francis should decide to do a first-ever papal visit to Sierra Leone, I would make it a point of duty to be there – that is the only other time or place I am keen for us to meet again. Before Heaven!

All this is from God, who reconciled us to Himself through Christ and gave us the ministry of reconciliation

(2 Corinthians 5:18)